ONLINE RESOURCES

We include online resources with the purchase of this study guide to help you fully prepare for your exam.

Practice Test
In addition to the practice test in the book, there is an online practice test.

Flash Cards
Our flash cards allow you to review important terms easily on your computer or smartphone.

Cheat Sheets
Review the core skills you need to master the exam with easy-to-read Cheat Sheets.

From Stress to Success Video
Watch "From Stress to Success," a brief but insightful video that offers the tip and tricks you need to score higher on your exam.

The instructions for accessing these materials are on the last page of this book.

CVRN Study Guide

CV-BC Test Prep and 2 Full-Length Practice Exams
for the Cardiac Vascular Nursing Certification
[Updated for the New Outline]

Jeremy Downs

Copyright ©2025 Trivium Test Prep

ISBN-13: 9781637989111

ALL RIGHTS RESERVED. By purchase of this book, you have been licensed on copy for personal use only. No part of this work may be reproduced, redistributed, or used in any form or by any means without prior written permission of the publisher and copyright owner. Trivium Test Prep; Accepted, Inc.; Cirrus Test Prep; and Ascencia Test Prep are all imprints of Trivium Test Prep, LLC.

TABLE OF CONTENTS

Introduction 1
    The ANCC Cardiac-Vascular Nursing Certification 1
    The ABCM Cardiovascular Nursing Certification 4
    Using This Book 5
    Ascencia Test Prep 5

Chapter 1 – Anatomy and Physiology of the Cardiovascular System 6
    The Heart 6
    Blood Vessels 10
    The Coagulation Process 11
    Answer Key 14

Chapter 2 – Cardiac Diseases and Risk Factors 15
    Risk Factors 15
    Acute Coronary Syndrome (ACS) 23
    Cardiomyopathies 27
    Dysrhythmias 28
    Heart Failure (HF) 34
    Hypertensive Crisis 37
    Infective Endocarditis 37
    Pericarditis 39
    Congenital Heart Defects 40
    Myocardial Conduction System Defects 44
    Congenital Conduction Defects 48
    Pulmonary Edema 49
    Pulmonary Hypertension (PH) 50
    Rheumatic Heart Disease (RHD) 51
    Shock 52
    Valvular Heart Disease 55
    Answer Key 56

Chapter 3 - Arterial and Venous Diseases 58
    Abdominal Aortic Aneurysm (AAA) 58
    Pseudoaneurysm 59
    Carotid Artery Occlusive Disease (CAOD) 60
    Chronic Venous Insufficiency (CVI) 61
    Deep Vein Thrombosis (DVT) 62
    Peripheral Vascular Insufficiency 64
    Cerebrovascular Accident (CVA) 66
    Answer Key 69

Chapter 4 – Patient Interviews and Cardiac and Vascular Assessment .. 70
    Taking a Focused Cardiovascular History 70
    Physical Examination 71
    Laboratory Tests 84
    Other Diagnostic Tools 88
    Electrocardiography and Telemetry 90
    Answer Key 100

Chapter 5 – Planning, Implementation, Evaluation, and Modification 101
    Developing an Individualized Plan of Care 101
    Coordinating Care Across the Continuum 103

Creating a Safe and Therapeutic Environment 104
Changes in Patient Condition 107
Outcomes Evaluations 107
Answer Key 110

Chapter 6 – The Professional Role of the Cardiac-Vascular Nurse 111

Communication 111
The Work Environment 115
Legal and Ethical Considerations 119
Answer Key 124

Chapter 7 - Cardiovascular Technologies and Procedures 125

Cardiac Monitoring 125
Care for Extremities 125
Cardiac Catheter Procedures 126
Surgical Interventions 131
Devices 136
Cardioversion and Defibrillation 142
Answer Key 144

Chapter 8 – Cardiovascular Pharmacology 145

Administering Medications 145
Angiotensin-Converting Enzyme (ACE) Inhibitors 146
Adrenergic Group - Alpha$_1$-Adrenergic Agonists 147
Adrenergic Group Alpha$_1$-Adrenergic Blockers 148
Alpha$_2$ -Adrenergic Agonists 149
Alpha$_2$-Adrenergic Blockers 150
Beta-Adrenergic Antagonists (Beta-Blockers) 151

Sympathomimetics 152
Angiotensin II Receptor Antagonists (ARBs) 153
Anticoagulants 154
Antidysrhythmics 156
Antiplatelets 157
Diuretics 158
Inotropic Agents - Cardiac Glycosides . 161
Inotropic Agents - Phosphodiesterase Inhibitors 162
Other Vasodilators - Nitrates 162
Other Vasodilators - Calcium Channel Blockers 164
Antihypertensive Vasodilators 165
Thrombolytics (Fibrinolytic Agents) 166
Drug Interactions 167
Answer Key 169

Chapter 9 – Patient and Community Education 171

The Learning Process 171
Education Plans 175
Factors That Influence Care 177
Outpatient Monitoring 180
Population Health Risk Management . 181
Answer Key 185

Practice Test 187

Answer Explanations 212

Appendix A – Signs and Symptoms Glossary 225

Appendix B - Abbreviations 227

Appendix C – Diagnostic Tests and Critical Values 232

Online Resources **239**

Introduction

Congratulations on choosing to earn your cardiac-vascular nursing board certification! Obtaining this certification is an important step forward in your nursing career, and we are excited to help prepare you to achieve this goal.

The ANCC Cardiac-Vascular Nursing Certification

What is the ANCC Cardiac-Vascular Nursing Certification?

Considered a subsidiary of the American Nurses Association (ANA), The American Nurses Credentialing Center (ANCC) is tasked with creating programs that allow nurses to participate in continuing education and earn various certifications for specific nursing specialties.

The Cardiac-Vascular Nursing Board Certification (CV-BC) exam is developed by the ANCC as part of its certification program for cardiac-vascular nurses. The cardiac-vascular exam measures the skills required to excel as a nurse who provides cardiac-vascular care. To qualify for the exam, you must meet the following criteria:

- have a current registered nurse license in the United States or its territories (or foreign equivalent)
- have practiced for two full years (or equivalent) as a registered nurse
- have at least 2,000 hours of practice as a cardiac-vascular nurse in the last three years
- have at least 30 hours of continuing education in cardiac-vascular nursing in the last three years

Once you have met the qualifications and passed the exam, you will have earned the credential *Cardiac-Vascular Nurse–Board Certified (CV-BC)*, which you may use as long as your certification remains valid. Your certification will need to be renewed every five years; this can be done by completing professional development requirements that may include a combination of continuing education hours, academic credits, research, or practice hours.

How many questions are on the ANCC CV-BC exam?

The exam consists of 150 questions; however, only 125 of these questions are scored—the remaining 25 questions are unscored questions that are used to gauge their appropriateness for future exams. You will not know which questions are unscored, so you must treat every question like it counts.

The questions are multiple-choice with four answer options. Some questions will include exhibits, such as ECG strips or laboratory results. There is no penalty for guessing on the exam. In other words, if you answer a question incorrectly, no points are deducted from your score; you simply do not get credit for that question. You should therefore always guess if you do not know the answer to a question. The computer testing system will allow you to go back to questions during the exam before submitting your final answers.

You will have three hours to complete the exam.

What is on the ANCC CV-BC exam?

The ANCC develops its exams based on feedback from cardiac-vascular nursing professionals about the nursing concepts and skills that are most important to their work. In addition to using this feedback to develop an exam framework, the ANCC performs periodic role delineation studies (i.e., job analyses) that inform updates to the contents of the exam. The most recent version of the exam was launched in December 2024. The following table describes the contents of the current exam.

Content Domain I: Assessment and Diagnosis		
Associated Knowledge	**Associated Skills**	**Exam Breakdown**
<ul><li>anatomy and physiology</li><li>pathophysiology</li><li>nursing diagnosis identification</li></ul>	<ul><li>patient interview (e.g., history, chief complaint, allergies)</li><li>cardiac-vascular assessment techniques and tools (e.g., Doppler, stroke scale)</li><li>data collection and interpretation (e.g., diagnostic tests, laboratory results)</li></ul>	27 questions (22% of exam)

Content Domain II: Planning and Implementation		
Associated Knowledge	**Associated Skills**	**Exam Breakdown**
<ul><li>evidence-based practice guidelines (e.g., ACC/AHA guidelines, quality measures)</li><li>scope and standards of practice (i.e., cardiac-vascular nursing, vascular nursing)</li><li>legal and ethical considerations (e.g., informed consent, advance directives)</li><li>invasive/non-invasive procedures (e.g., peripheral)</li><li>surgeries (e.g., coronary bypass, transplant)</li><li>pharmacologic therapies</li><li>non-pharmacologic and complementary therapies</li><li>risk-reduction measures (e.g., venous thromboembolism prophylaxis)</li></ul>	<ul><li>prioritization and care coordination (e.g., discharge planning, interdisciplinary teams)</li><li>interventions (e.g., cardioversion)</li></ul>	44 questions (35% of exam)

Content Domain III: Evaluation and Modification		
Associated Knowledge	Associated Skills	Exam Breakdown
• expected outcomes • drug interactions (e.g., drug-drug, drug-food)	• adverse reactions and events (e.g., heparin-induced thrombocytopenia, hypotension) recognition and treatment • urgent conditions (e.g., pseudoaneurysm) recognition and treatment • emergent condition (e.g., STEMI) recognition and treatment	23 questions (18% of exam)

Content Domain IV: Patient and Community Education		
Associated Knowledge	Associated Skills	Exam Breakdown
• cardiac-vascular risk factors (e.g., ethnicity, smoking) • chronic disease management • cardiac-vascular education topics (e.g., procedures, medications) • self-management strategies (e.g., daily weights, blood pressure logs) • community resources (e.g., cardiac rehabilitation, anticoagulation clinic)	• individualized education planning and implementation (e.g., addressing barriers) • outpatient monitoring (e.g., remote telemetry, point-of-care testing) • health promotion (e.g., wellness counseling, health fairs)	31 questions (25% of exam)

Where is the ANCC CV-BC exam administered?

The ANCC Cardiac-Vascular Nursing Board Certification (CV-BC) exam is administered at Prometric testing centers. To register for the exam, you must first apply through the ANCC website (https://www.nursingworld.org/our-certifications/cardiac-vascular-nurse/). After your application is accepted, you will receive an Authorization to Test. You can then officially register for the exam at www.prometric.com/ANCC. You will have 90 days from the date you receive your Authorization to Test to take the exam.

On test day, you should plan to arrive at the testing site 30 minutes early. You will need to bring an appropriate government-issued ID (driver's license, state ID card, military ID, or passport). If you do not have any of these IDs, you may bring two IDs: one with a signature and one with a photograph.

You will not be allowed to bring any personal items into the testing room, such as calculators or phones. You may not bring pens, pencils, or scratch paper, but the testing center will provide a personal whiteboard for note-taking. Most testing centers provide lockers for valuables.

After you check in, you will receive instructions for your exam. You will then be allotted time to practice with the computer testing program before beginning the exam.

When will I know the results of my ANCC CV-BC exam?

Once you have completed your test, the staff at the Prometric testing center will give you a score report. The score report will include your raw score (the number of questions you answered correctly) and a scaled score. A minimum scaled score of 350 is required to pass the exam. The number of correct answers needed for a scaled score of 350 will vary depending on the questions that appear in your version of the test. (If you take a version of the test with harder questions, the passing raw score will be lower.)

If you fail the exam, you will receive scoring information for each separate content area. You may reapply and retake the test after 60 days. You have three chances to pass the exam within a twelve-month period.

The ABCM Cardiovascular Nursing Certification

What is the ABCM Cardiovascular Nursing Certification exam?

The American Board of Cardiovascular Medicine (ABCM) offers the Cardiovascular Nursing Level I and Cardiovascular Nursing Level II Board Certification (CVRN-BC) examinations as part of its certification process. To qualify for either exam, you must have a current registered nurse license as well a minimum of one year of cardiac nursing experience:

- The Cardiovascular Nursing Level I exam is designed for nursing roles that take place in cardiac rehab units, heart clinics, and other cardiac settings that are not considered acute.
- The Cardiovascular Nursing Level II exam is designed for nursing roles that take place in cath labs, transplant units, and other acute-care cardiac settings.

You can apply for the exam through the ABCM website (https://abcmcertification.com/exams). Once your application has been approved, you will receive an email with instructions for exam registration. The exam can be taken on a home computer or at an approved testing facility.

How many questions are on the ABCM CVRN-BC exam?

During the exam you will have three hours to answer 150 questions.

What is on the ABCM CVRN-BC exam?

Questions cover nursing concepts from the following content areas:

1. Bedside Assessment (14.5% of exam)
2. Basic ECG Concepts (18% of exam)
3. Coronary Artery Disease & ACS (9.5% of exam)
4. Hypertension (9.5% of exam)
5. Heart Failure (9.5% of exam)

6. Cardiomyopathy (6.5% of exam)
7. Cardiovascular Pharmacology (11.5% of exam)
8. Pacemakers/ICDs (6.0% of exam)
9. Noninvasive and Interventional Cardiology (15% of exam)

When will I know the results of my ABCM CVRN-BC exam?

After the exam, you will receive an email with your score and a pass/fail designation. You will need to answer 105 questions (70%) correctly to pass the exam. If you fail the exam, you can pay a fee to retake it. There is no limit to the number of times you may take the exam.

Using This Book

This book is divided into two sections: content areas and practice exams.

In the content areas, you will find a review of the knowledge and skills necessary to pass the exam. Throughout each chapter, you will have the opportunity to answer Quick Review Questions in order to reinforce important concepts and terms.

The book also includes two full-length practice tests: one appears in the book, and the other appears online. Each exam includes answer rationales. These practice tests can be used to gauge your readiness for the exam and to identify content areas you may need to review more thoroughly.

Ascencia Test Prep

With health care fields such as nursing, pharmacy, emergency care, and physical therapy becoming the fastest-growing industries in the United States, individuals looking to enter the health care industry or rise in their fields needs high-quality, reliable resources. Ascencia Test Prep's study guides and test preparation materials are developed by credentialed industry professionals with years of experience in their respective areas of expertise. Ascencia Test Prep recognizes that health care professionals nurture bodies and spirits, and save lives. Ascencia Test Prep's mission is to help health care workers grow in their careers.

Chapter 1 – Anatomy and Physiology of the Cardiovascular System

The Heart

The heart has four chambers: the left atrium, the right atrium, the left ventricle, and the right ventricle:

- The **right atrium** collects blood from the body.
- The **right ventricle** pumps blood to the lungs.
- The **left atrium** collects blood from the lungs.
- The **left ventricle** pumps blood to the body.
- The atria are separated by the **atrial septum**, and the ventricles by the **ventricular septum**.

Figure 1.1. Anatomy of the Heart

The **atrioventricular valves** are located between the atria and ventricles and cause the first heart sounds (S1) when they close:

- The **tricuspid valve** separates the right atrium and right ventricle.

- The **mitral valve** separates the left atrium and left ventricle.

The two **semilunar valves** are located between the ventricles and great vessels, and they cause the second heart sound (S2) when they close:

- The **pulmonic valve** separates the right ventricle and pulmonary artery.
- The **aortic valve** separates the left ventricle and aorta.

Blood flows through the cardiac valves in the following order:

- tricuspid → pulmonic → mitral → aortic
- The mnemonic, *Tissue Paper My Assets*, can be used to remember this order.

The heart is formed by layers of tissue:

- **pericardium:** the outermost protective layer of the heart, which contains a lubricative liquid
- **epicardium:** the deepest layer of the pericardium, which envelops the heart muscle
- **myocardium:** the heart muscle
- **endocardium:** the innermost, smooth layer of the heart walls

The pericardium is divided into two layers: the **fibrous pericardium** and the **serous pericardium**. The serous pericardium is further divided into the **visceral** and **parietal** layers. The space between these two layers is the **pericardial space**, which contains pericardial fluid.

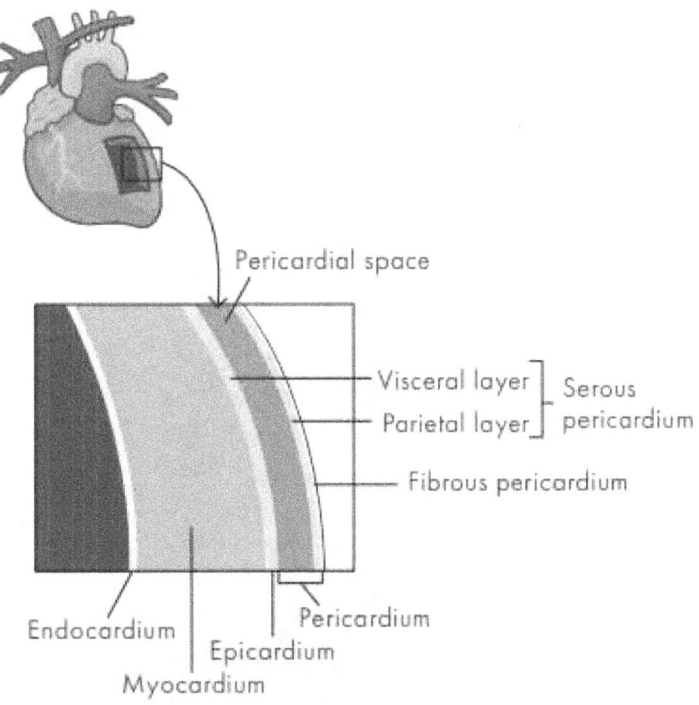

Figure 1.2. Layers of the Heart

Blood is supplied to the heart by coronary arteries: the **right coronary artery (RCA)**, **left anterior descending (LAD) artery**, and **left circumflex artery**. The heart's pumping action is regulated by the **cardiac conduction system**, which produces and conducts electrical signals in the heart:

- The **sinoatrial (SA) node** sets the heart's pace by sending out electrical signals that cause the atria to contract. It is located in the anterior wall of the right atrium.
- The **atrioventricular (AV) node** relays the electrical impulse of the sinoatrial node to the ventricles. The impulse is delayed to allow the atria to fully contract and fill the ventricles. The node is located at the base of the right atrial wall.
- The **bundle of His** carries the electrical signal from the AV node to the right and left bundle branches.
- The endpoint of the conduction system are **Purkinje fibers** in the endocardial layer that depolarize muscle cells, causing contraction of the ventricles.

Figure 1.3. Coronary Arteries

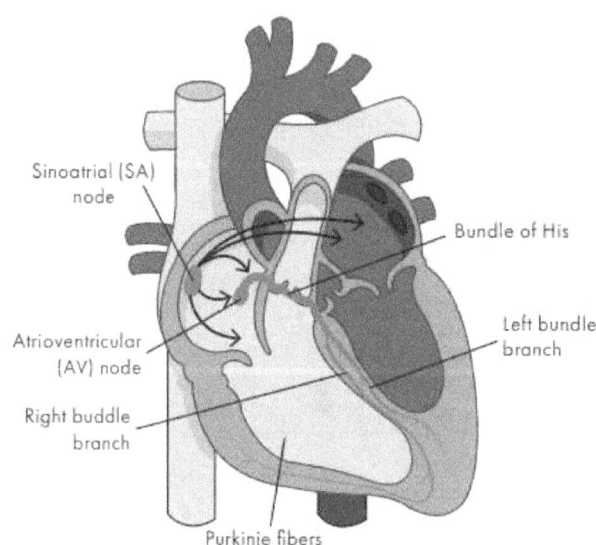

Figure 1.4. The Cardiac Conduction System

The circulatory system is a closed double loop:

- In the **pulmonary loop**, deoxygenated blood leaves the heart and travels to the lungs, where it loses carbon dioxide and becomes rich in oxygen. The oxygenated blood then returns to the heart.

- The heart then pumps blood through the **systemic loop**, which delivers oxygenated blood to the rest of the body and returns deoxygenated blood to the heart.

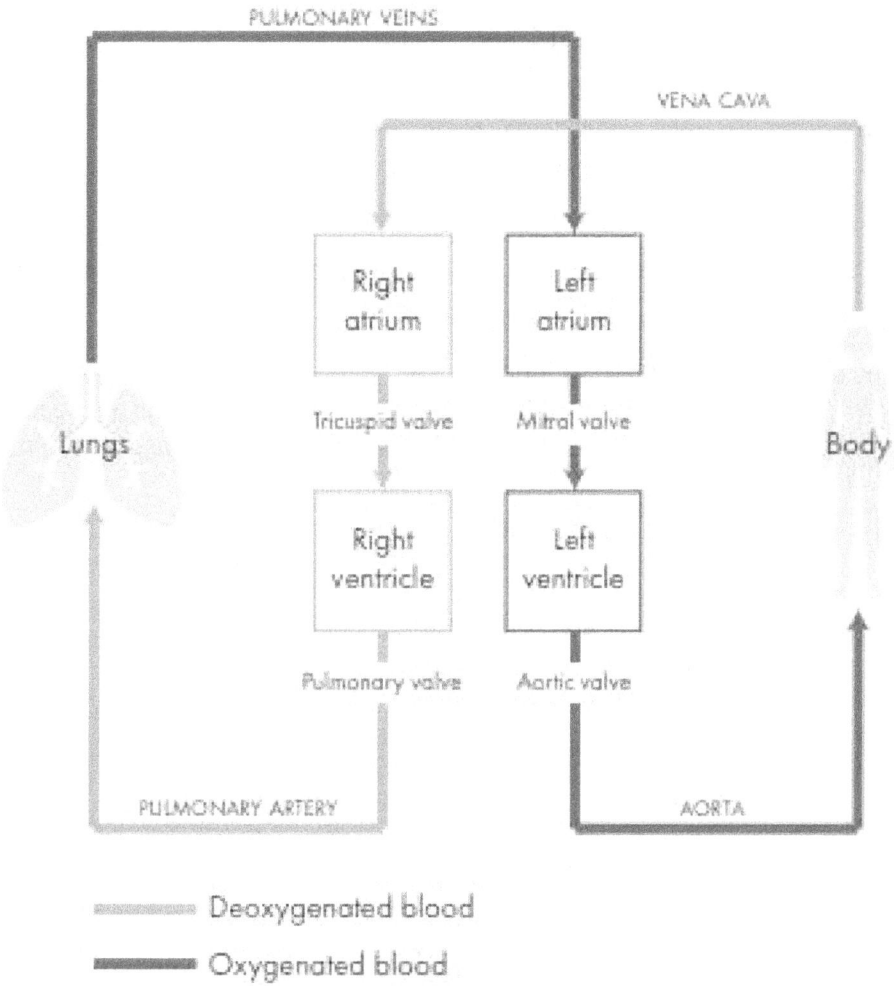

Figure 1.5. The Pulmonary and Systemic Loops

During the **cardiac cycle**, the heart alternates between diastole (relaxation) and systole (contraction) to move blood:

- When both chambers are in diastole, the atria passively fill the ventricles.
- During **atrial systole**, the atria force blood into the ventricles.
- During **ventricular systole**, the ventricles force blood into the arteries.

Quick Review Question

1. Left-sided heart failure can cause pulmonary edema, while right-sided heart failure is more likely to cause edema in the abdomen and extremities. How does the anatomy of the heart produce this difference?

Blood Vessels

The cardiovascular system circulates blood, which carries nutrients, waste products, hormones, and other important substances dissolved or suspended in liquid plasma:

- **Red blood cells (RBCs)** transport oxygen throughout the body.
- RBCs contain **hemoglobin**, a large molecule with iron atoms that bind to oxygen.
- **White blood cells (WBCs)** fight infection.

Blood leaves the heart and travels throughout the body in **blood vessels**, which decrease in diameter as they move away from the heart and toward the tissues and organs. Blood exits the heart through **arteries**, which branch into **arterioles** and then **capillaries**, where gas exchange between blood and tissue takes place.

Figure 1.6. Major Arteries

Deoxygenated blood travels back to the heart through **veins**; some veins have valves that prevent deoxygenated blood from flowing back to the extremities. Blood vessels have three layers:

- the **tunica adventitia**, the outer layer, composed of connective tissue
- the **tunica media**, the middle layer, composed of smooth muscle
- the **tunica intima**, the thin inner layer

> **Helpful Hint**
>
> **Carotid intima-media thickness** is a measure of the width of the tunica intima and tunica media in the carotid artery. It is used to evaluate atherosclerosis and cardiovascular risk.

The **lumen** is the interior space of the blood vessel, through which blood flows.

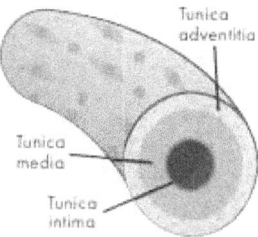

Figure 1.7. Structure of Blood Vessels

Quick Review Question

2. A patient presents with weak popliteal and pedal pulses and intermittent claudication in the left calf muscle. The nurse should suspect an occlusion in which artery?

The Coagulation Process

Hemostasis is the process of stopping blood loss from a damaged blood vessel. Blood loss is stopped through **coagulation**, the process of turning liquid blood into a semisolid clot composed of platelets and red blood cells held together by the protein **fibrin**. The process of coagulation is a complex cascade of reactions involving proteins called **clotting factors**:

- Platelet aggregation is initiated by the exposure to **von Willebrand factor (vW)** and **tissue factor (TF)**.

- During coagulation, the protein **fibrinogen (factor I)** is converted to fibrin by the enzyme **thrombin (factor IIa)**.
- **Prothrombin (factor II)** is a precursor to thrombin.

Figure 1.8. The Coagulation Cascade

Coagulation can follow two possible pathways:

- The **intrinsic pathway** is activated via damage within a blood vessel:
    - This pathway is monitored by measuring the activated partial thromboplastin time (aPTT).
    - Heparin disrupts the intrinsic pathway.
- The **extrinsic pathway** is activated by damage outside the vasculature.
    - This pathway is monitored by measuring the prothrombin time (PT).
    - Warfarin disrupts the extrinsic pathway.
- Both pathways activate clotting factor X and produce a fibrin clot; **fibrinolysis** is the disintegration of the blood clot.

Helpful Hint

Most clotting factors are designated by Roman numerals. These numerals give the order in which factors were discovered—not the order in which they are activated.

Helpful Hint

The liver is highly involved in the synthesis and removal of clotting components. Chronic liver disease often leads to coagulation disorders caused by the decreased synthesis of clotting factors and the poor clearance of activated factors.

Quick Review Question

3. Congenital hypofibrinogenemia is an inherited condition characterized by low circulating levels of fibrinogen (150 mg/dL). What abnormal laboratory values should a nurse expect in a patient with severe hypofibrinogenemia?

Answer Key

1. Blood from the lungs is returned to the left side of the heart. When the left side cannot pump this blood back out to the body, fluid builds up in the lungs, resulting in pulmonary edema. Blood from the body is returned to the right side of the heart, so right-sided failure causes fluid to build up in the abdomen and extremities.

2. The nurse should suspect an occlusion in the femoral artery, which is located proximal to the weak pulses and the site of claudication.

3. Fibrinogen (clotting factor I) is a substrate necessary for coagulation. Patients with very low fibrinogen levels are at risk for severe bleeding and will have prolonged PTs, INRs, PTTs, and aPTTs.

Chapter 2 – Cardiac Diseases and Risk Factors

Risk Factors

Atherosclerosis

<u>Pathophysiology</u>

Atherosclerosis, also called **atherosclerotic cardiovascular disease (ASCVD)**, is a progressive condition in which plaque builds up in the tunica intima of arteries. Plaque deposits begin in childhood and may grow larger throughout adulthood. The initial stage of atherosclerosis includes fatty streaks composed of macrophages that have absorbed lipids. Over decades, more lipids are deposited and older cells become calcified, creating an atheroma. This **atheroma**, or plaque, may eventually become fibrous, creating **fibroatheroma** (also called **fibrous plaque**).

The presence of advanced atherosclerosis places patients at a high risk for several cardiovascular conditions:

- Arteries may become **stenotic**, or narrowed, limiting blood flow to specific areas of the body (e.g., carotid stenosis).

- When a plaque **ruptures**, the plaque and the clot that forms around it (**superimposed thrombus**) can quickly lead to complete occlusion of the artery (e.g., myocardial infarction [MI]).

- The clots or loosened plaque released by a rupture may also move through the bloodstream and occlude smaller vessels (e.g., ischemic stroke).

Atherosclerosis is also a cause of **aneurysms** (widened arteries), which weaken arterial walls, increasing the risk of arterial dissection or rupture (e.g., abdominal aortic aneurysm). Atherosclerosis can occur in any artery and is categorized according to the location of the plaque buildup:

- **coronary artery disease (CAD):** narrowing of the coronary arteries
- **peripheral artery disease (PAD):** narrowing of the peripheral arteries
- **renal artery stenosis:** narrowing of the renal arteries
- **cerebrovascular disease:** dysfunction in the cerebrovascular system; most commonly caused by atherosclerosis

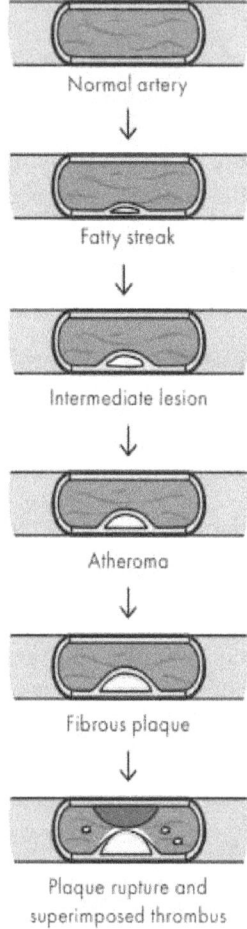

Figure 2.1. Progression of Atherosclerosis

Demographics

- some degree of atherosclerosis common in people older than age 65
- more common in males
- 75% of all acute MIs caused by plaque rupture

Risk Factors

- dyslipidemia
- hypertension
- smoking
- diabetes
- obesity
- family history
- poor diet
- sedentary lifestyle

Quick Review Question

1. A patient recovering from an atherectomy asks the nurse what to do to prevent further buildup of plaque in the arteries. What should the nurse tell the patient?

Diabetes

Pathophysiology

Diabetes mellitus is a metabolic disorder affecting insulin production and insulin resistance. It requires long-term management with insulin or oral hypoglycemic drugs. Diabetes mellitus is classified as type 1 or type 2:

- **Type 1 diabetes** is an acute-onset autoimmune disease predominant in children, teens, and adults under the age of 30. Beta cells in the pancreas are destroyed and unable to produce sufficient amounts of insulin, causing blood sugar to rise.
- **Type 2 diabetes** is a gradual-onset disease predominant in adults over age 40, but it can develop in individuals of all ages. Type 2 diabetes is not an autoimmune disease; instead, the person develops insulin resistance, which prevents the cellular uptake of glucose and causes blood sugar to rise.

Diabetes is highly correlated with CVD:

- At least 68% of people over the age of 65 with diabetes die from CVD.
- Approximately 16% of people over age 65 with diabetes die from stroke.
- People with diabetes develop CVD at a younger age than do those without diabetes.

Demographics

- affects over 11% of US population
- can occur in any ethnicity but is most common in Americans of African descent
- type 1 most common in childhood
- type 2 most common in adults over age 40

Symptoms, Physical Findings, and Diagnostic Tests

- the 3 Ps of diabetes:
  - polyuria
  - polydipsia
  - polyphagia
- elevated blood sugar: fasting blood glucose levels (> 126mg/dL)
- elevated glucose tolerance test: (blood glucose level > 200mg/dL)
- elevated HgbA1C (HbA1C):
  - normal (no diabetes): 4% – 5.6%
  - at risk for diabetes: 5.7% – 6.4%
  - diabetes: ≥6.5%

Management

People with type 1 diabetes need insulin injections or continuous insulin infusions through a pump. The various types of insulin and information concerning their onset, peak, and duration are described in Table 2.1.

Table 2.1. Types of Insulin

Type of Insulin	Onset	Peak	Duration
rapid acting [insulin lispro injection (Humalog);insulin aspart injection (Novolog)]	15 – 30 minutes	1 – 2 hours	3 – 6 hours
short acting (regular insulin)	30 minutes – 1 hour	2 – 4 hours	3 – 6 hours
intermediate acting [neutral protamine Hagedorn insulin (NPH)]	2 – 4 hours	8 – 10 hours	10 – 18 hours
Long-acting [insulin glargine (Lantus); insulin detemir (Levemir)]	1 – 2 hours	None	19 – 24 hours

People with type 2 diabetes may be able to control the disease with lifestyle changes, such as dietary improvements and exercise routines; however, some people with type 2 diabetes may require medication management with oral hypoglycemic drugs, including the following:

- sulfonylureas (e.g., glipizide, glimepiride)
- meglitinides (repaglinide and nateglinide)
- thiazolidinediones (pioglitazone and rosiglitazone)
- metformin

- alpha-glucosidase inhibitors (acarbose [Precose] and miglitol [Glyset])

Quick Review Question

2. A patient with diabetes has a fasting blood glucose level of 98 mg/dL, but an HgbA1C of 7.0. The patient asks why the diabetes is not considered under control, since the fasting blood glucose is with the normal range. How should the nurse respond?

Dyslipidemia

Pathophysiology

Dyslipidemia is an abnormal level of lipids, including cholesterol and triglycerides, in the blood. The most common form of dyslipidemia is **hyperlipidemia**, or elevated lipids within the blood. Dyslipidemia is usually asymptomatic but is correlated with heart disease. There are several types of cholesterol, each of which plays a different role in predicting CVD:

- High levels of **low-density lipoprotein (LDL)** are a risk factor for atherosclerosis. LDL is measured as LDL cholesterol (LDL-C).
- High levels of **high-density lipoprotein (HDL)** are inversely correlated with cardiovascular risk. HDL is measured as HDL cholesterol (HDL-C).
- High levels of **triglycerides** are correlated with cardiovascular risk related to atherosclerosis.

Demographics

- more common in Asian Indians, Filipinos, and US Hispanics/Latinos than in other ethnicities
- more common in males
- more common with advancing age

Risk Factors

- heredity
- chronic medical conditions (e.g., diabetes, renal failure)
- lifestyle factors (e.g., high-fat diet, smoking)
- medications (e.g., beta blockers, corticosteroids, antivirals)

Diagnostic Tests

- normal LDL-C: 100 mg/dL
- normal HDL-C: >60 mg/dL
- normal cholesterol: 200 mg/dL

Management

Dyslipidemia is initially managed through lifestyle changes, including weight loss, dietary changes, regular exercise, and smoking cessation. Medications are usually considered for patients with high cholesterol (>200 mg/dL) or high LDL-C (>190 mg/dL) levels that have not been lowered by lifestyle changes. Medications are also considered for patients with LDL-C >70 mg/dL when the individual also has certain other conditions (e.g., atherosclerosis, diabetes):

- **Statins** [e.g., atorvastatin (Lipitor), simvastatin (Zocor)] are a class of medications used to lower cholesterol.
- Nonstatin medications may also be used to lower cholesterol and include ezetimibe (Zetia) and fenofibrate (Fenoglide).
- Niacin may also be prescribed to increase HDL alongside other medications for hyperlipidemia.

Quick Review Question

3. A patient diagnosed with hyperlipidemia tells the nurse that, despite following a healthy diet, she has high cholesterol levels and wants to know why. How should the nurse respond?

Hypertension

Pathophysiology

Hypertension is blood pressure >120/80 mm Hg. Because blood pressure readings can vary, at least 2 readings on separate days must be taken to diagnose hypertension. **Primary (essential) hypertension** occurs with no known cause; it is highly correlated with lifestyle factors, including smoking, inactivity, obesity, high alcohol intake, and a high-sodium diet.

Secondary hypertension has a known primary cause, such as medication or an endocrine disorder. Persistent hypertension can cause organ damage and is a risk factor for other cardiac disease processes.

Table 2.2. Assessing for Hypertension	
Category	Description
Elevated blood pressure	systolic BP 120 – 129 mm Hg
	diastolic BP 80 mm Hg
Stage 1 hypertension	systolic BP 130 – 139 mm Hg
	diastolic BP 80 – 90 mm Hg
Stage 2 hypertension	systolic BP ≥140 mm Hg
	diastolic BP ≥90 mm Hg
Hypertensive urgency	systolic BP >180/110 mm Hg without evidence of organ dysfunction
Hypertensive crisis	systolic BP >180 mm Hg and/or a diastolic BP >120 mm Hg, accompanied by evidence of impending or progressive organ dysfunction

Demographics

- affects >30% of US population
- more common in Americans of African descent than in other ethnicities
- more common in males 50
- more common in females >50

Management

Initial management of chronic hypertension includes the following types of lifestyle changes:

- decreased salt intake
- DASH diet (high in fruits, vegetables, and lean meats; low in sugar and red meat)
- increased exercise
- weight loss
- reduced caffeine intake

First-line pharmacological treatments include the following:

- ACE inhibitors
- ARBs
- calcium channel blockers
- thiazide diuretics

> **Helpful Hint**
> Statin-associated muscle symptoms are a common side effect of statin use. Symptoms include muscle weakness, aches, and cramps. In rare cases, statin use may lead to rhabdomyolysis or muscle necrosis.

> **Helpful Hint**
> **White coat syndrome** is hypertension with no other symptoms that occurs only when an individual is in a clinical setting in the presence of health care providers.

Quick Review Question

4. A patient has an initial blood pressure reading of 160/95 mm Hg and expresses concern about being diagnosed with hypertension and needing to be on lifelong hypertensive medications. What actions should the nurse take?

Lifestyle Factors

Certain lifestyle choices can increase a person's risk for CVD. These choices are referred to as **modifiable risk factors** because people can lower their risks by modifying their behaviors. The main modifiable risk factors for CVD are discussed below.

Smoking

- Smoking is a strong risk factor for many cardiovascular conditions, including MI, stroke, atherosclerosis, and heart failure.
- Smoking increases mortality after cardiovascular catheterization and other surgical interventions.

- Smoking is estimated to account for one-third of all cardiovascular deaths in the United States.
- Smoking just 1 cigarette a day increases the risk of CVD by 50%.
- Cardiovascular risk increases with the duration and number of cigarettes smoked.
- All patients with acute or chronic cardiovascular conditions should be asked about tobacco use and offered support for smoking cessation.

Diet

The relationship between diet and CVD is complex, and our understanding of it continues to improve. Across countries, increases in the consumption of refined carbohydrates, trans fatty acids, and meat is linked to dramatic increases in CVD. Patients diagnosed with cardiovascular conditions should be educated on the components of a healthy diet that lowers CVD risk. A healthy diet has the following components:

- includes foods with a low glycemic index
- involves moderate alcohol consumption or abstinence
- is high in fruits and vegetables
- is high in lean protein
- is high in fiber
- is low in trans fatty acids
- avoids red meat
- avoids processed foods

> **Helpful Hint**
>
> Some OTC cold and cough medicines contain decongestants like pseudoephedrine, which may increase blood pressure.

Patients with hypertension should also be encouraged to follow a low-salt diet.

Exercise

It is estimated that a lack of physical activity increases the risk of CVD twofold. Exercise offers numerous potential cardiovascular benefits:

- weight loss
- increased overall cardiovascular fitness
- increased HDL
- reduced blood pressure

Only moderate levels of exercise are needed to see cardiovascular benefits. Patients diagnosed with cardiovascular conditions should be educated on aspects of a healthy exercise program:

- Adults should try to get 150 minutes of moderate aerobic activity or 75 minutes of intense aerobic activity every week.
- Exercise programs should also include muscle-strengthening activities and activities to improve mobility.

- Patients with coronary heart disease should undergo cardiac rehabilitation under professional supervision to rebuild exercise tolerance.

Obesity

Obesity is linked to morbidity from many conditions (e.g., CVD, hypertension, stroke) and is categorized according to BMI [$BMI = body\ weight$ (in kg) $\div height$ (in meters^2)]:

- underweight: 18.5 kg/m^2
- normal weight: 18.5 – 24.9 kg/m^2
- overweight: 25.0 – 29.9 kg/m^2
- obesity, class I: 30.0 – 34.9 kg/m^2
- obesity class II: 35.0 – 39.9 kg/m^2
- obesity class III: ≥40 kg/m^2 (also referred to as severe, extreme, or massive obesity)

A large waist circumference is considered a good indicator of cardiovascular risk:

- ≥102 cm (40 in) for males
- ≥88 cm (35 in) for females

Quick Review Question

5. A patient diagnosed with hypertension asks the nurse if a different diet could lower the risk of having a heart attack. How should the nurse respond?

Acute Coronary Syndrome (ACS)

Pathophysiology

Acute coronary syndrome (ACS) is an umbrella term for cardiac conditions in which thrombosis impairs blood flow in coronary arteries. **Angina pectoris** (commonly just called **angina**) is chest pain caused by narrowed coronary arteries and presents with negative troponin, an ST depression, and T wave changes:

- Stable angina usually resolves in about 5 minutes, is resolved with medications or with rest, and can be triggered by exertion, large meals, and extremely hot or cold temperatures.
- Unstable angina can occur at any time and typically lasts longer (>20 minutes). The pain is usually rated as more severe than stable angina and is not easily relieved by the administration of nitrates.
- **Variant angina** (also called **Prinzmetal angina** or **vasospastic angina**) describes episodes of angina and temporary ST elevation caused by spasms in the coronary artery; chest pain is easily relieved by nitrates.

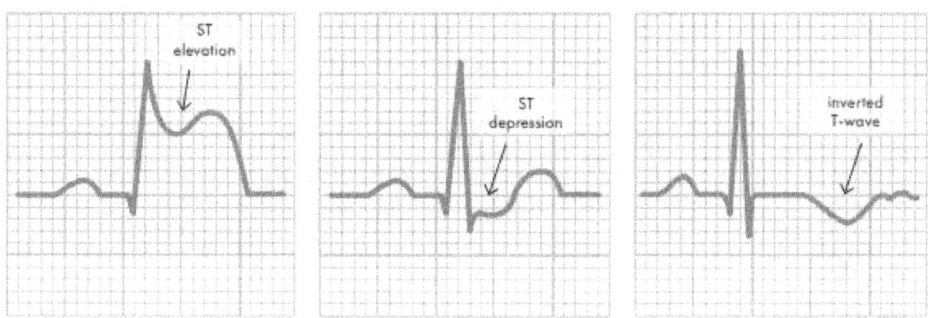

Figure 2.2. ECG Changes Associated with ACS

A **myocardial infarction (MI)**, or ischemia of the heart muscle, occurs when the coronary arteries are partly or completely occluded. MI is diagnosed via positive troponin and ECG changes; it is classified by the behavior of the ST wave. A **non-ST-elevation myocardial infarction (NSTEMI)** includes an ST depression and a T wave inversion. An **ST-elevation myocardial infarction (STEMI)** includes an elevated ST (> 1 mm), indicating a complete occlusion of a coronary artery. Signs, symptoms, and diagnostic findings for MI vary depending on which coronary artery is occluded:

- **anterior-wall MI:** occlusion of the LAD artery, which supplies blood to the anterior of the left atrium and ventricle:
    - ST changes in V1 – V4
    - increased risk of left ventricular failure (and subsequent cardiogenic shock)
    - increased risk of second-degree, type II heart block and bundle branch blocks
    - increased risk of ventricular septal rupture (usually 2 – 7 days post-MI)
- **inferior-wall MI:** occlusion of the RCA, which supplies blood to the right atrium and ventricle, the SA node, and the AV node:
    - ST changes in II, III, aVF
    - presents with bradycardia and hypotension
    - increased risk of AV heart blocks (e.g., first-degree AV block)
    - increased risk for papillary muscle rupture
    - cautious use of beta blockers and nitrates to avoid reducing preload
- **right ventricular infarction:** may occur with inferior-wall MI
    - ST changes in V4R – V6R
    - presents with tachycardia, hypotension, and jugular vein distention (JVD)
    - treated with positive inotropes
    - avoid preload-reducing medications (beta blockers, diuretics, morphine, nitrates)
- **lateral-wall MI:** occlusion of the left circumflex artery, which supplies blood to the left atrium and the posterior/lateral walls of the left ventricle (ST changes may be seen in I, aVL, V5, or V6)

- **posterior-wall MI:** occlusion of the RCA or left circumflex artery, with ST elevation in V7 – V9 and ST depression in V1 – V4

Demographics

- angina
    - experienced by >9 million individuals in the United States each year
    - more common in females, especially females of African descent
    - common in individuals with CAD
    - in males, most common between ages 55 and 65
- MI
    - more common in males
    - occurs most often in the early morning hours and on Mondays
    - >1.5 million MIs occurring every year (in the United States)

> **Helpful Hint**
> Papillary muscle rupture is a rare but serious complication that occurs 2 – 8 days post MI. Patients will present with hemodynamic compromise; pulmonary edema, new, loud systolic murmur; and a large V wave in PAOP. Papillary muscle rupture usually requires immediate surgical repair.

Symptoms and Physical Findings

- continuous chest pain that may radiate to the back, arm, or jaw (possible Levine's sign)
- upper abdominal pain (more common in adults >65, people with diabetes, and females)
- dyspnea
- nausea or vomiting
- dizziness or syncope
- diaphoresis and pallor
- palpitations

Diagnostic Tests

- elevated troponin (>0.01 ng/mL)
- elevated CK-MB (>2.5%)

Management

- 160 – 325 mg aspirin (chewed and swallowed); clopidogrel for patients who cannot take aspirin
- NSTEMI: continual monitoring; may require PCI; initially treated with medication:
    - nitroglycerin for vasodilatation of coronary arteries
    - beta blockers or calcium channel blockers to reduce myocardial oxygen demand
    - heparin to improve blood flow
    - morphine if pain is not relieved by nitroglycerin

- STEMI: immediate fibrinolytic therapy or PCI
    - goal for door to balloon time: 90 minutes
    - goal for door to fibrinolytic therapy: 30 minutes

Quick Review Question

6. A patient with a new complaint of chest pain and left arm pain is found clutching his chest. He is in bed and appears pale and diaphoretic. His heart rate is 55 bpm. What priority interventions should the cardiac nurse take?

Cardiomyopathies

Cardiomyopathy is abnormal functioning of the heart muscles. Symptoms and physical findings of cardiomyopathy are similar to those of HF and vary with the location and degree of dysfunction. Types of cardiomyopathies include dilated, hypertrophic, and restrictive.

Figure 2.3. Dilated Congestive Cardiomyopathy

Figure 2.4. Hypertrophic Cardiomyopathy

Figure 2.5. Restrictive Cardiomyopathy

Table 2.3. Pathophysiology and Management of Cardiomyopathy	
Type of Cardiomyopathy	**Management**
• **Dilated congestive cardiomyopathy (DCCM)** occurs • when damage to the myofibrils causes dilation in the • ventricles, causing enlargement and systolic impairment (40% ejection fraction). • DCCM has a high mortality rate: the 2-year survival rate is 50%, and most patients will die within 10 years of diagnosis. • See Figure 2.3.	• beta blockers, ACE inhibitors (ARBs if patient is ACE intolerant), and diuretics • implantable defibrillator or cardiac resynchronization therapy
• **Hypertrophic cardiomyopathy (HCM)** is an inherited disorder characterized by left ventricular hypertrophy and diastolic dysfunction. • In **obstructive HCM**, cardiac output (CO) is decreased.	• beta blockers, calcium channel blockers, and antidysrhythmic agents • implantable defibrillator

Chapter 2 – Cardiac Diseases and Risk Factors

Table 2.3. Pathophysiology and Management of Cardiomyopathy

Type of Cardiomyopathy	Management
• The stiffening of the ventricle septum obstructs the left ventricle outflow tract and disrupts mitral valve function, resulting in a decreased preload and an increased afterload. • Hypertrophic cardiomyopathy is one of the most common causes of sudden death in adolescent athletes. • See Figure 2.4.	• **contraindicated:** ACE inhibitors, digoxin, vasodilators, and diuretics
• **Restrictive cardiomyopathy (RCM)** occurs when fibrous tissue builds up within the ventricles, resulting in diastolic dysfunction and decreased CO. • Systolic function is usually normal. • Unlike other cardiomyopathies, in RCM the ventricles will not be enlarged or hypertrophic. • See Figure 2.5.	• diuretics; beta blockers and calcium channel blockers used cautiously • **contraindicated:** digoxin, nitrates
• **Ischemic cardiomyopathy** is impaired left ventricular functioning caused by CAD and the resulting ischemia and ventricular remodeling.	• ACE inhibitors • beta blockers

Quick Review Question

7. The nurse is completing a medication reconciliation on a patient admitted with HF symptoms and a history of HCM. The home medications include metoprolol, diltiazem (Cardizem), and digoxin. Which medication should the nurse be concerned about?

Dysrhythmias

A **cardiac dysrhythmia** is an abnormal heartbeat or rhythm. Dysrhythmias are typically caused by a malfunction in the heart's cardiac conductions system. Most dysrhythmias of clinical importance are caused by **reentry**: the re-excitation of the heart by an electrical impulse that did not die out. Reentry dysrhythmias include A-fib, atrial flutter, V-tach, and V-fib. Treatment is based on whether the patient is deemed hemodynamically stable or unstable:

- stable patients: noninvasive interventions or drugs to correct an abnormal rhythm
- unstable patients: appropriate electrical therapy

> **Helpful Hint**
>
> When treating dysrhythmias, medical staff should always consider a hypotensive patient to be unstable.

Bradycardia

Pathophysiology

Bradycardia is a heart rate of 60 bpm. It results from a decrease in the sinus node impulse formation (automaticity). Bradycardia is normal in certain individuals and does not require an intervention if the patient is stable. Symptomatic patients, however, need immediate treatment to address the cause of bradycardia and to correct the dysrhythmia.

Symptoms and Physical Findings

- hypotension
- syncope
- confusion
- dyspnea

Management

- stable, asymptomatic patients: no intervention required; may be monitored for the development of symptoms
- symptomatic, hemodynamically stable patients: monitor while determining underlying cause
- symptomatic, hemodynamically unstable patients: medication
    - first line: atropine 0.5 mg for first dose, with a maximum of 3 mg total
    - second line: dopamine or epinephrine if atropine is ineffective or if maximum dose of atropine already given and patient is still stable
    - patients with bradycardia and who have had a heart transplant: administer isoproterenol; atropine is ineffective in these patients
    - unstable patients who do not respond to medication: TCP

Figure 2.6. ECG: Bradycardia

Quick Review Question

8. A patient presents with complaints of confusion, dizziness, and dyspnea. The patient's blood pressure is 72/40 mm Hg, with a heart rate of 32 bpm and O_2 saturation of 92% on room air. What priority intervention should the nurse prepare for?

Narrow-Complex Tachycardias

Pathophysiology

Narrow-complex tachycardias (also called **supraventricular tachycardias [SVTs]**) are dysrhythmias with >100 bpm and a narrow QRS complex (0.12 seconds). The dysrhythmia originates at or above the bundle of His (supraventricular), resulting in rapid ventricular activation. Narrow-complex tachycardias are often asymptomatic.

Symptoms and Physical Findings

- palpitations
- chest pain
- hypotension
- dyspnea

Management

- first-line treatment for SVT: vagal maneuvers
- rapid bolus dose of adenosine (6 mg) to restore sinus rhythm if dysrhythmia continues; second dose (this time 12 mg) may be administered if chemical cardioversion does not occur within 1 – 2 minutes
- for refractory SVT:
    - stable patients: calcium channel blockers, beta blockers, or digoxin may also be given
    - unstable patients and patients for whom medications are ineffective: synchronized cardioversion required

Quick Review Question

9. A patient in SVT is unresponsive to vagal maneuvers. What intervention is likely to be ordered next?

Atrial Fibrillation And Flutter

Pathophysiology

Atrial fibrillation (A-fib) is an irregular narrow-complex tachycardia. During A-fib, the heart cannot adequately empty, causing blood to pool and clots to form, increasing stroke risk. The irregular atrial

> **Helpful Hint**
>
> A-fib is the most common cardiac dysrhythmia. It occurs in approximately 2 – 6 million individuals in the United States annually.

contractions also decrease CO. The ECG in A-fib will show an irregular rhythm with no P waves and an undeterminable atrial rate (Figure 2.7.).

Figure 2.7. ECG: Atrial Fibrillation (A-fib)

During **atrial flutter**, the atria beat regularly but too fast (240 – 400 bpm), causing multiple atrial beats in between the ventricular beat. Atrial flutter can be regular or irregular. The ECG in atrial flutter will show a saw-toothed flutter and multiple P waves for each QRS complex (Figure 2.8.).

Figure 2.8. ECG: Atrial Flutter

Management

- adenosine: slows the rhythm so that it may be identified; will not convert dysrhythmia to a sinus rhythm
- hemodynamically stable patients:
  - calcium channel blockers, beta blockers, or cardiac glycoside to slow the rhythm
  - antidysrhythmics to convert to sinus rhythm
  - hemodynamically unstable patients: cardioversion required
  - anticoagulants to lower risk of stroke
  - cardiac ablation may be used to correct A-fib and atrial flutter

Quick Review Question

10. A patient presents with A-fib. Vital signs are as follows:
    - BP 125/80 mm Hg
    - HR 150 bpm
    - RR 23

What intervention should the nurse anticipate?

Ventricular Tachycardia And Fibrillation

Pathophysiology

Ventricular tachycardia (V-tach) is tachycardia originating below the bundle of His, resulting in slowed ventricular activation. During V-tach, ≥3 consecutive ventricular beats occur at a rate >100 bpm. V-tach is often referred to as a wide-complex tachycardia because of the width of the QRS complex.

> **Helpful Hint**
>
> **Torsades de pointes**, a type of V-tach with irregular QRS complexes, occurs with a prolonged QT interval. It can be congenital or caused by antidysrhythmics, antipsychotics, hypokalemia, or hypomagnesemia.

Because the ventricles cannot refill before contracting, patients in this rhythm may have reduced CO, resulting in hypotension. V-tach may be short and asymptomatic, or it may precede V-fib and cardiac arrest.

Figure 2.9. ECG: Monomorphic Ventricular Tachycardia (V-tach)

During **ventricular fibrillation (V-fib)**, the ventricles contract rapidly (300 – 400 bpm) with no organized rhythm. There is no CO. The ECG will initially show coarse V-fib with an amplitude >3 mm (Figure 2.10.). As V-fib continues, the amplitude of the waveform decreases, progressing through fine V-fib (3 mm) and eventually reaching asystole.

Figure 2.10. ECG: Ventricular Fibrillation (V-fib)

Management

- priority intervention for V-tach: check for pulse
    - for pulseless V-tach: follow ACLS protocols
    - for V-tach with a pulse, patient stable: administer amiodarone
    - for V-tach with a pulse, patient unstable (hypotensive): synchronized cardioversion
    - patients with recurrent V-tach: may require implantable defibrillator or radiofrequency ablation
- for V-fib: follow ACLS protocols:
    - immediately initiate high-quality CPR at 100 – 120 compressions per minute
    - defibrillation ASAP, before administration of any drugs
    - defibrillation doses: 200 J → 300 J → 360 J (biphasic)
    - ≥ 2 defibrillation attempts should be made for patients in V-fib before giving any medications
    - first line: epinephrine 1 mg every 3 – 5 minutes
    - shock-refractory V-fib: amiodarone (300 mg as first dose and 150 mg for second dose)

Quick Review Question

11. The nurse is participating in a cardiac resuscitation attempt of a patient found in V-fib. A total of two defibrillation attempts have been made, and 1 dose of epinephrine has been given 2 minutes earlier. What priority action should the nurse take next?

Pulseless Electrical Activity (PEA)/Asystole

Pathophysiology

Pulseless electrical activity (PEA) is an organized rhythm in which the heart does not contract with enough force to create a pulse. **Asystole**, also called a "flat line," occurs when there is no electrical or mechanical activity within the heart (Figure 2.11). Both PEA and asystole are nonshockable rhythms with poor survival rates.

Figure 2.11. ECG: Asystole

Chapter 2 – Cardiac Diseases and Risk Factors

Management

- immediate, high-quality CPR
- epinephrine 1 mg every 3 – 5 minutes until circulation returns or a shockable rhythm emerges
- immediate attempts to determine and treat underlying cause, particularly H's and T's (common causes of PEA and asystole):
  - hypovolemia
  - hypoxia
  - hydrogen ion (acidosis)
  - hyperkalemia/hypokalemia
  - hypothermia
  - toxins
  - tamponade
  - tension pneumothorax
  - thrombosis (coronary or pulmonary)

Quick Review Question

12. A patient is found in bed and unresponsive to commands. The person appears cyanotic, and the nurse determines there is no pulse and no breathing present. What should the nurse do first?

Heart Failure (HF)

Pathophysiology

Heart failure (HF) occurs when either one or both of the ventricles in the heart cannot efficiently pump blood, resulting in decreased CO. The condition is typically due to another disease or illness, most commonly CAD. **Acute decompensated heart failure** is the sudden onset or worsening of HF symptoms. The American Heart Association classifies HF into four stages:

- Stage A: high risk of developing heart failure
- Stage B: diagnosis of left systolic ventricular failure with no symptoms
- Stage C: diagnosis of heart failure, with symptoms
- Stage D: advanced symptoms that have not improved with treatment

HF is classified according to the left ventricular ejection fraction. Impairment of systolic function results in **heart failure with reduced ejection fraction (HFrEF, or systolic HF)**, classified as an ejection fraction of 50%. **Heart failure with preserved ejection fraction (HFpEF, or diastolic HF)** is characterized by an ejection fraction of >50% and diastolic dysfunction.

Table 2.4. Systolic Versus Diastolic Heart Failure

Systolic HF (HFrEF)	Diastolic HF (HFpEF)
• reduced ejection fraction (50%) • dilated left ventricle • S3 heart sound • hypotension	• normal ejection fraction • no enlargement of heart • S4 heart sound • hypertension

HF can also be categorized as left-sided or right-sided, depending on which ventricle is affected. **Left-sided HF** is usually caused by cardiac disorders (e.g., MI, cardiomyopathy) and produces symptoms related to pulmonary function. **Right-sided HF** is caused by right ventricle infarction or pulmonary conditions (e.g., PE, COPD) and produces symptoms related to systemic circulation. Unmanaged left-sided HF can lead to right-sided HF.

Demographics

- in the United States, >500,000 new cases of HF every year
- more common in Americans of African descent than in other ethnicities
- equally common in males and females

Risk Factors

- CAD
- MI
- congenital heart disease
- cardiomyopathy
- alcohol abuse

> **Helpful Hint**
>
> **Cor pulmonale**, or impaired functioning of the right ventricle, is caused by pulmonary disease or pulmonary hypertension.

Symptoms and Physical Findings

Table 2.5. Symptoms and Physical Findings of Right- and Left-Sided Heart Failure (HF)

Left-Sided HF	Right-Sided HF
• increased LVEDP and left atrial pressures • increased PAP • dyspnea or orthopnea • pulmonary edema • tachycardia • bibasilar crackles	• increased right ventricular end-diastolic pressure (RVEDP) and right atrial pressures • increased CVP • increased PAP • dependent edema (usually in lower legs); ascites • jugular vein distention (JVD)

Table 2.5. Symptoms and Physical Findings of Right- and Left-Sided Heart Failure (HF)	
Left-Sided HF	**Right-Sided HF**
• cough, frothy sputum, hemoptysis • left-sided S3 sound • diaphoresis • pulsus alternans • oliguria	• hepatomegaly • right-sided S3 sound • weight gain • nausea, vomiting, abdominal pain • nocturia

Diagnostic Tests

- BNP >100 pg/mL
- echocardiogram to assess ejection fraction, ventricular hypertrophy, valve dysfunction
- chest X-ray to show cardiomegaly or pulmonary congestion

Management

- varying patient needs for pharmacological and surgical interventions, depending on the type and degree of HF
- improve CO and CI
- medications:
    - inotropic agents
    - vasodilators
    - ACE inhibitors, ARBs
    - digoxin
    - diuretics
    - beta blockers (decrease the risk of sudden cardiac death)
- other interventions: implantable cardioverter-defibrillator (ICD), a permanent pacemaker, an IABP, a ventricular assist device (VAD), or a transplant

Quick Review Question

13. A patient presents with sudden onset dyspnea, JVD, and peripheral edema. What laboratory test would confirm a diagnosis of acute decompensated heart failure?

Hypertensive Crisis

Pathophysiology

Hypertensive crises include hypertensive urgency and hypertensive emergencies. **Hypertensive urgency** occurs when BP is >180/110 mm Hg without evidence of organ dysfunction. A **hypertensive emergency** occurs when systolic BP is >180 mm Hg or when diastolic BP is >120 mm Hg and when either of these is accompanied by evidence of impending or progressive organ dysfunction. Hypertensive crises increase the risk of cerebral infarction, and prolonged hypertension can lead to heart or renal failure.

Symptoms and Physical Findings

- usually asymptomatic
- headache
- blurred vision
- dizziness
- dyspnea
- retinal hemorrhages
- epistaxis
- chest pain

Management

- blood pressure reduction: limited to a decrease of ≤25% within the first 2 hours to maintain cerebral perfusion
- labetalol, hydralazine, clonidine, or metoprolol (first-line medications)
- quiet, non-stimulating environment for relaxation
- oxygen administration

Quick Review Question

14. A patient is found to be alert and oriented with a BP of 200/100 mm Hg and is asymptomatic. What priority intervention should the nurse take?

Infective Endocarditis

Pathophysiology

Infective endocarditis occurs when an infection causes inflammation of the endocardium. The inflammation impairs valve function and may also disrupt the electrical conduction system. The most common cause of infection is bacterial, but the infection may also be fungal or viral. Staphylococcus aureus and Streptococcus account for about half of all cases. Infective endocarditis can occur secondary to surgical valve replacement; these cases have high mortality rates.

Demographics
- more common in males
- more common in people of European descent than in other ethnicities
- affects > 30,000 individuals each year in the United States

Risk Factors
- heart-valve problems or surgery involving heart valves
- recent implantation of cardiac device
- immunocompromised individuals
- poor dental health or recent dental work
- central venous line access
- rheumatic heart disease
- IV drug abuse

Symptoms and Physical Findings
- general signs and symptoms of infection (e.g., fever, chills, anorexia)
- petechiae
- splinter hemorrhages under fingernails
- Janeway lesions, Osler nodes, or Roth spots
- arthralgias
- dyspnea

Diagnostic Tests
- ECG may show dysrhythmias (A-fib or AV block most common)
- echocardiogram to assess valves
- blood cultures showing bacteria present in the bloodstream
- possibly elevated WBC

Management
- aggressive treatment with IV antimicrobials
- pharmacologic management of symptoms: antipyretics, diuretics, or dysrhythmics
- surgical repair of valves if necessary

Quick Review Question

15. A patient is admitted with signs of infective endocarditis. What priority interventions should the nurse expect to perform?

Pericarditis

Pathophysiology

Pericarditis is the inflammation of the pericardium, the lining that surrounds the heart. When inflammation occurs, fluid can accumulate, resulting in pericardial effusion. When the effusion is large enough to impair the ability of the heart to pump blood sufficiently, the condition is called **pericardial tamponade**.

Pericarditis can be classified into 3 categories: acute, subacute, or chronic:

- **Acute pericarditis** occurs quickly (6 weeks).
- **Subacute pericarditis** usually occurs over a few months.
- **Chronic pericarditis** occurs for >6 months.

Demographics

- more common in males
- more common in individuals 20 – 50 years old
- more common in Americans of African descent than in other ethnicities

Risk Factors

- mostly idiopathic
- secondary to MI, cardiac surgery, or thoracic trauma

Symptoms and Physical Findings

- chest pain:
    - sudden and severe
    - increases with movement, lying flat, and inspiration
    - decreases by sitting up or learning forward
    - radiates to neck
    - pericardial friction rub
    - tachycardia (usually the earliest sign)
    - tachypnea or dyspnea
    - fever, chills, and cough

Diagnostic Tests

- ECG:
    - ST elevation possible, usually in all leads except aVR and V1
    - tall, peaked T waves
- chest X-ray showing "water bottle" silhouette in pericardial effusion

- echocardiogram that may show pericardial effusion, thickening, or calcifications

Management

- symptoms management:
  - pain not relieved by nitroglycerin or rest
  - NSAID [e.g., ibuprofen or indomethacin (Indocin)]
  - placing patient in comfortable position (e.g., leaning over a bedside table)
  - bed rest
  - oxygen
- treat underlying conditions (e.g., antibiotics, steroids, or corticosteroids)
- pericardiocentesis or pericardial window if effusion needs to be drained
- complications: dysrhythmias, cardiac tamponade, heart failure

Quick Review Question

16. A patient with acute pericarditis complains of sudden chest pain, and a pericardial friction rub can be heard on auscultation. What interventions should the nurse expect to perform to treat this patient?

Congenital Heart Defects

Congenital heart defects are heart structure abnormalities that exist at birth.

Table 2.6. Pathophysiology and Management of Congenital Heart Defects	
Defect	**Management**
Atrial septal defect (ASD), an abnormal opening in the atrial septum, results from a lack of formation of septal tissue: • Oxygen-rich blood flows through the hole from the left atrium to the right atrium (left-to-right shunting) instead of flowing normally into the left ventricle. • This shunting can lead to increased pulmonary hypertension and enlargement of the right atrium. • The most common symptom in children is a midsystolic pulmonary flow or ejection murmur. • See Figure 2.12.	• monitoring; intervention only required when symptomatic • defects 6 mm: high likelihood of spontaneous closure • surgical or endovascular repair when ASD does not close • symptomatic patients: beta blockers, anticoagulants, diuretics, and digoxin

Table 2.6. Pathophysiology and Management of Congenital Heart Defects

Defect	Management
Patent ductus arteriosus (PDA) occurs when the fetal ductus arteriosus does not close within the first few weeks of life: • Without closure, blood flows from the aorta to the pulmonary artery. • This alteration in blood flow increases the workload of the left side of the heart and causes pulmonary congestion. • Symptoms include murmur with a characteristic machine-like sound and poor feeding/weight gain. • See Figure 2.13.	• preterm infants: indomethacin and ibuprofen to close patent ductus • monitoring; intervention only required when symptomatic • PDA closed surgically or percutaneously when infant is at safe weight
The foramen ovale is an opening that allows oxygen-rich blood to move from the right to left atrium in the fetus, bypassing the fetus's lungs (which are nonfunctional): • The foramen ovale normally closes after birth because of increased blood pressure from the left side of the heart. • A **patent foramen ovale (PFO)** is when this hole fails to close.	• do not normally need to be closed; managed with medication to prevent blood clots • catheter closure when necessary
Tetralogy of Fallot consists of 4 defects within the heart (**PROVe** mnemonic): 1. **P**ulmonic stenosis 2. **R**ight ventricular hypertrophy 3. **O**verriding aorta 4. **Ve**ntricular septal defect Patients may experience transient cyanotic episodes (tet spells). See Figure 2.14.	• open surgery before 1 year of age • pharmacological management of cyanosis and HF symptoms before surgery
Transposition of the great arteries, sometimes called dextro-transposition of the great arteries, occurs when the vessels that carry blood from the heart to the lungs are reversed: • The aorta is attached to the right-sided ventricle instead of the left, and the	• immediate pharmacological or surgical intervention to ensure adequate oxygenation • surgery (atrial switch procedure) when infant is 3 – 5 days old

Chapter 2 – Cardiac Diseases and Risk Factors

Table 2.6. Pathophysiology and Management of Congenital Heart Defects

Defect	Management
pulmonary artery is attached to the left-sided ventricle instead of the right. • This type of heart defect is cyanotic in nature, meaning that deoxygenated blood is pumped into circulation.	
A **ventricular septal defect (VSD)** is an abnormal opening or hole between the right and left ventricles: • Blood flows through the opening into the pulmonary artery. • The increased blood volume into the lungs can cause increased pulmonary vascular resistance. See Figure 2.15.	• monitoring and possible closure (as with ASD) • pharmacological management for symptoms • high-calorie nutrition for infants

Figure 2.12. Atrial Septal Defect (ASD)

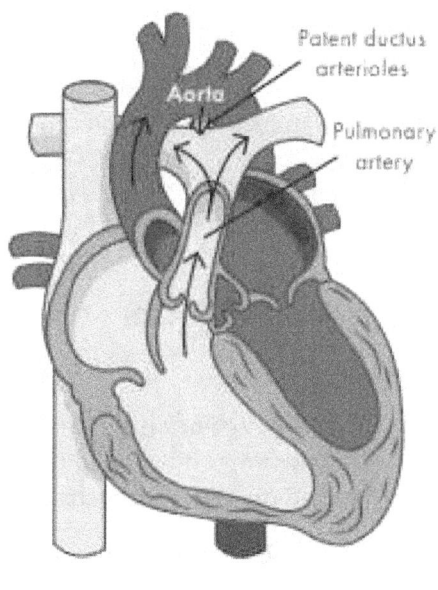

Figure 2.13. Patent Ductus Arteriosus (PDA)

Figure 2.14. Tetralogy of Fallot

Figure 2.15. Ventricular Septal Defect (VSD)

Chapter 2 – Cardiac Diseases and Risk Factors

Quick Review Question

17. The parents of a child diagnosed with a large ASD ask why their child will need a catheter procedure even though the child has no symptoms. How should the nurse respond?

Myocardial Conduction System Defects

Atrioventricular Blocks

Pathophysiology

An **atrioventricular (AV) block** is the disruption of electrical signals between the atria and the ventricles. The electrical impulse may be delayed (first-degree block), intermittent (second-degree block), or completely blocked (third-degree block).

A **first-degree AV block** occurs when the conduction between the SA and the AV nodes is slowed, creating a prolonged PR interval. A first-degree AV block is a benign finding that is usually asymptomatic, but it can progress to a second-degree or third-degree block.

The ECG in a first-degree AV block will show a prolonged PR interval of >0.20 seconds (Figure 2.16.).

Figure 2.16. ECG: First-Degree Atrioventricular (AV) Block

A **second-degree AV block**, type 1 (Wenckebach or Mobitz type 1), occurs when the PR interval progressively lengthens until the atrial impulse is completely blocked and does not produce a QRS impulse. This dysrhythmia occurs when the atrial conduction in the AV node or bundle of His is either being slowed or blocked. This type of block is cyclic; after the dropped QRS complex, the pattern will repeat itself.

The ECG in second-degree AV block, type 1, will show progressively longer PR intervals until a QRS complex completely drops (Figure 2.17.).

Helpful Hint

If the R is far from P, then you have a **first degree**. Longer, longer, longer, drop; this is how you know it's a *Wenckebach*. If some Ps just don't go through, then you know it's a **type 2**. If Ps and Qs don't agree, then you have a third degree.

A **second-degree AV block, type 2** (Mobitz type 2), occurs when the PR interval is constant in length but not every P wave is followed by a QRS complex. This abnormal rhythm is the result of significant conduction dysfunction within the His-Purkinje system.

Figure 2.17. ECG: Second-Degree AV Block, Type 1

The ECG in second-degree AV block, type 2, will show constant PR intervals and extra P waves, with dropped QRS complexes (Figure 2.18.).

Figure 2.18. ECG: Second-Degree AV Block, Type 2

A **third-degree AV block**, sometimes referred to as a **complete heart block**, is characterized by a complete dissociation between the atria and the ventricles. There are effectively 2 pacemakers within the heart, so there is no correlation between the P waves and the QRS complexes. The most common origin of the block is below the bundle of His, but the block can also occur at the level of the bundle branches of the AV node.

The ECG for third-degree AV block will show regular P waves and QRS complexes that occur at different rates. There will be more P waves than QRS complexes, with P waves possibly buried within the QRS complex (Figure 2.19.).

Figure 2.19. ECG: Third-Degree AV Block

Symptoms and Physical Findings

- first- and second-degree AV blocks usually asymptomatic
- may show symptoms of reduced CO (e.g., hypotension, dyspnea, chest pain)
- bradycardia

Management

- symptomatic patients: TCP possibly needed to manage symptoms
- implantable pacemaker if underlying cause cannot be resolved
- hypotensive patients: dopamine or epinephrine may be needed
- discontinue medications that slow electrical conduction in the heart (e.g., antidysrhythmic drugs)

Quick Review Question

18. A patient begins to complain of dizziness and weakness and appears diaphoretic. The nurse notes from the telemetry monitor that the patient is in a third-degree AV block, and the blood pressure reads 71/55 mm Hg, with a heart rate of 30 bpm. What interventions does the nurse expect?

Sinus Node Dysfunction (SND)

Pathophysiology

Sinus node dysfunction (SND), also known as **sick sinus syndrome (SSS)**, refers to dysrhythmias caused by a dysfunction in the SA node. An individual with SND can have bouts of bradycardia or tachycardia, or can alternate between the two. SND can also arise from an SA block or sinus arrest. Because of these irregular and usually unpredictable signals, most people with SND will need a permanent pacemaker. The ECG for SND will show alternating bradycardia, tachycardia, and sinus arrest (Figure 2.20.).

- Figure 2.20. ECG: Sinus Arrest

Symptoms and Physical Findings

- syncope
- fatigue
- dyspnea
- palpitations
- confusion

> **Helpful Hint**
>
> Atropine is ineffective for Mobitz type 2 and third-degree AV block. It only increases the firing of the SA node, and the block prevents the SA node from influencing ventricular contraction.

Management

- hemodynamically unstable patients: atropine and temporary pacing to correct bradycardia
- stable, asymptomatic patients: monitoring only
- symptomatic patients with recurrent episodes of bradycardia: implantable pacemaker required

Helpful Hint

Use non-dihydropyridine calcium channel blockers, beta blockers, and antidysrhythmic drugs with caution because they may worsen SA node dysfunction.

Quick Review Question

19. A patient with recurring episodes of bradycardia due to SND tells the nurse that she does not want to have surgery for a pacemaker, since she currently has no symptoms. What is the nurse's best response?

Bundle Branch Block (BBB)

Pathophysiology

Right bundle branch block (RBBB) and **left bundle branch block (LBBB)** are interruptions in conduction through a bundle branch. Bundle branch blocks (BBB) usually occur secondary to underlying cardiac conditions, including MI, hypertension, and cardiomyopathies. LBBB in particular is associated with progressive underlying structural heart disease and poor outcomes post-MI; however, both RBBB and LBBB may occur in the absence of heart disease.

Ischemic heart disease is the most common cause of both RBBB and LBBB. LBBB can also arise from other heart diseases, hyperkalemia, or digoxin toxicity. Other causes of RBBB include cor pulmonale, pulmonary edema, and myocarditis.

Helpful Hint

LBBB may mask the characteristic signs of MI on an ECG.

If the patient with a BBB is asymptomatic, no treatment is necessary. Patients with syncopal episodes may need to have a pacemaker inserted.

Figure 2.21. ECG: Bundle Branch Blocks (BBB)

Quick Review Question

20. A patient with HF develops a new-onset LBBB. What medication would be important to consider as a possible cause of the LBBB?

Congenital Conduction Defects

- **Wolff-Parkinson-White syndrome**, caused by an early excitation of an extranodal accessory pathway, results in tachycardia:
    - asymptomatic, or presents as sudden A-fib or paroxysmal tachycardia (HR>150)
    - ECG: short PR interval (0.12 seconds) with slurred QRS upstroke and wide QRS (>0.12 seconds)
    - treatment: synchronized cardioversion; unstable patients may require catheter ablation
    - contraindications: adenosine, digoxin, amiodarone, beta blockers, calcium channel blockers
- **Long QT syndrome** is a cardiac electrical disturbance that causes a prolonged ventricular repolarization (seen as a QT interval > 0.44 seconds on ECG):
    - asymptomatic, or presents with dysrhythmias (especially torsades de pointes), syncope, seizure, or sudden cardiac death
    - management: beta blockers and placement of an ICD
    - contraindications: medications likely to prolong the QT interval
- **Brugada syndrome** is a genetically inherited cardiac electrical pathway syndrome that is linked to 4 – 12% of all sudden cardiac deaths:
    - characteristic ECG findings with sudden cardiac arrest, ventricular tachydysrhythmias, or syncopal episodes to diagnose
    - ECG: pseudo-RBBB and persistent ST-segment elevation
    - ECG abnormalities may be unmasked by sodium channel blockers
    - treat with medication (quinidine or flecainide) or ICD placement
    - contraindications: medications likely to prolong the QT interval

> **Helpful Hint**
>
> Caution should be exercised when administering antipsychotics, antidepressants, and anticonvulsants if the QT is >0.45 seconds.

Quick Review Question

21. A combative patient with schizophrenia develops torsades de pointes in the ICU. What medications may have caused this dysrhythmia?

Pulmonary Edema

Pathophysiology

Pulmonary edema is characterized by fluid accumulation in the lungs and is caused by extravasation of fluid from pulmonary vasculature into the interstitium and alveoli of the lungs. The fluid impairs respiration and may lead to acute respiratory failure.

Cardiogenic pulmonary edema develops secondary to a decrease in left ventricular function. The decrease in left-side function increases pulmonary venous pressure and capillary pressure in the lungs, forcing fluid from the vasculature into interstitial spaces. Common causes of acute cardiogenic pulmonary edema (ACPE) include acute decompensated HF, MI, severe dysrhythmias, hypertensive crises, valvular disease, or complications of cardiopulmonary bypass.

Symptoms and Physical Findings

- severe, sudden onset of dyspnea
- blood-tinged sputum
- orthopnea (requiring high-Fowler's positioning)
- anxiety, irritability, or restlessness
- tachycardia
- inspiratory fine crackles, rales, or wheezing
- other symptoms and physical findings of right-sided HF

Diagnostic Tests

- chest X-ray that shows intestinal edema
- PAOP >25 mm Hg

Management

- immediate objective: to improve oxygenation and reduce pulmonary congestion
- O_2 therapy: noninvasive (e.g., BiPAP) preferred; intubation possibly required
- morphine to reduce anxiety and afterload
- diuretic therapy [e.g., furosemide (Lasix)] to reduce fluid overload
- vasodilator therapy (e.g., nitroglycerin) to reduce preload and afterload
- medication to improve contractility (digoxin, dopamine, dobutamine)
- aminophylline to prevent associated bronchospasm (may increase risk of tachycardic dysrhythmias)
- identification and treatment of the underlying cause

Quick Review Question

22. A patient being treated for refractory V-tach develops severe orthopnea and dyspnea; the lung sounds are coarse, with rales throughout. What is the probable cause of these symptoms and physical findings, and what testing is likely to be ordered to confirm the diagnosis?

Pulmonary Hypertension (PH)

Pathophysiology

Pulmonary hypertension (PH) is a mean pulmonary arterial pressure >25 mm Hg at rest or >30 mm Hg while exercising. (A normal pulmonary arterial pressure is 15 mm Hg.) PH is caused by increased pulmonary vascular resistance and increased pulmonary venous pressure. These increases can lead to right ventricular hypertrophy, which can ultimately cause heart failure. PH is classified by the World Health Organization into five groups based on etiology:

- Group I: pulmonary arterial hypertension (PAH) that is inherited or caused by congenital disorders, drug use, or conditions not included in other groups
- Group II: PH associated with left-sided heart disease
- Group III: PH associated with lung disease or hypoxemia
- Group IV: PH associated with chronic thrombotic or embolic disease
- Group V: PH with an unidentified etiology

Demographics

- more common in females
- much more common in people of European descent than in those of other ethnicities
- symptoms most commonly begin at age 30 – 50 years

Symptoms and Physical Findings

- dyspnea, worsening with activity
- dizziness
- syncope
- fatigue
- poor appetite
- right upper quadrant pain due to liver involvement
- possible hoarseness due to compression of laryngeal nerve by pulmonary artery
- JVD
- edema of lower extremities and abdomen

- midsystolic ejection murmur
- S4 sound

Diagnostic Tests

- right heart catheterization
- echocardiogram possibly needed to visualize heart chambers and blood flow

Management

- diuretics to reduce edema and congestion
- vasodilators (e.g., epoprostenol) to improve blood flow
- anticoagulants to prevent blood clots
- sildenafil (Viagra) or tadalafil (Cialis) to expand the blood vessels within the lungs
- calcium channel blockers to relax blood vessel walls

Quick Review Question

23. A patient is diagnosed with PAH and prescribed sildenafil (Viagra). The patient questions this medication, knowing that it is used for erectile dysfunction. How should the nurse respond to the patient's question?

Rheumatic Heart Disease (RHD)

Pathophysiology

Rheumatic heart disease (RHD) is an autoimmune reaction to rheumatic fever. It is triggered by infections of group A beta hemolytic streptococci, most commonly from untreated strep throat. RHD is characterized by carditis and valvulitis, especially in the mitral and aortic valves. Having RHD greatly increases the risk of developing mitral stenosis because of valve damage.

Demographics

- common cause of HF in developing countries; rare in populations with access to high-quality health care
- globally, >30 million individuals diagnosed with RHD
- more common in females
- rheumatic fever most common in children 5 – 15 years old
- RHD symptoms usually appear in adults between ages 20 – 50

Symptoms and Physical Findings

- fatigue
- dyspnea
- tachycardia

- chest pain
- joint pain
- cardiomegaly
- syncope
- murmurs related to mitral or aortic regurgitation

Diagnostic Tests

- echocardiogram

Management

- antibiotics to treat infected heart valves (possibly long term)
- anti-inflammatories to reduce heart-valve inflammation
- heart valve replacement if necessary

Quick Review Question

24. What combination of physical findings and medical history should cause a nurse to suspect RHD?

Shock

Cardiogenic Shock

Pathophysiology

Cardiogenic shock, a cyclical decline in cardiac function, results in decreased CO in the presence of adequate fluid volume. A lack of coronary perfusion causes or escalates ischemia/infarction by decreasing the ability of the heart to pump effectively. The heart rate increases in an attempt to meet myocardial oxygen demands; however, the reduced pumping ability of the heart reduces CO and CI, and demands for coronary or tissue perfusion are not met. LVEDP increases, which leads to stress in the left ventricle and an increase in afterload. This distress results in lactic acidosis. Cardiogenic shock is most commonly seen after an MI but can be associated with trauma, infection, or metabolic disease.

Symptoms and Physical Findings

- tachycardia and sustained hypotension (SBP 90 mm Hg)
- oliguria (30 mL/hr or 0.5 mL/kg/hour output)
- crackles
- tachypnea and dyspnea
- pallor
- JVD
- altered LOC

> **Helpful Hint**
>
> Left ventricular dysfunction caused by an anterior MI is the most common cause of cardiogenic shock.

- cool, clammy skin
- S3 heart sound possible

Diagnostic Tests

- CI 2.2 L/min/m^2
- PAOP >15 mm Hg
- elevated SVR, CVP
- decreased SvO_2, MAP
- elevated lactate
- ABG shows metabolic acidosis and hypoxia

Management

- main treatment goal: to identify and treat underlying cause, reduce cardiac workload, and improve myocardial contractility
- immediate IV fluids
- medications:
  - dobutamine or norepinephrine (to increase contractility and CO)
  - antiplatelet drugs (e.g., aspirin or clopidogrel)
  - thrombolytic drugs [e.g., alteplase (Activase) or reteplase]
  - morphine
  - nitroprusside (Nipride)
- other interventions:
  - IABP to reduce afterload and increase coronary perfusion
  - cardiac catheterization to improve myocardial perfusion and increase contractility
  - LVAD
- monitor patient for cardiac dysrhythmias

Quick Review Question

25. A patient presents with tachycardia, pallor, JVD, and crackles after emergent PCI for anterior MI. What hemodynamic findings for this patient would indicate cardiogenic shock?

Hypovolemic Shock

Pathophysiology

Hypovolemic shock (hypovolemia) occurs when rapid fluid loss decreases the circulating blood volume and cardiac output, resulting in inadequate tissue perfusion. **Hemorrhagic shock** is a type of hypovolemic shock in which blood is lost rapidly.

Risk Factors

- most common cause of hypovolemic shock: trauma
- in cardiac care setting, most common causes of hypovolemic shock: postoperative bleeding and diuresis

Symptoms and Physical Findings

- tachycardia
- hypotension
- tachypnea
- oliguria
- dizziness
- confusion
- weakness
- headache
- nausea
- diaphoresis
- cool, clammy skin

Diagnostic Tests

- electrolyte imbalances:
    - hyperkalemia
    - increased magnesium
    - hypernatremia
- increased BUN/creatinine:
    - increased lactate
- increased urine specific gravity and urine osmolality

> **Helpful Hint**
>
> Patients in early shock are often normotensive. Narrowed pulse pressure can be a better indicator of the patient's level of shock.

Management

- oxygen
- volume resuscitation with isotonic crystalloid (i.e., normal saline or lactated Ringer's)
- transfusion of blood products for hemorrhagic shock
- dopamine, epinephrine, norepinephrine, or dobutamine for refractory
- hypotension
- monitor for cardiac dysrhythmias

Quick Review Question

26. A patient recovering from a CABG begins to show signs of hemorrhagic shock, including tachycardia, tachypnea, hypotension, and oliguria. What interventions should the nurse expect?

Valvular Heart Disease

- In **aortic stenosis (AS)**, blood flow from the left ventricle to the aorta is impeded:
  - The pressure load on the left ventricle is increased, eventually leading to left ventricular hypertrophy and decreased CO and HF.
- Aortic regurgitation (AR) occurs when blood flows backward from the aorta to the left ventricle.
- Volume overload in the left ventricle leads to left ventricular hypertrophy and systolic dysfunction with a lowered ejection fraction.
- In mitral stenosis (MS), blood flow from the left atrium to the left ventricle is impeded, resulting in an enlarged atrium:
  - Almost all cases of mitral stenosis are caused by rheumatic heart disease, with most patients showing symptoms ≥15 years after the initial infection.
  - Mitral regurgitation (MR) occurs when the blood flows backward from the left ventricle to the left atrium.
  - This backward flow increases the preload and decreases the afterload.
  - Aortic and mitral valve disease presents with symptoms and physical findings similar to HF; they include dyspnea, exercise intolerance, angina, and dizziness or syncope.
- Symptomatic patients will require surgical valve repair or replacement (e.g., transcatheter aortic valve replacement).

> **Helpful Hint**
> Diuretics, beta blockers, and vasodilators should be avoided in patients with AS because they can worsen symptoms.

Quick Review Question

27. What heart sound is associated with aortic stenosis?

Answer Key

1. The nurse should tell the patient that some lifestyle choices can slow the progression of atherosclerosis. Topics to discuss with the patient include a healthy diet and exercise regimen, smoking cessation, and the management of dyslipidemia.

2. The nurse should explain that a blood glucose result gives an accurate representation of the blood sugar at that specific moment, but an HgbA1C result shows how well controlled the blood sugar has been over approximately 3 months; therefore, the best way to determine compliance and the plan of care is based on the HgbA1C result.

3. The nurse should inform the patient that diet is only one risk factor for dyslipidemia. Lack of exercise or a sedentary lifestyle, along with smoking or excessive alcohol use, can also contribute to dyslipidemia. Additionally, some individuals have a genetic predisposition for dyslipidemia and may have elevated cholesterol levels even with regular exercise and a healthy diet.

4. The nurse should make sure that the correct cuff size is being used and should check the blood pressure a second time, preferably on the opposite arm unless contraindicated. The nurse can also inform the patient that a diagnosis of hypertension must be made after 2 separate elevated blood pressures are confirmed on 2 separate days.

5. The nurse should provide the patient with educational materials on how to build a healthy diet. The patient should be encouraged to try a diet low in fat and red meat and high in fruits, vegetables, lean protein, and fiber. The nurse should also tell the patient that reducing sodium intake can help lower blood pressure.

6. The main priority for this patient is obtaining a 12-lead ECG to rule out a STEMI. Additional priorities include obtaining labs, specifically a troponin and electrolyte panel; monitoring the patient's vital signs; applying oxygen if the person is hypoxic; and placing the patient on telemetry to continuously monitor cardiac rhythm.

7. Digoxin is contraindicated with hypertrophic cardiomyopathy (HCM), as the medication is a positive inotropic and can reduce LV filling and increase obstruction of the left ventricular outflow tract. The medication should be verified with the patient, and the admitting physician should be notified immediately.

8. This patient is hemodynamically unstable because of bradycardia. The nurse should prepare to push IV atropine.

9. If the patient in SVT does not respond to vagal maneuvers, the patient will likely be administered 6 mg of adenosine to terminate the dysrhythmia.

10. The nurse should expect a hemodynamically stable patient with A-fib to receive calcium channel blockers, beta blockers, or cardiac glycosides to decrease the heart rate.

11. After two defibrillation attempts and the first dose of epinephrine has been given, the nurse should prepare the first dose of amiodarone (300 mg) to be given next.

12. The nurse should activate the code team and begin high-quality compressions immediately. (CPR should not be delayed to administer epinephrine.)

13. A BNP lab value of >100 pg/mL indicates heart failure (HF).

14. After confirming that the BP reflects a hypertensive crisis, the nurse should administer an antihypertensive medication but should aim for a reduction of no more than 25% within the first 2 hours.

15. The nurse should expect orders to get an ECG and draw labs to monitor the patient's WBC count, sedimentation rate, and C-reactive protein; the nurse should also expect to collect at least 2 sets of blood cultures. The nurse should plan to administer antibiotics after the blood cultures have been drawn.

16. The nurse should obtain a 12-lead ECG and then have the patient sit up and lean forward, a position that can help reduce the pain. The nurse can also administer an NSAID such as ibuprofen or indomethacin to assist with pain control and reduce inflammation.

17. The nurse should explain that the hole between the atria allows oxygenated blood to flow back into the right atrium. The increased blood volume in the right atrium causes the muscles of the heart to enlarge. While the child has no symptoms now, an enlarged heart will eventually lead to dysrhythmias and heart failure when the child is an adult. Closing the hole early allows the heart muscle to regain normal size and prevents future symptoms.

18. The nurse should prepare the patient for TCP. Dopamine and epinephrine may be appropriate medications to administer for a third-degree block as they will increase the overall heart rate.

19. The nurse should explain that the absence of symptoms does not mean that underlying conditions are gone. Without the pacemaker, the patient risks developing additional dysrhythmias or could go into cardiac arrest without warning.

20. Digoxin, often administered for the treatment of HF, has a narrow therapeutic index. Digoxin toxicity may manifest itself as an LBBB. Labs would need to be drawn to assess for digoxin toxicity.

21. There is a strong association between antipsychotic medication use and torsades de pointes in patients with prolonged QT. The patient may have been administered haloperidol, which is one of the most commonly used medications in the ICU associated with torsades de pointes.

22. Because of the patient's dysrhythmia and the presented symptoms, pulmonary edema should be suspected. Confirmation through a chest X-ray will reveal anomalies, especially pleural effusions and basal congestion due to accumulation of fluid within the alveolar space.

23. The nurse should explain that sildenafil (Viagra) can be used to treat erectile dysfunction but that it is also used to treat PAH because it relaxes and widens the blood vessels within the lungs, which allows for better activity tolerance.

24. A patient with RHD will have a history of untreated rheumatic fever and usually will have had untreated strep throat. The patient will also show symptoms and physical findings related to valve dysfunction, including fatigue, dyspnea, and regurgitation murmurs.

25. Cardiogenic shock is characterized by symptoms and physical findings of hypoperfusion combined with a systolic BP of 90 mm Hg, a CI of 2.2 L/min/m^2, and a normal or elevated PAOP (> 15 mm Hg).

26. The nurse should expect to provide IV fluids or blood products to the patient and to prepare the patient to return to the operating theater.

27. In aortic stenosis, an S4 heart sound may be heard. This extra heart sound, heard before S1, is caused by the atrial contraction of blood into a noncompliant ventricle.

Chapter 3 - Arterial and Venous Diseases

Abdominal Aortic Aneurysm (AAA)

Pathophysiology

An **abdominal aortic aneurysm (AAA)**, often called a **triple A**, occurs when the lower aorta is enlarged. The AAA is the most common type of aneurysm. Other common aneurysms include thoracic aneurysms and thoracoabdominal aortic aneurysms.

An **aortic rupture**, a complete tear in the wall of the aorta, rapidly leads to hemorrhagic shock and death. An **aortic dissection** is a tear in the aortic intima; the tear allows blood to enter the aortic media. Both aortic rupture and dissection will lead to hemorrhagic shock and death without immediate intervention.

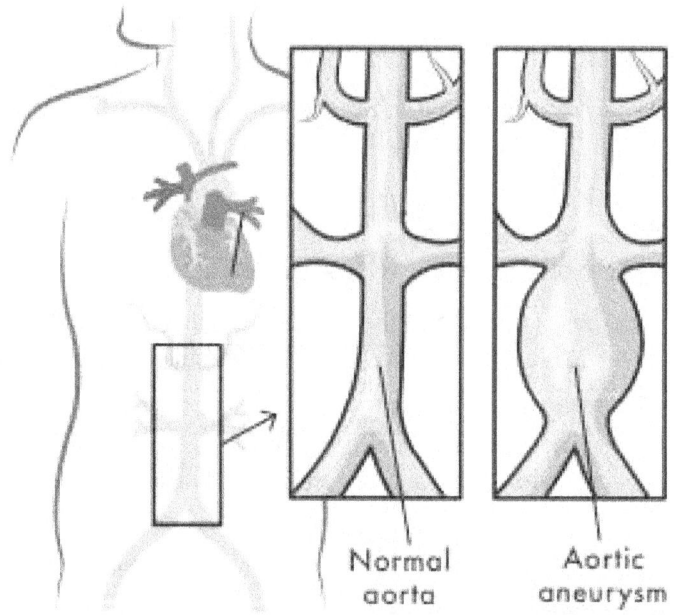

Figure 3.1. Abdominal Aortic Aneurysm (AAA)

Demographics

- more common in males
- affects approximately 4 – 8% of US population
- most common in patients aged 60 and older
- more common in Caucasians than in other ethnicities

Symptoms and Physical Findings

- usually asymptomatic unless rupture or dissection occurs
- rupture or dissection:
    - sharp, severe pain in the chest, back, abdomen, or flank; often described as "tearing"
    - a blood pressure difference of ≥20 mm Hg between the left and right arms
    - new-onset murmur
    - signs and symptoms of hypovolemic shock

Diagnostic Tests

- CT scan
- TEE
- Angiogram
- chest MRI

Management

- treatment determined by size of aneurysm
- small aneurysms: monitoring, medications, and/or lifestyle changes:
    - maintain normal BP and low cholesterol
    - smoking cessation
    - beta blockers
    - follow-up CTs at 3- or 6-month intervals
- aneurysms >5 cm or rapidly enlarging aneurysm: surgery or endovascular repair
- aneurysm dissection or rupture: emergency surgery

Quick Review Question

1. A patient is in the cardiology clinic for monitoring of a previously diagnosed AAA that has remained 4 cm in size. The patient asks the nurse if the AAA will need to be surgically repaired. How should the nurse respond?

Pseudoaneurysm

Pathophysiology

Pseudoaneurysms may be aortic, cardiac, femoral (the most common), or visceral. They most often occur as the result of trauma (e.g., from endovascular procedures, mitral valve surgery, congenital heart surgery); penetrating lesions (e.g., atherosclerotic, myocardial infarction); or infection (e.g., endocarditis, pancreatitis with pseudocyst fistula).

An **aneurysm** is a ballooning of the vascular wall with the blood contained in the dilated vessel wall, whereas a **pseudoaneurysm** results from a disruption (e.g., a puncture) of the vascular wall that allows blood to leak into surrounding tissues. This blood forms a hematoma that is encased in a capsule formed by fibrin and platelets. The capsule is usually round or oval shaped, different from the fusiform or saccular shape of a true aneurysm.

Symptoms and Physical Findings

- pain and swelling at the site
- a pulsatile mass with bruit
- skin discoloration or ischemia if the blood flow is compromised

Management

- watchful waiting
- compression
- thrombin injection (ultrasound guided, although surgical repair or endovascular embolization may be indicated for a large pseudoaneurysm)

Quick Review Question

2. If a patient develops a small (2 cm) asymptomatic pseudoaneurysm after a femoral catheterization, what is the most likely treatment?

Carotid Artery Occlusive Disease (CAOD)

Pathophysiology

Carotid artery occlusive disease (CAOD), or **stenosis**, is a narrowing or hardening of the carotid arteries, usually caused by atherosclerosis. The artery may be occluded, or plaque may break off and travel to the brain, causing a TIA or an ischemic stroke. Carotid artery stenosis may be asymptomatic and is usually diagnosed after a CVA. It is the most common cause of ischemic strokes.

Demographics

- more common in males
- more common in Native Americans and people of European descent than in other ethnicities

Symptoms and Physical Findings

- can be asymptomatic
- carotid bruits
- diminished carotid pulse
- dizziness
- blurry vision

> **Helpful Hint**
>
> Positive inotropes are contraindicated in patients with aortic dissection because the medications increase stress on the aortic wall.

Diagnostic Tests

- arteriography
- carotid ultrasound to examine blood flow

Management

- carotid artery 50% blocked: lifestyle changes and medications
  - maintain normal BP and low cholesterol
  - antiplatelet or anticoagulant
- carotid artery >50% blocked: surgical intervention [carotid artery angioplasty or carotid endarterectomy (CEA)]

Quick Review Question

3. A patient is diagnosed with carotid artery stenosis and asks the nurse why this condition puts a person at greater risk for having a stroke. How should the nurse respond?

Chronic Venous Insufficiency (CVI)

Pathophysiology

Chronic venous insufficiency (CVI) occurs when the veins within the legs do not move blood effectively because of inadequate muscle pump function, damaged venous valves, or thrombosis. Blood then pools within the veins, and blood flow to the heart is diminished.

Demographics

- more common in females
- more common in adults >50 years of age
- approximately 6 – 7 million Americans with CVI

Risk Factors

- immobility
- prolonged sitting or standing
- DVT
- obesity
- pregnancy
- family history

Symptoms and Physical Findings

- distended vessels
- varicose veins
- lower extremity edema

Chapter 3 - Arterial and Venous Diseases

- pain that increases with movement
- a feeling of tightness or stretching of the legs
- itching feeling in lower extremities
- skin discoloration
- leg muscle cramps or spasms
- venous ulcers

Helpful Hint

Patients with CVI should be educated on proper skin hygiene to prevent skin infections.

Diagnostic Tests

- venous duplex ultrasound

Management

- most patients managed without medication or invasive procedures:
  - elevation of legs to promote blood flow back to the heart
  - compression stockings to apply pressure to legs and keep blood flowing
  - exercise to increase circulation
  - higher-fiber diet to help control CVI
  - reduced-sodium diet to prevent excess fluid accumulation
- surgical or endovascular procedures (vein ablation or venous bypass) for patients who do not respond to noninvasive management

Quick Review Question

4. A nurse is caring for a patient with CVI. What type of diet should the nurse teach the patient to follow?

Deep Vein Thrombosis (DVT)

Pathophysiology

A **deep vein thrombosis (DVT)** is the most common form of acute venous occlusion; it occurs when a thrombus forms within a deep vein. DVT is most common in the lower extremities.

Risk Factors

- Virchow's triad
  - hypercoagulability (e.g., due to estrogen, contraceptive use, or malignancy)
  - venous stasis (bed rest or any other activity that results in decreased physical movement)
  - endothelial damage (damage to the vessel wall from trauma, drug use, inflammatory processes, or other causes)

- pregnancy, hormone replacement therapy, oral contraceptives
- recent surgery

Demographics

- most common in adults >45 years of age
- more common in males

Symptoms and Physical Findings

- pain localized to a specific area (usually the foot, ankle, calf, or behind the knee)
- unilateral edema, erythema, and warmth
- positive Homans sign

Diagnostic Tests

- elevated D-dimer
- venous duplex ultrasonography to diagnose

Management

- anticoagulants (first-line treatments)
- thrombolytics; may be administered when anticoagulants are ineffective
- possible requirement for surgical or endovascular thrombectomy
- possible placement of inferior vena cava filter to avoid a pulmonary embolism in patients who cannot tolerate anticoagulants

Quick Review Question

5. A patient diagnosed with a DVT complains of dyspnea. What is the priority intervention for this patient?

Peripheral Vascular Insufficiency

Pathophysiology

Atherosclerosis that occurs in peripheral arteries leads to **peripheral vascular insufficiency** [also called **peripheral arterial disease (PAD)**]. **Acute peripheral vascular insufficiency** (also called **acute arterial occlusion**) occurs when a thrombus or an embolus occludes a peripheral artery and causes ischemia and possibly the loss of a limb. This condition is a medical emergency requiring prompt treatment to prevent tissue necrosis.

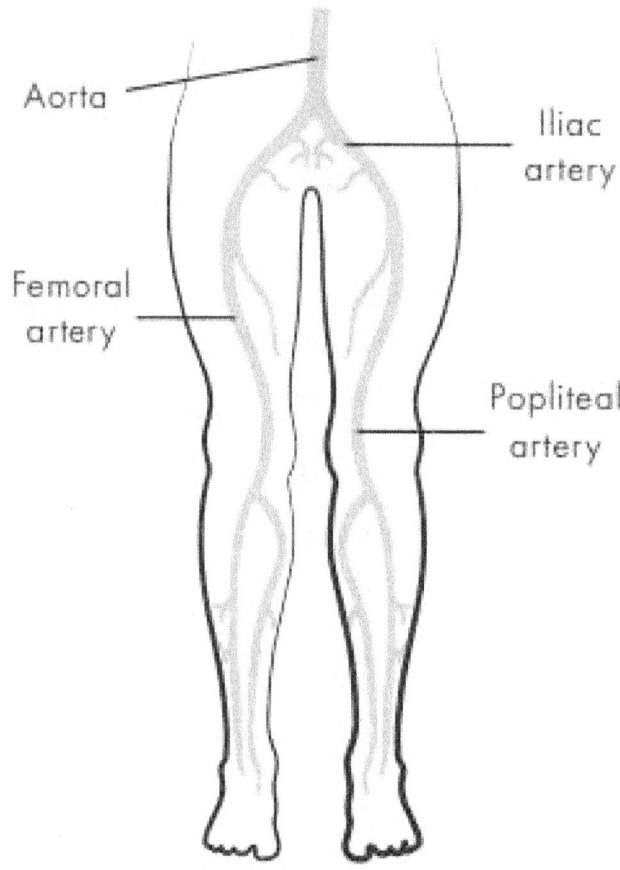

Figure 3.2. Common Locations of Acute Peripheral Vascular Insufficiency

Demographics

- approximately 10% of US population affected by lower extremity arterial disease
- more common in males
- more prevalent with age
- more prevalent in Americans of African descent than in those of other ethnicities

Risk Factors

- valvular heart disease

- trauma
- fractures and compartment syndrome
- circumferential burns
- A-fib
- heart failure

Symptoms and Physical Findings

- the 6 Ps (hallmark signs) of an arterial occlusion:
    - pain (intermittent claudication)
    - pallor
    - pulselessness
    - paresthesia
    - paralysis
    - poikilothermia
- petechiae (visible with microemboli)
- ABI 0.30 (indicating poor outcome of limb survivability)

Diagnostic Tests

- duplex ultrasonography, CT angiography, or catheter-based arteriography
- elevated D-dimer

Management

- pharmacological management: thrombolytics, anticoagulants (e.g., heparin), and antiplatelet agents
- other interventions: embolectomy, catheter-directed thrombolysis, or bypass surgery
- nursing considerations for arterial occlusion:
    - frequent pulse and neurovascular checks to monitor for worsening of condition or other changes
    - do not elevate extremity or apply heat
    - thrombolytic therapy, typically for 4 – 24 hours; reevaluation via angiogram; monitoring for symptoms and physical findings of bleeding

Quick Review Question

6. Catheter-directed thrombolysis is performed on a patient with an acute arterial occlusion in the lower right leg. What are the most important nursing interventions?

Cerebrovascular Accident (CVA)

A **cerebrovascular accident (CVA)**, also known as a **stroke**, is a neurological emergency where blood flow to the brain is stopped or blocked. There are 2 types of stroke: hemorrhagic and ischemic.

Hemorrhagic Stroke

Pathophysiology

A **hemorrhagic stroke** occurs when a vessel ruptures in the brain or when a brain aneurysm bursts. The blood that accumulates in the brain leads to increased intracranial pressure (ICP) and edema, both of which damage brain tissue and cause neurological impairment. Hemorrhagic stroke is an emergent condition that requires immediate and aggressive care in order to prevent further bleeding.

Demographics

- more common in males
- accounts for approximately 10% – 20% of strokes
- more common in Americans of African descent and Hispanics/Latinos

Risk Factors

- hypertension
- trauma
- blood thinners
- oral contraceptives
- excessive consumption of alcohol
- cocaine use

Symptoms and Physical Findings

- severe, sudden headache
- sudden onset of weakness
- difficulty speaking
- difficulty walking
- lethargy
- altered LOC, or coma (using Glasgow Coma Scale [GCS])

Diagnostic Tests

- immediate CT scan necessary to show location of bleed

Management

- protect patient's airway; intubation and mechanical ventilation may be required
- common complications: hypertension, increased ICP, seizures

- immediately discontinue and/or reverse anticoagulants and antiplatelets
- possible need for surgery or a thrombectomy
- contraindicated: NSAIDs, fibrinolytics, lumbar puncture

Quick Review Question

7. What is the nursing priority for a patient experiencing a hemorrhagic stroke?

Ischemic Stroke

Pathophysiology

An **ischemic stroke** occurs when blood flow within an artery in the brain is blocked, leading to ischemia and damage to brain tissue. The lack of blood flow can be caused by a thrombosis or an embolus.

Demographics

- accounts for approximately 80% of strokes
- twice as common in Americans of African descent than in other groups
- more common in males

Risk Factors

- history of previous strokes or TIA
- atherosclerosis or CAD
- history of A-fib
- sickle cell disease
- cocaine and/or amphetamine use
- vasculitis

Symptoms and Physical Findings

- facial drooping, usually on one side
- numbness, paralysis, or weakness on one side of the body
- slurred speech or inability to speak
- confusion
- vision changes
- dizziness or loss of balance control
- sudden onset of severe headache
- arm drift possible

- **National Institutes of Health Stroke Scale (NIHSS)** to quantitatively measure the patient's neurological deficits:
  - lowest score: 0 (no deficits)
  - highest score: 42 (severe stroke)

Diagnostic Tests

- CT scan without contrast a priority to exclude hemorrhage
- bedside glucose test to rule out hypoglycemia as cause of symptoms

Management

- administer tissue plasminogen activator (tPA) if CT scan is negative for hemorrhage:
  - within 3 – 4.5 hours of the last time patient was seen as normal
  - dosing: 0.9 mg/kg, with a maximum dose of 90 mg, with 10% of dose given as an IV push bolus and the remainder given through infusion
  - BP strictly controlled: 185 mm Hg systolic and 110 mm Hg diastolic
  - monitor for bleeding
- tPA contraindicated in patients with hemorrhagic stroke, head trauma, or recent neurosurgery or stroke
- frequent neurological checks
- possible thrombectomy to remove clot

Quick Review Question

8. Upon entering a patient's room, the nurse notices that the patient, who previously had a GCS of 15, now has slurred speech, a left-sided facial droop, and seems confused. What interventions should the nurse prioritize?

Answer Key

1. The nurse should explain that an AAA that remains at 4 cm has a low risk of rupture and does not need surgical intervention. The medical provider will likely recommend surgical repair if the aneurysm grows to >5 cm or if it begins to enlarge rapidly.

2. Small asymptomatic pseudoaneurysms (i.e., 2 cm) often require no treatment other than watchful waiting with ultrasound exams to monitor blood flow. If there is still bleeding, compression may be applied.

3. The nurse should explain that the plaque within the carotid artery can become dislodged and travel through the vessels to the brain, where pieces of plaque can block blood vessels. This blockage prevents blood flow to the brain, causing a stroke.

4. The patient with CVI should follow a low-sodium, high-fiber diet to reduce fluid buildup.

5. Patients with DVT and dyspnea should immediately have a CT scan ordered to rule out a pulmonary embolism (PE). A PE is an emergent condition that needs immediate treatment.

6. The nurse should ensure strict bedrest and make sure that the affected extremity is kept straight. The nurse should also assess the site frequently and notify the physician for bleeding, coldness, increased pain, or decreased pulse. NPO status should be initiated 8 hours before reevaluation.

7. The nursing priority is to manage complications from the stroke (especially hypertension, ICP, and seizures) and to prepare the patient for possible surgery.

8. The nurse should prioritize preparing the patient for an immediate CT scan to rule out a hemorrhagic stroke and to see if the patient meets the criteria for tPA administration. The nurse should also assess the patient's neurological deficits using the NIHSS. The patient's blood pressure and heart rhythm should also be closely monitored.

Chapter 4 – Patient Interviews and Cardiac and Vascular Assessment

Taking a Focused Cardiovascular History

The following topics should be covered when taking a focused cardiovascular history:

- signs and symptoms
- current medications (including over-the-counter medications, recreational drugs, herbal remedies, and topical treatments)
- allergies (food and medications)
- lifestyle habits (nutrition, exercise, tobacco use, alcohol use)
- medical history
- surgical history
- family history

Common cardiac and vascular symptoms to look for include the following:

- chest, jaw, or arm pain
- upper abdominal or lower back pain (more common in adults >65 years of age, people with diabetes, and women)
- nausea or vomiting
- diaphoresis
- light-headedness, dizziness, or syncope
- weakness or fatigue
- dyspnea
- palpitations
- numbness or tingling

When taking a focused cardiovascular history, you should also ask the patient about preceding events that could have triggered the onset of symptoms, such as the following:

- extreme temperatures
- stress
- intercourse
- smoking

- eating

When assessing a patient's pain, use the acronym **PQRST**:

- **P**rovoking: What was happening when the pain started? What makes the pain better or worse?
- **Q**uality: What does the pain feel like (e.g., sharp, stabbing, dull, aching, burning)?
- **R**egion: Where is the pain located? Does the pain radiate or move to another area of the body?
- **S**everity: On a scale of 0 – 10 (10 being the worst pain imaginable), how bad is the pain?
- **T**iming: How long have you been experiencing this pain? When did it start? How long does it typically last?

Assess the patient's psychosocial status. The following are just some of the factors that can affect a patient's psychosocial status:

- psychiatric history
- current/past work history
- financial situation
- educational history
- spiritual/cultural preferences
- violence assessment
- coping skills

Quick Review Question

1. An 80-year-old female patient with a history of angina states during her interview that she has been experiencing constipation, headaches, and severe lower back pain for the last twenty-four hours. Why would these symptoms require immediate follow-up from the nurse?

Physical Examination

Initial Survey

The **initial survey** is a rapid assessment to identify any life-threatening conditions:

- Assess the general appearance of the patient:
  - obvious wounds
  - level of consciousness (LOC)
  - signs of distress
  - skin color (e.g., rubor, pallor, jaundice, cyanosis)

- race and gender
- Evaluate **ABCs** (**a**irway, **b**reathing, and **c**irculation):
  - Airway: Ensure the patient has a patent airway.
  - Breathing: Assess the patient's breathing status and the need for any interventions.
  - Circulation: Assess for signs of cyanosis or decreased blood flow.
  - Whether the patient is unresponsive or not breathing: look, listen, and feel for 10 seconds or less, and then start CPR/ACLS protocols.

Quick Review Question

2. Upon entering a patient's room for assessment, the nurse notices that the patient appears newly diaphoretic and out of breath. What should the nurse's priority be, and what actions need to be taken?

Vital Signs

- Pulse: A normal pulse should be 60 – 100 bpm and regular:
  - The apex (or apical) pulse is heard using a stethoscope at the fifth intercostal space midclavicular.
  - Peripheral pulses are taken by palpating arteries in the extremities (see Figure 4.1.).

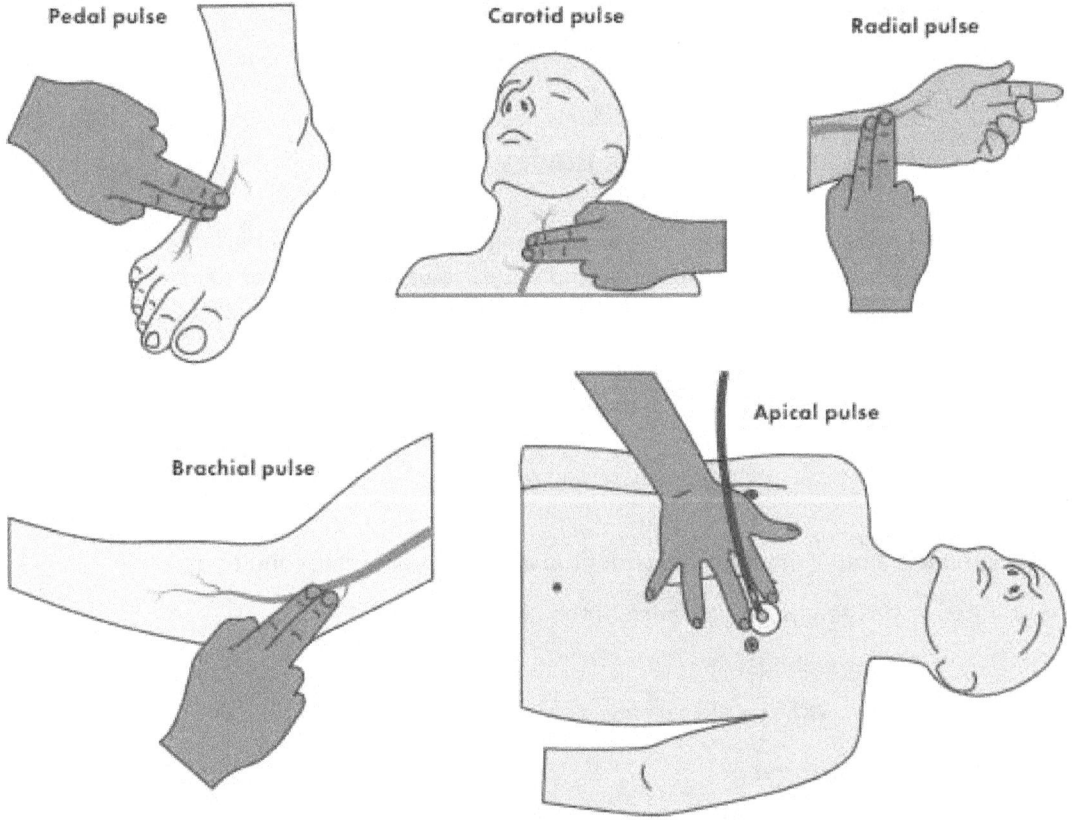

Figure 4.1. Location of Pulses

- Respirations: Normal respirations are 12 – 20 breaths per minute.
- **Blood pressure (BP)** is the pressure exerted by blood on the inside of blood vessels:
  - **Systolic blood pressure (SBP)** is the pressure that occurs while the heart is contracting.
  - **Diastolic blood pressure (DBP)** occurs while the heart is relaxed.
- The **pulse pressure** is the difference between the systolic and diastolic blood pressures (e.g., BP 120/80 = pulse pressure of 40).
- **Orthostatic blood pressure** is taken when the patient stands after having been lying down. A drop of 20 mm Hg in systolic blood pressure or 10 mm Hg after the patient has stood up from a lying position is considered abnormal.
- A **pulse deficit** is the difference between the patient's pulse rate and heart rate.
- The **ankle-brachial index (ABI)** is a ratio of the BP taken at the ankle and the BP taken at the brachial artery (upper arm):
  - $ABI = \dfrac{\text{systolic ankle BP}}{\text{systolic arm BP}}$
  - Normal ABI is 0.9 – 1.3. Lower values indicate occluded arteries caused by peripheral vascular disease (PVD); higher values are caused by abnormally hardened blood vessels.

> **Helpful Hint**
> Pulse deficits are often seen in patients with cardiac arrhythmias.

- **Oxygen saturation (blood oxygen)** is a measurement of the ratio of oxygen-saturated hemoglobin (red blood cells carrying oxygen) to unsaturated hemoglobin. Normal blood oxygen level is 94 – 100 percent.

Figure 4.2. Classifying Blood Pressure

Chapter 4 – Patient Interviews and Cardiac and Vascular Assessment

Quick Review Question

3. During a physical exam, the nurse finds that a patient's ABI is 0.55. The nurse should expect further testing for what condition?

Neurological Assessment

- Assess the patient's mental status, including LOC, alertness, orientation, and speech.
- The **Glasgow Coma Scale (GCS)** is the most commonly used, systematic, objective scoring tool for judging a patient's LOC.

Table 4.1. Scoring on the Glasgow Coma Scale

Eye Opening (E)	Verbal Response (V)	Motor Response (M)
4 = spontaneous 3 = to sound 2 = to pressure 1 = none NT = not testable	5 = orientated 4 = confused 3 = to words 2 = to sounds 1 = none NT = not testable	6 = obeys commands 5 = localizes 4 = normal flexion 3 = abnormal flexion 2 = extension 1 = none NT = not testable

- Assess the patient's motor function. Special attention should be paid to nonsymmetrical findings:
    - muscle tone and coordination (bilateral hand squeeze and foot press, moving fingers and toes)
    - facial symmetry (patient's ability to lift eyebrows and smile)
    - **PERRLA** (**P**upils **E**qual, **R**ound, and **R**eactive to **L**ight and **A**ccommodation)
- Assess patient's response to stimulus (light touch on an area).
- Assess cranial nerve function. (See Table 4.2.)

> **Helpful Hint**
>
> Determine if slurred or incoherent speech is due to altered mental status (**aphasia**) or impairment of muscular control (**dysarthria**).

Table 4.2. Cranial Nerve and Function Assessment	
Cranial Nerve	**Assessment**
I. Olfactory: sense of smell	Have patient identify a smell with eyes closed, using each nostril individually.
II. Optic: central and peripheral vision	Have patient read something; assess peripheral vision.
III. Oculomotor: constriction of pupils and extraocular movement	Test pupil response with penlight; make a large "H" with a finger and have the patient follow it with his eyes.
IV. Trochlear: downward eye movement	Have the patient follow your finger as it moves toward her nose.
V. Trigeminal: face	Check sensation on the patient's forehead, cheeks, and jaw; test jaw strength; have patient clench teeth.
VI. Abducens: sideways eye movement	Have patient look toward each ear and complete the 6 cardinal fields of gaze.
VII. Facial: movement and expression	Assess facial symmetry; have patient puff cheeks, pucker, raise eyebrows, and smile.
VIII. Vestibulocochlear: hearing and equilibrium	Assess gait; hold a ticking watch by patient's ear, have them close their eyes, and ask them what they hear.
IX. Glossopharyngeal: tongue, throat, and uvula	Assess ability to taste sweet and sour on the back of the tongue; assess gag reflex.
X. Vagus: sensory and motor	Have patient swallow while speaking; have patient say "ah."
XI. Accessory: head and shoulder movement	Have patient shrug shoulders and turn head against resistance.
XII. Hypoglossal: tongue position	Have patient stick tongue out midline and then side to side.

Quick Review Question

4. A patient is being prepared for cardiac ablation to treat atrial fibrillation (A-fib). During assessment, the nurse notes that the patient has slurred speech and a left-sided facial droop. What priority intervention should the nurse anticipate?

Respiratory and Chest Assessment

- Perform respiratory inspection. Look for abnormalities in the shape of the chest, and assess the rate, depth, and effort of breathing:
    - tachypnea: rapid breathing
    - bradypnea: slow breathing
    - dyspnea: difficulty breathing
    - hyperventilation: an increase in the rate or volume of breaths; which can cause excessive elimination of CO_2
    - Kussmaul breathing: type of hyperventilation characterized by deep, labored breathing that is associated with metabolic acidosis
    - Cheyne-Stokes breathing: deep breathing alternating with apnea or a faster rate of breathing; associated with left heart failure or sleep apnea
- Perform lung percussion; tone indicates where lungs are solid or filled with air or fluid:
    - Normal air-filled structures have a resonant note (tympanic or drum-like sound).
    - Fluid or tissue-filled cavities (e.g., pneumonia) have a dull sound.
    - Air-filled tissues (e.g., emphysema, pneumothorax) have a hyperresonant sound (more pronounced, drum-like noise).
- Perform lung auscultation:
    - **Vesicular breath sounds** are heard over the lungs.
    - **Bronchial breath sounds** are heard over the trachea and bronchi.

Table 4.3. Lung Sounds

Sound	Description	Etiology
wheezes	continuous musical-like sound; can occur upon inspiration or expiration	air being forced through narrowed passages in the airway (e.g., asthma, COPD)
rhonchi	low-pitched, coarse rattling lung sounds	secretions in the airway (e.g., pneumonia, cystic fibrosis)
stridor	high-pitched wheezing sound	air moving through narrowed or obstructed passages in the upper airway (e.g., aspiration, laryngospasm)
rales (crackles)	crackling, rattling sound that can be coarse or fine	fluid in the small airways of the lung (e.g., pulmonary edema, pneumonia)
pleural friction rub	a grating, creaking sound	inflamed pleural tissue (e.g., pleuritis, pulmonary embolism)

Table 4.3. Lung Sounds		
Sound	**Description**	**Etiology**
diminished or absent breath sounds	decreased intensity of breath sounds due to lack of air in lung tissues	air or fluid around the lungs (e.g., pleural effusion, pneumothorax) or blocked airway
egophony	an "e" sound heard as "a" due to increased resonance of sound traveling across fluid	fluid in the lungs (e.g., pleural effusion, pneumonia)
bronchophony	increased volume of spoken voice over areas of lung consolidation	
whispered pectoriloquy	increased volume of whispered voice over areas of lung consolidation	

Quick Review Question

5. A patient is admitted to the cardiac care unit with pleural effusion secondary to right-sided heart failure. What sound should the nurse expect to hear when auscultating over the area of effusion?

Cardiovascular Assessment

- Inspect and palpate **carotid arteries** with the patient positioned at a 45-degree angle with their head turned away.
- Inspect and palpate the **jugular veins**:
    - Have the patient relax the sternocleidomastoid muscle so that pulsations in the interior jugular vein can be observed.
    - **Jugular venous distention (JVD)** can be used to estimate central venous pressure (CVP): JVD indicates an elevated CVP.
- Observe the temperature, size, and color of extremities; palpate peripheral pulses simultaneously. Special attention should be paid to asymmetrical findings.
- To perform cardiac percussion, the nurse taps on the patient's chest to identify cardiac margins and underlying structures. (Although percussion is useful to identify cardiac margins and underlying structures, this outdated process has been replaced by X-ray.)

- Perform cardiac auscultation from the apex of the heart to the base of the heart using a stethoscope:
    o **mitral valve:** found at the fifth left intercostal space at the midclavicular line
    o **tricuspid valve:** found at the fifth left intercostal space at the left sternal border
    o **Erb's point:** found at the third left intercostal space at the left sternal border
    o **pulmonic valve:** found at the second left intercostal space at the left sternal border
    o **aortic valve:** found at the second right intercostal space at the right sternal border

Helpful Hint
Palpate one carotid artery at a time; do not occlude both arteries at the same time.

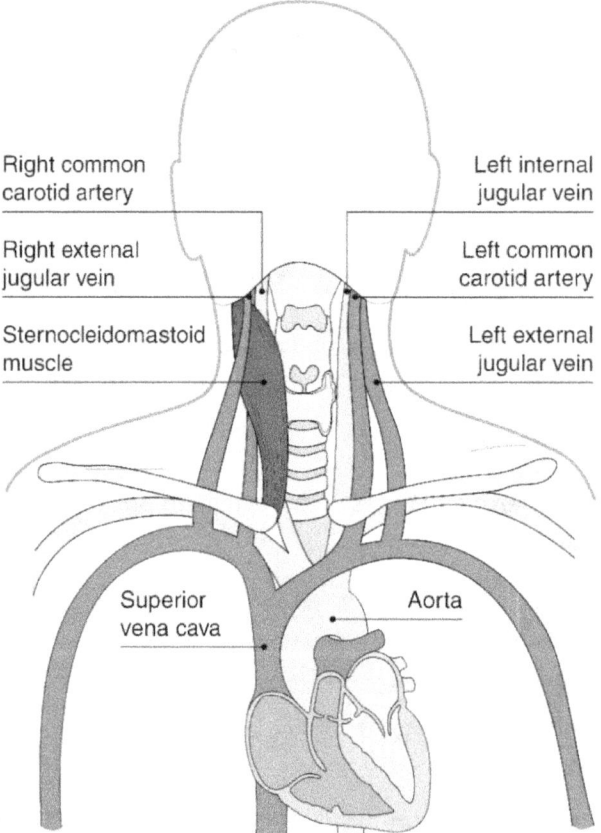

Figure 4.3. Vasculature of the Neck

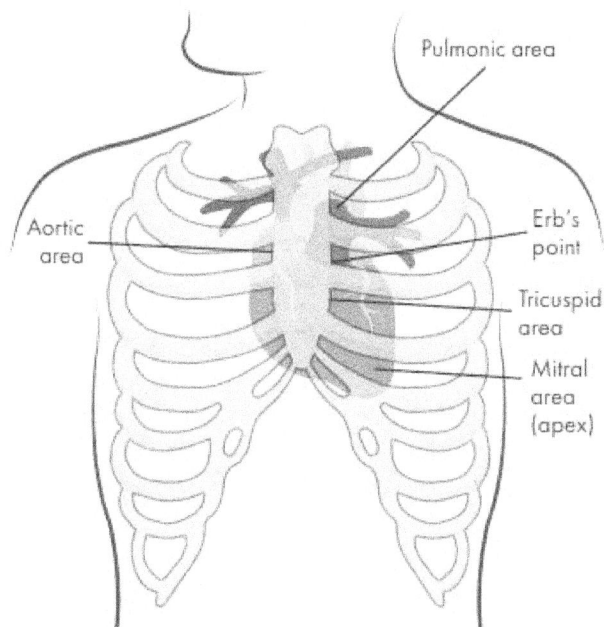

Figure 4.4. Locations for Cardiac Auscultation

- **Heart sounds** are produced as blood moves through the heart:
    - **S1:** caused by the closure of the AV valves; indicates the end of diastole and the beginning of systole
    - **S2:** caused by the closure of the semilunar valves; indicates the end of systole and the beginning of diastole
    - **S3 (ventricular gallop):** an extra heart sound heard after S2; caused by a rush of blood into a ventricle; a normal finding in children and young adults
    - **S4 (atrial gallop):** an extra heart sound heard before S1; caused by the atrial contraction of blood into a noncompliant ventricle; can be a normal finding in older adults

> **Helpful Hint**
> S3 heart sound is associated with ventricular dysfunction or volume overload in the ventricles (e.g., MI, systolic HF, dilated cardiomyopathy, or mitral valve regurgitation). S4 heart sound is associated with decreased ventricular compliance (e.g., hypertrophic cardiomyopathy, hypertension, or aortic stenosis).

- **Murmurs** are the sounds made by turbulent blood flow in and around the heart:
    - Murmurs can be **systolic** (occurring during ventricular contraction) or **diastolic** (occurring during ventricular filling).
    - Murmurs caused by increased blood flow across a normal valve are soft and systolic; they are commonly caused by anemia, pregnancy, hyperthyroidism, fever, or exercise.
    - Abnormal murmurs can be caused by septal defects, infections, or structural damage (e.g., stenosis or endocarditis).

- **Pericardial friction rub** is a high-pitched, leathery sound that is a characteristic of pericarditis:
    - heard loudest at the fourth and fifth intercostal spaces, with patient leaning forward
    - will continue even if patient is holding breath
- **Carotid bruits** are abnormal sounds heard over the carotid artery caused by turbulent blood flow. They can be heard with a Doppler or stethoscope and may indicate carotid artery disease.

Quick Review Question

6. Which abnormal heart sound might a nurse expect to hear in a patient with heart failure?

Abdominal and Gastrointestinal Assessment

- Perform bowel auscultation:
    - High-pitched gurgling sounds are normal. Normal bowel sounds can be documented as normal, hypoactive, or hyperactive.
    - Borborygmi: loud, rumbling sounds caused by shifting of fluids or gas within the intestines; a normal finding
    - High-pitched bowel sounds are often described as tinkling or rushing sounds; they may indicate an early bowel obstruction.

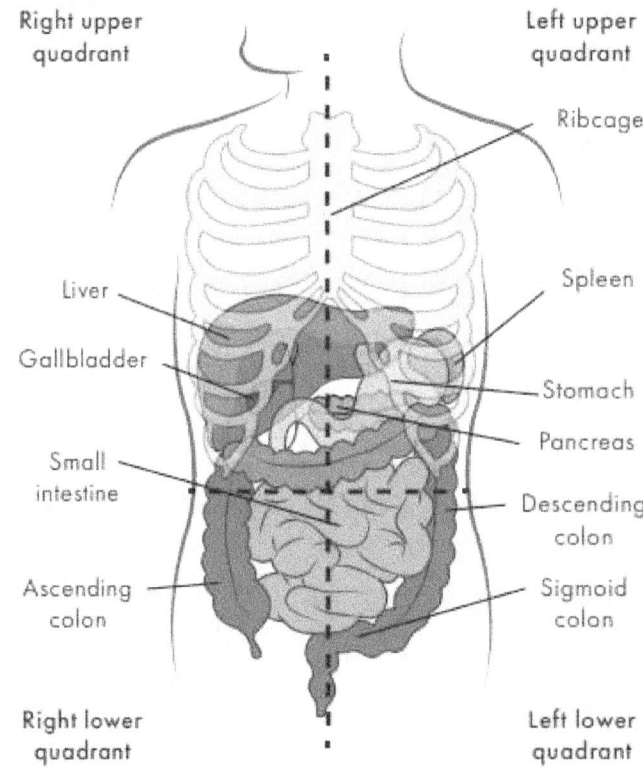

Figure 4.5. Abdominopelvic Quadrants

- **Absent bowel sounds** are an indication of an ileus where no peristalsis is occurring; bowel sounds may be temporarily absent in certain cases (e.g., after surgery), but their absence, combined with abdominal pain, indicates a serious condition.
- Palpate abdomen; ask the patient where the pain is being experienced, and palpate this area last.
- Perform abdominal percussion:
    o Start at the umbilicus and move downward.
    o **Tympanic sounds** indicate air-filled intestines.
    o **Dull sounds** indicate organomegaly, masses, or fluid.

Quick Review Question

7. A patient has been admitted to the cardiac care unit with right-sided heart failure. What is the most likely reason a nurse would note dullness when percussing the abdomen?

Skin and Nail Assessment

- Inspect skin for abnormalities.
- Assess the extent of **skin edema** by pressing firmly into the skin and grading the indentation.

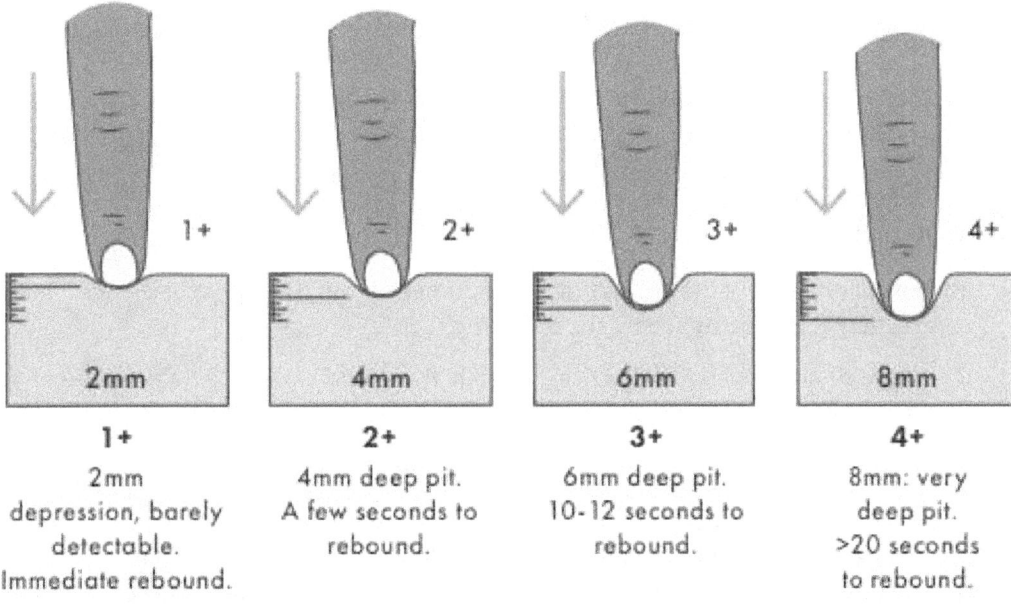

Figure 4.6. Grading Skin Edema

- Observe the color and the temperature of the skin:
    - **cyanosis:** a blue or purplish skin color caused by hypoxia
    - **pallor:** paleness associated with anemia, shock, and other disorders
    - **rubor:** redness of the skin; often caused by inflammation
    - **hemosiderin staining:** brown skin color caused by iron deposits within cells; associated with chronic venous insufficiency and iron overload
    - **shiny skin in the extremities:** a potential sign of peripheral vascular disease
- Observe skin for signs of bleeding (hematoma, ecchymosis, petechiae, or purpura).
- Inspect nails for abnormalities:
    - **clubbing:** an enlargement of the tissue at the distal phalange; occurs over a long period and is associated with many chronic cardiovascular and respiratory disorders
    - **capillary refill time (CRT):** how long it takes for blood to return to the skin under the nail after pressure is applied. Normal time is 3 seconds or less.

> **Helpful Hint**
>
> In patients with **ascites** (collections of fluid in the peritoneal cavity), the location of the dull sound will shift as the fluid shifts when the patient changes position between supine or lying on their side.

Quick Review Question

8. A patient presents to the clinic with complaints of left calf tenderness. During assessment, the nurse notes cyanosis of the left foot with no palpable pulse. What diagnosis do these findings support?

Hemodynamics

- **Stroke volume (SV)** is the volume of blood pumped from the left ventricle during one contraction; it is determined by the following:
    - **preload:** how much the ventricles stretch at the end of diastole (a measure of ventricular end-diastolic volume)
    - **afterload:** resistance the heart must overcome during systole to pump blood into circulation (a measure of aortic pressure and systemic vascular resistance [SVR])
    - **contractility:** the force of the heart independent of preload and afterload

Table 4.4. Hemodynamic Parameters

Parameter	Description	Normal Range
Blood pressure (BP)	• vascular BP given as systolic pressure [(SBP)—the top number] and diastolic pressure [(DBP)—the bottom number]	90/60 – 120/80 mm Hg

Table 4.4. Hemodynamic Parameters

Parameter	Description	Normal Range
Central venous pressure (CVP), or right atrial pressure (RAP)	• pressure in the vena cava; used to estimate preload	2 – 6 mm Hg
Pulmonary artery pressure (PAP)	• pressure in the pulmonary artery	8 – 20 mm Hg
Stroke volume (SV)	• volume of blood forced from the left ventricle with each contraction	60 – 100 mL/beat
Cardiac output (CO)	• volume of blood pumped in a unit of time (usually per minute) • $CO = SV \times HR$	4 – 8 mL/min
Cardiac index (CI)	• CO relative to patient size • $CI = \frac{CO}{BSA}$	2.5 – 4 L/min/m²
Mean arterial pressure (MAP)	• average BP during a complete cardiac cycle • $MAP = SBP + \frac{2 \times DBP}{3}$	70 – 100 mm Hg
Systemic vascular resistance (SVR)	• total peripheral vascular system resistance to blood flow • $SVR = 80 \times \frac{MAP - CVP}{CO}$	700 – 1200 dynes sec/cm⁵
Pulmonary artery occlusion pressure (PAOP), or pulmonary capillary wedge pressure (PCWP)	• indirect measurement of left atrial pressure • uses Swan-Ganz catheter to "wedge" inflated balloon into a branch of the pulmonary artery	6 – 12 mm Hg
Pulmonary vascular resistance (PVR)	• vascular resistance to blood flow in the lungs • $PVR = 80 \times \frac{MPAP - PAOP}{CI}$	255 – 285 dynes sec/cm⁵
Left ventricular end diastolic pressure (LVEDP)	• pressure in the left ventricle before systole	5 – 12 mm Hg
Arterial oxygen saturation (SaO_2)	• fraction of oxygen-saturated hemoglobin in arteries	95 – 100%

Table 4.4. Hemodynamic Parameters

Parameter	Description	Normal Range
Mixed venous saturation (SvO_2)	• fraction of oxygen-saturated hemoglobin in veins (taken from PAC)	60 – 80%
Central venous oxygen saturation ($ScvO_2$)	• fraction of oxygen-saturated hemoglobin in veins • surrogate for SvO_2 (taken from central venous catheter)	>70%
Arterial oxygen content (CaO_2)	• volume of oxygen delivered to tissue per unit of blood	16 – 22 mL/dL
Oxygen delivery (DO_2)	• volume of blood oxygen being transported to tissues per unit of time	arterial = 1000 mL/min venous = 775 mL/min
Oxygen consumption (VO_2)	• volume of oxygen used by the body per unit of time	200 – 250 mL/min

Quick Review Question

9. The nurse is reassessing a patient with severe sepsis after a fluid bolus and the administration of vasopressors. What hemodynamic value would indicate an improvement?

Laboratory Tests

Table 4.5. Common Laboratory Tests

Test: Cardiac Biomarkers	Description	Normal Range
Troponin I (cTnI) and troponin T (cTnT)	• proteins released when the heart muscle is damaged • high levels can indicate an MI but may also be due to other conditions that stress the heart (e.g., renal failure, HF, PE) • levels peak 24 hours post-MI and can remain elevated for up to 2 weeks	cTnI: 0.04 ng/mL cTnT: 0.01 ng/mL
Creatine kinase (CK)	• responsible for muscle cell function • an increase indicates cardiac or skeletal muscle damage	22 – 198 U/L

Table 4.5. Common Laboratory Tests

Creatine kinase–muscle/brain (CK-MB)	• cardiac marker for damaged heart muscle • often used to diagnose a second MI or ongoing cardiovascular conditions • high ratios of CK-MB to CK (high CK-MB/CK) indicate damage to heart muscle (as opposed to skeletal muscle)	normal CK-MB: 5 – 25 IU/L CK-MB/CK suggesting possible MI: 2.5 – 3
Test: Complete Blood Count (CBC)		
white blood cells (WBCs)	high WBC count can indicate inflammation or infection	4,500 – 10,000 cells/μL
red blood cells (RBCs)	cells that carry oxygen throughout the body and filter carbon dioxide	men: 5 – 6 million cells/μL women: 4 – 5 million cells/μL
hemoglobin (HgB)	protein that binds oxygen in the blood	men: 13.8 – 17.2 g/dL women: 12.1 – 15.1 g/dL
hematocrit (Hct)	percentage of the blood composed of red blood cells	men: 41% – 50% women: 36% – 44%
mean corpuscular volume (MCV)	average size of RBCs	MCV: 80 – 95 fL
mean corpuscular hemoglobin (MCH)	average amount of HgB in RBCs	27.5 – 33.2 pg
mean corpuscular hemoglobin concentration (MCHC)	average concentration of HgB in RBCs	334 – 355 g/L
platelets	blood components that play a role in clotting	150,000 – 450,000 platelets/μL
white blood cells (WBCs)	a high WBC count can indicate inflammation or infection	4,500 – 10,000 cells/μL
Test: WBC Differential	**Description**	**Normal Range**
neutrophils	first responders that quickly migrate to the site of infections to destroy bacterial invaders	2,000 – 7,000/μL (40 – 60%)
band neutrophils	immature neutrophils (also called "bands")	700/μL (5%)
lymphocytes	B cells, T cells, and natural killer cells; all of which develop from common lymphoid progenitors	1,000 – 3,000/μL (20 – 40%)

Table 4.5. Common Laboratory Tests

monocytes	foreign substance cells that engulf and destroy microbes and cancer cells	200 – 1,000/µL (2 – 8%)
eosinophils	cells that attack parasites and regulate inflammation	20 – 500/µL (1 – 4%)
basophils	cells responsible for inflammatory reactions, including allergies	20 – 100/µL (0 – 2%)
Test: Coagulation Studies and Clotting Factors		
prothrombin time (PT)	how long it takes blood to clot	10 – 13 seconds
international normalized ratio (INR)	standardized PT for patients taking warfarin	healthy adults: 1.1 patients receiving anticoagulants: 2.0 – 3.0
partial thromboplastin time (PTT)	the body's ability to form blood clots	60 – 70 seconds
activated partial thromboplastin time (aPTT)	the body's ability to form blood clots using an activator to speed up the clotting process	20 – 35 seconds
D-dimer	protein fragment produced during fibrinolysis	Negative
fibrin split products (FSP) or fibrin degradation products (FDP)	components produced during fibrinolysis	10 mg/L
fibrinogen	amount of fibrinogen (clotting factor I)	200 – 400 mg/dL
plasminogen	substrate involved in fibrinolysis	10 – 16 mg/dL
Test: Kidney Function	**Description**	**Normal Range**
BUN	by-product of ammonia metabolism; filtered by the kidneys; high levels can indicate insufficient kidney function	7 – 20 mg/dL
creatinine	product of muscle metabolism; filtered by the kidneys; high levels can indicate insufficient kidney function	0.6 – 1.2 mg/dL
BUN-to-creatinine ratio	increased ratio indicates dehydration, AKI, or GI bleeding; decreased ratio indicates renal damage	10:1 – 20:1

Table 4.5. Common Laboratory Tests

GFR	volume of fluid filtered by the renal glomerular capillaries per unit of time; decreased GFR indicates decreased renal function	• men: 100 – 130 mL/ min/1.73 m^2 • women: 90 – 120 mL/ min/1.73 m^2 • GFR 60 mL/min/1.73 m^2 common in adults >70 years
potassium (K+)	helps with muscle contraction and regulates water and acid-base balance	3.5 – 5.2 mEq/L
sodium (Na+)	maintains fluid balance and plays a major role in muscle and nerve function	135 – 145 mEq/L
calcium (Ca2+)	plays an important role in skeletal function and structure, nerve function, muscle contraction, and cell communication	8.5 – 10.3 mg/dL
Chloride (Cl–)	plays a major role in muscle and nerve function	98 – 107 mEq/L
magnesium (Mg2+)	regulates muscle, nerve, and cardiac function	1.8 – 2.5 mg/dL
Test: Liver Function	**Description**	**Normal Range**
albumin	protein made in the liver; low levels may indicate liver damage	3.5 – 5.0 g/dL
alkaline phosphatase (ALP)	enzyme found in the liver and bones; increased levels indicate liver damage	45 – 147 U/L
alanine transaminase (ALT)	enzyme in the liver; helps metabolize protein; increased levels indicate liver damage	7 – 55 U/L
aspartate transaminase (AST)	enzyme in the liver; helps metabolize alanine; increased levels indicate liver or muscle damage	8 – 48 U/L
total protein	low levels may indicate liver damage	6.3 – 7.9 g/dL
total bilirubin	produced during the breakdown of heme; increased levels indicate liver damage or anemia	0.1 – 1.2 mg/dL
gamma-glutamyltransferase (GGT)	enzyme that plays a role in antioxidant metabolism; increased levels indicate liver damage	9 – 48 U/L
L-lactate dehydrogenase (LD or LDH)	enzyme found in most cells in the body; increased levels may indicate liver damage, cancer, or tissue breakdown	adults: 122 – 222 U/L
Test: Urinalysis	**Description**	**Normal Range**

Table 4.5. Common Laboratory Tests

leukocytes	presence of WBCs in urine indicates infection	negative
nitrate	presence in urine indicates infection by gram-negative bacteria	negative
protein	presence in urine may indicate diabetic neuropathy, nephritis, or eclampsia	negative
pH	decreased (acidic) pH may indicate systemic acidosis or diabetes mellitus; increased (alkali) pH may indicate systemic alkalosis or UTI	4.5 – 8
blood	presence in urine may indicate infection, renal calculi, a neoplasm, or coagulation disorders	negative
specific gravity	concentration of urine; decreased concentration may indicate diabetes insipidus or pyelonephritis; increased concentration may indicate dehydration or SIADH	1.010 – 1.025
urine osmolality	concentration of urine; more accurate than specific gravity	300 – 900 mOsm/kg
ketones	produced during fat metabolism; presence in urine may indicate diabetes, hyperglycemia, starvation, alcoholism, or eclampsia	negative

Helpful Hint

An elevated BUN:creatinine ratio is associated with decreased kidney function and increased breakdown of protein. It is often seen with upper GI bleeds (due to the digestion of blood) but not with lower GI bleeds.

Quick Review Question

10. A female patient is admitted with an RBC count of 2.8 million. What signs and symptoms should the nurse expect her to present with?

Other Diagnostic Tools

- A **chest X-ray** is used to diagnose abnormalities in the lungs, heart, and bones.
- A **CT (computed tomography)** scan is a type of X-ray that produces a 3-D picture of organs, bones, and tissues. IV or oral contrast can be used for this test; kidney function needs to be checked before the procedure.

- **MRI (magnetic resonance imaging)** uses large magnets and radiofrequencies to produce detailed pictures of the body. MRA (magnetic resonance angiography) uses large magnets and radiofrequency to view and identify abnormalities in blood vessels.

- A **PET (positron emission tomography)** scan uses a radioactive dye that helps identify areas of high chemical activity that could represent disease. Check for iodine allergies before testing.

- A **TEE (transesophageal echocardiogram)** uses a specialized probe that passes through the patients' esophagus to view the heart structure and record images. Check for gag reflex after the procedure; patient must remain NPO for at least 60 minutes after the procedure (or until numbness subsides) to prevent choking.

> **Helpful Hint**
> Some PET scans require patients to be on a no sugar, low-carb diet for twenty-four hours before the scan.

- A **TTE (transthoracic echocardiogram)** is a noninvasive test that uses ultrasound to view the heart. The ultrasound probe is placed on the chest or stomach to obtain the necessary images.

- During **electrophysiology studies (EPS)**, a small catheter is guided through the femoral vein to the heart to test the electrical system of the heart and identify dysrhythmias.

- During a **diagnostic cardiac catheterization**, a small catheter is threaded through the radial, brachial, or femoral artery and guided to the heart; dye is then injected through the catheter, and X-ray pictures are taken of the heart.

- **Stress testing** is used to assess the cardiovascular system's response to strenuous work. They can be physical (via treadmill) or chemical.

- The **Borg scale** is used to assess a patient's perception of exertion during physical activity. The rating goes from 6 (no exertion) to 20 (maximum exertion).

- The **six-minute walk** test assesses how far a patient can walk in six minutes. The procedure is done on a hard, flat service, and the patient is able to set the pace.

Quick Review Question

11. A patient has returned to the cardiac vascular unit after undergoing a diagnostic cardiac catheterization. A priority concern for this patient is a risk of bleeding. Why is this a concern, and what should be done if bleeding occurs?

Electrocardiography and Telemetry

ECG Basics

- A 12-lead **electrocardiogram (ECG)** is a noninvasive diagnostic tool that records the heart's electrical activity. This diagnostic test can help determine a patient's cardiac rhythm and rate.

Figure 4.7. Twelve-Lead ECG Electrode Placement Diagram

Table 4.6. Twelve-Lead ECG Electrode Placement	
Electrode	Placement
V1	fourth intercostal space to the right of the sternum
V2	fourth intercostal space to the left of the sternum
V3	midway between V2 and V4
V4	fifth intercostal space at the midclavicular line
V5	anterior axillary line at the same level as V4
V6	midaxillary line at the same level as V4 and V5
RA	between right shoulder and right wrist
LA	between left shoulder and left wrist

Table 4.6. Twelve-Lead ECG Electrode Placement	
Electrode	**Placement**
RL	above right ankle and below the torso
LL	above left ankle and below the torso

- A 12-lead ECG includes 3 types of leads:
  - 3 bipolar (leads I, II, and III)
  - 3 unipolar (leads aVR, aVL, and aVF)
  - 6 precordial (leads V1 – V6)

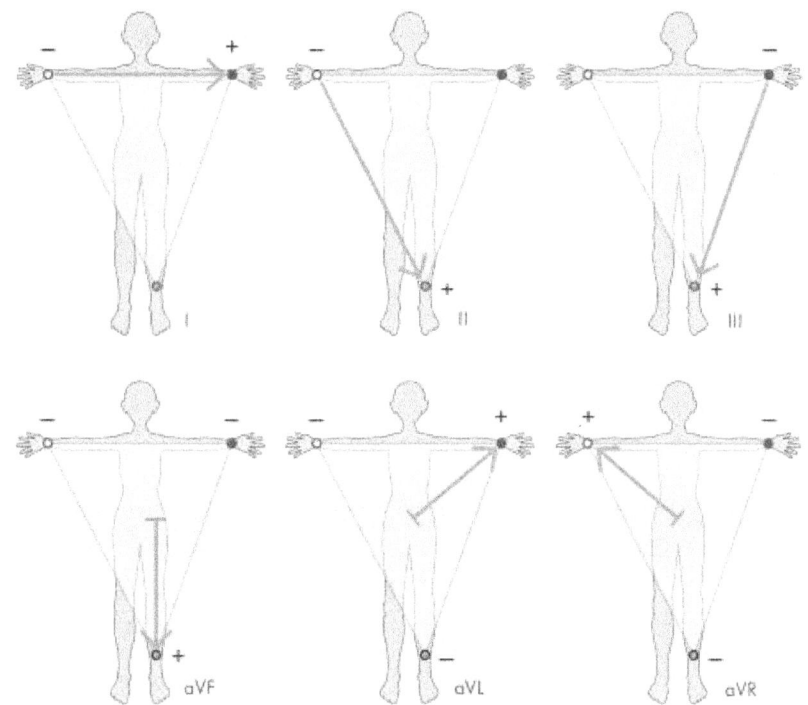

Figure 4.8. Bipolar and Unipolar Leads in a 12-Lead ECG

- The leads show activity in different areas of the heart:
  - The inferior portion of the heart can be seen through leads II, III, and aVF.
  - The anterior portion of the heart can be seen in leads V3 and V4.
  - The lateral portion of the heart can be seen in leads I, aVL, V5, and V6.
  - The septal region can be seen in leads V1 and V2.
- Additional leads may be used when the patient is suspected of having damage to the posterior of the heart or the right ventricle.
  - **Posterior leads** (V7, V8, and V9) are placed on the patient's back when a posterior infarction is suspected.

- o **Right-side leads** (V3R, V4R, V5R, and V6R) are placed on the patient's right side in a mirror image of V3 – V6 when a right ventricular infarction is suspected.
- Damage to coronary arteries can be seen in changes to specific leads (see Table 4.7.).

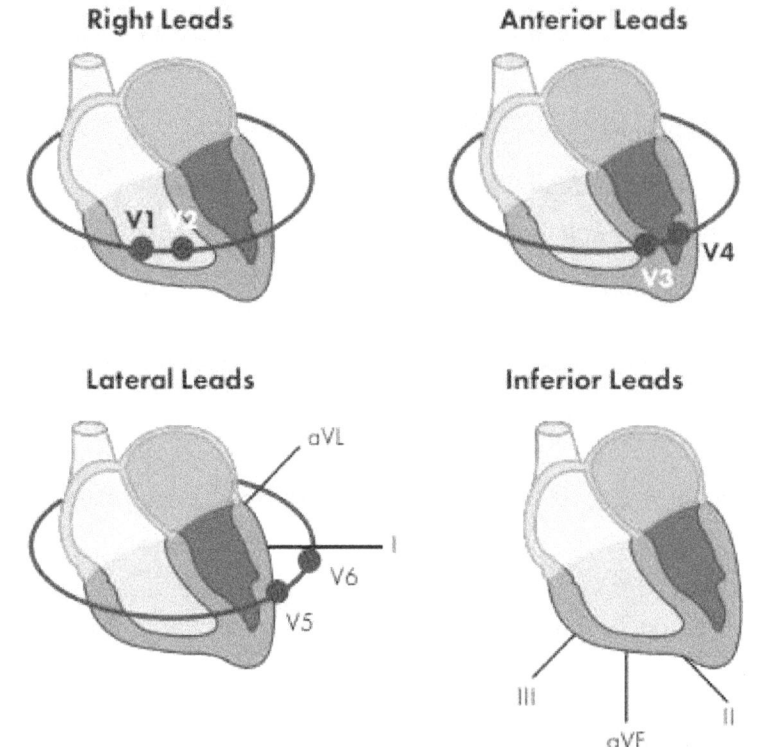

Figure 4.9. Portion of Heart Corresponding to ECG Leads

Table 4.7. Lead Changes and Affected Coronary Artery by Location of MI

Location of MI	Lead with ST Changes	Affected Coronary Artery
anteroseptal	V1 – V4	LAD
anterior	V2 – V4	LAD
lateral	I, aVL, V5, V6	circumflex artery
inferior	II, III, aVF	RCA
posterior	V7 – V9	RCA
right ventricular	V4R – V6R	RCA

Quick Review Question

12. A 12-lead ECG is performed on a patient with chest pain. The ECG shows ST elevations in leads II, III, and aVF. Which medications are contraindicated for this patient?

Reading The ECG

The cardiac rhythm is assessed by reading, or reviewing, the electrocardiogram (ECG) rhythm strip. These strips may be collected with various numbers of leads (discussed above), from 3 to 12, and contain the following basic measurements:

- **QRS complex:** The QRS complex is measured from the end of the PR interval until the end of the **S wave** (a negative wave that appears after a positive wave); the spike should be measured. The QRS complex represents ventricular depolarization and should measure 0.08 – 0.10 seconds.

- **RR interval:** The RR interval is the distance between QRS complexes. See Figure 4.11.

- **P wave:** The P wave is the small bump seen before a QRS complex. It represents atrial depolarization and should measure 0.06 – 0.11 seconds.

- **PR interval:** The PR interval is measured from the start of the P wave to the start of the QRS interval. It represents the AV conduction time and should measure between 0.12 and 0.20 seconds.

- **T wave:** The T wave is the small bump directly following the QRS complex and represents the repolarization of the ventricles.

- **U wave:** This is another small bump that, when visible, will follow the T wave.

These basic measurements can be assessed to determine the following information:

- Heart rate:

    o **Atrial rate** is calculated by counting the number of P waves in a 6-second strip and multiplying by 10. See Figure 4.12.

    o **Ventricular rate** is calculated by counting the number of R waves in the strip and multiplying by 10. Verify the rate with auscultation. **Bradycardia** is indicated in ventricular rates of 60 beats per minute (bpm); **tachycardia** is indicated at rates of >100 bpm. See Figure 4.12.

- **Regularity:** Assess the regularity of the interval from R wave to R wave to determine if there are irregular rhythms; irregular intervals; or, in the case of atrial fibrillation and atrial flutter, no distinct P waves. Ventricular fibrillation, another irregular rhythm (bradyarrhythmia), is chaotic with no discernible QRS wave or P wave. See Figure 4.13.

- **Atrial activity:** Assess the presence and appearance of the P waves before each QRS complex. P waves are indistinct with atrial fibrillation, and they are have a sawtooth pattern with atrial flutter (see Figures 2.7. and 2.8. in Chapter 2).

- **AV node conduction:** Assess the PR interval (normal is 0.12 to 0.20 seconds). A prolonged PR interval occurs with heart block, and it is shortened with preexcitation syndromes in which electrical impulses bypass the AV node. See Figure 4.14.

- **Ventricular repolarization:** Assess the T waves: peaked T waves may indicate hyperkalemia, and inverted T waves may indicate ischemia or a history of infarction. See Figure 4.15.

- **Ventricular depolarization:** Assess the QRS duration (normal is 0.06 to 0.12 seconds). A rapid heart rate with a wide QRS complex indicates life-threatening ventricular tachycardia. See Figure 4.16.

- **ST segment:** The ST segment is measured from the end of the QRS complex to the start of the T wave. On the rhythm strip, this segment will appear elevated if there is a myocardial infarction and depressed if there is a cardiac ischemia and/or myocardial injury. See Figure 4.10.

- **QT interval:** The QT interval is measured from the beginning of the QRS complex until the end of the T wave and represents the total time of ventricular activity (depolarization and repolarization). The QT segment shows the early part of ventricular repolarization. A normal QT interval should be 0.36 – 0.44 seconds. The QT interval is prolonged with life-threatening arrhythmias and shorted with hypercalcemia. See Figure 4.10.

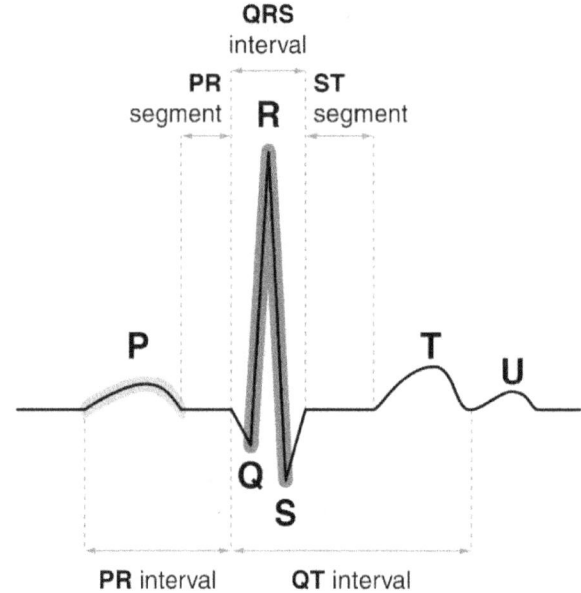

Figure 4.10. Waveforms and Intervals on an ECG

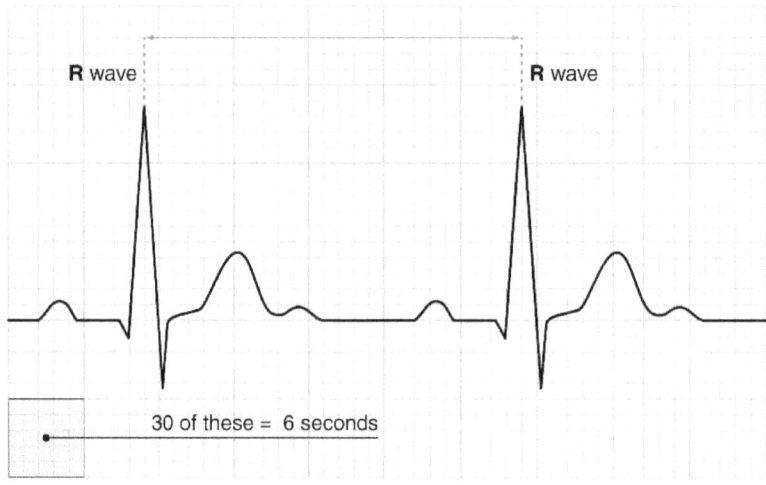

Figure 4.11. The RR Interval on an ECG

Atrial rate

is calculated by counting the number of P waves in a 6-second strip and multiplying by 10

Ventricular rate

is calculated by counting the number of R waves in the strip and multiplying by 10.

Verify the rate with auscultation. **Bradycardia** is indicated in ventricular rates of **<60 beats per minute (bpm)**; **tachycardia** is indicated at rates of **>100 bpm**.

Figure 4.12. Atrial and Ventricular Rates on an ECG (Note: A 6-second strip is the equivalent of 30 large squares on the ECG.)

Normal sinus rhythm
60-100 bpm

Bradyarrhythmia
< 60 bpm

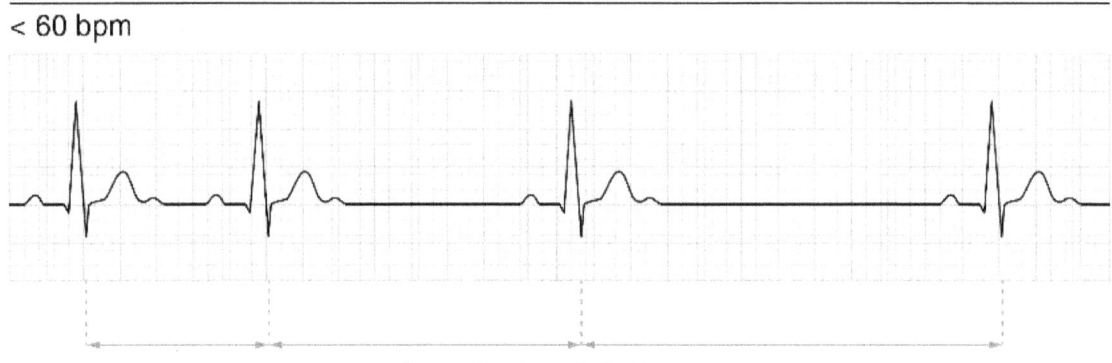

Figure 4.13. Normal Sinus Rhythm (Regular) and Bradyarrhythmia (Irregular)

Figure 4.14. AV Node Conduction

Ventricular repolarization

Assess the T waves: **peaked T waves** may indicate **hyperkalemia**, and **inverted T waves** may indicate **ischemia or a history of infarction**.

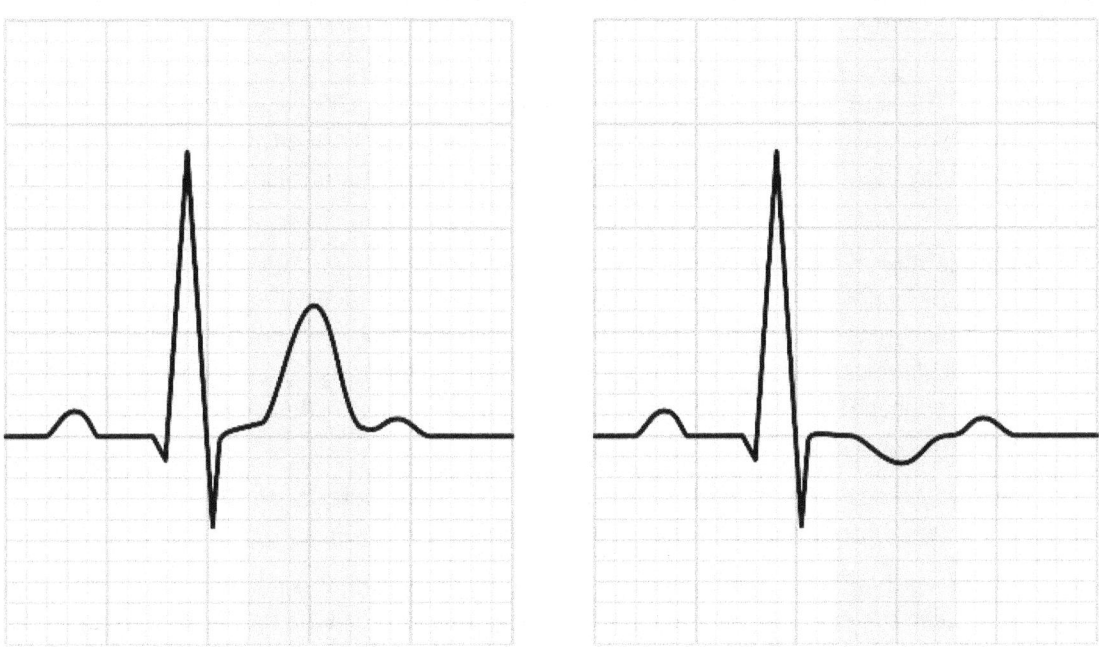

Figure 4.15. Ventricular Repolarization

Ventricular depolarization

Normal

Ventricular tachycardia

Figure 4.16. Ventricular Depolarization (Normal Depolarization and Ventricular Tachycardia)

Quick Review Question

13. An EKG strip shows a regular atrial and ventricular rate of 108 bpm, with a normal P wave, and a PR interval of 0.12. The QRS complex is 0.10 seconds with a regular appearance, a normal T wave, and a QT interval of 0.38 seconds. How is this interpreted?

Echocardiography

Doppler ultrasound uses high-frequency sound waves emitted by a transducer to assess the movement of red blood cells. The sound waves are reflected at different frequencies based on the speed and direction of the blood flow. The frequency increases when the blood flow is toward the transducer, and it decreases when the blood flow is away from the transducer. Doppler ultrasound use is indicated for the following:

- **Echocardiography:** Doppler ultrasonography monitors blood flow through the heart; measures valve function; assesses heart failure, left ventricular systolic function, and diastolic function; allows visualization of heart structures; and allows estimation of left ventricular ejection fraction. Echocardiography may be transthoracic (noninvasive) or transesophageal. The transesophageal echocardiogram provides more detailed images than the transthoracic echocardiogram.

- **Arterial/venous assessment:** Doppler ultrasonography detects stenosis or blockage, deep vein thrombosis, and venous reflux in arteries and veins.

- **Ankle-brachial index (ABI):** Doppler ultrasonography evaluates peripheral arterial disease in the extremities. The ankle systolic pressure is divided by the brachial systolic pressure to determine the ABI.

- **Fetal heart monitoring:** Doppler ultrasonography monitors the blood flow in the umbilical artery and the fetal heart.

Quick Review Question

14. If the ankle systolic pressure is 85 and the brachial systolic pressure is 110, what is the ABI?

Stroke Scale

The **National Institutes of Health Stroke Scale (NIHSS)** is a standardized instrument used to assess the severity of a stroke. It focuses on functional impairment, the need for thrombolytic therapy, and progress during recovery. The NIHSS should be administered as soon as possible after the onset of symptoms. Scores correlate with long-term prognoses: high scores indicate poor prognoses.

Eleven items are scored from 0 (no impairment) to 4 (no movement). The range of scores and their meanings differ between items, with some items being scored on a scale of 0 – 2 and other items being scored on a scale of 0 – 4; in some cases, a score of "UN"—meaning "untestable" may be given. These items—and the scores associated with them—are described in Table 4.8. Complete scoring information for each item can be found at https://www.ninds.nih.gov/health-information/stroke/assess-and-treat/nih-stroke-scale.

Table 4.8. Items Evaluated During National Institutes of Health Stroke Scale		
Item and Item Number	Description	Score Scale
1. Level of consciousness (divided into levels 1a, 1b, and 1c)	alert, not alert, unresponsive or responds with reflex motor or autonomic effects	1a: 0 – 3 1b: 0 – 2 1c: 0 – 2
2. Best gaze	normal, partial palsy, forced deviation	0 – 2
3. Visual fields	partial, complete, bilateral hemianopia	0 – 3
4. Facial palsy	minor, partial, or complete paralysis	0 – 3
5. Motor function (arms)	degree of drift	0 – 4 or "UN"
6. Motor function (legs)	degree of drift	0 – 4 or "UN"
7. Limb ataxia	absent or present	0 – 2 or "UN"
8. Sensory	response to pinprick, noxious stimulus	0 – 2
9. Best language	presence or absence of aphasia	0 – 3
10. Dysarthria	mild to severe	0 – 2 or "UN"
11. Extinction and inattention	response to sensory (visual, tactile, auditory, spatial, personal) stimulation	0 – 2

Quick Review Question

15. When administering the NIHSS and assessing facial palsy, the patient is unable to move the right side of his face. What is the appropriate score for that item of the scale?

Answer Key

1. Lower back pain is a symptom of ACS often seen in women and the elderly. Because the patient has a history of angina, the nurse should assess the patient for other signs and symptoms of ACS and expect that an ECG will be administered.

2. The nurse's priority should be the patient's breathing. The nurse should elevate the head of the bed, apply oxygen, and notify the physician.

3. Low ABI values (≤0.9) indicate a likely arterial occlusion.

4. The patient is showing signs of an ischemic stroke, possibly caused by A-fib. The nurse should alert the medical provider and prepare for the patient to have an immediate, non-contrast CT scan of the head.

5. The nurse should expect to hear decreased or absent breath sounds in the area of effusion. The nurse may also hear bronchial breath sounds and egophony.

6. S3 gallops are heard with heart failure.

7. Right-sided heart failure can cause edema in the extremities and abdomen. When fluid collects in the peritoneal cavity (ascites), it creates a dull sound during percussion of the abdomen.

8. The patient's foot is cyanotic and pulseless, which indicates arterial occlusion. The occluded artery has resulted in hypoxia in the patient's foot, giving it a blue color.

9. The nurse should focus on CVP as CVP is an indirect measure of right ventricular pressure and is highly influenced by fluid status. In sepsis, CVP is 2 mmHg because of profound systemic vasodilation. Both treatments would be expected to increase preload, thereby increasing CVP.

10. The patient will have decreased O_2 levels, increased CO_2 levels, and show signs of anemia, including dyspnea, fatigue, and palpitations.

11. Because a cardiac catheterization is performed by gaining access to a patient's artery, the procedure puts the patient at a high risk of bleeding. If bleeding occurs, the nurse should apply pressure at the catheterization site and notify the physician.

12. The symptoms indicate right-sided MI. When treating patients with right ventricular infarction, nitrates, diuretics, and morphine are to be avoided due to their preload-reducing effects.

13. This EKG strip represents sinus tachycardia because the only abnormality is the heart rate, which is >100. The P wave, PR interval, QRS complex, T wave, and QT intervals are within normal parameters.

14. The ABI is calculated by dividing the ankle systolic pressure by the brachial systolic pressure. In this case, the calculation is:

$$86 \div 110 = 0.78$$

Normal values are 1 to 1.1; values 0.95 indicate narrowing of the vessel; 0.6 to 0.8, borderline perfusion; 0.5 to 0.75, severe disease, 0.5, pain at rest/limb threatening; and 0.25, severe/critical limb threatening.

15. During administration of the NIHSS and assessment facial palsy, if the patient is only able to move half of his face, the appropriate score for that item would be 1 (partial facial palsy) on the NIHSS.

Chapter 5 – Planning, Implementation, Evaluation, and Modification

Developing an Individualized Plan of Care

A **nursing care plan** is a comprehensive overview of a patient's condition and required nursing care. The cardiac vascular nurse is responsible for initiating and updating the plan of care for patients from arrival through discharge:

- The **ADPIE model** is used to develop nursing care plans:
    - **Assessment:** Gather data about the client's physiological, psychological, and emotional conditions.
    - **Diagnosis:** Use clinical judgment to identify the patient's condition and medical needs.
        - **NANDA-I diagnoses:** guide clinical care planning for patients under the care of the cardiac vascular nurse
        - While it is not in the cardiac vascular nurse's scope of practice to diagnose a specific disease or ailment, it is within the scope to identify a general cause of symptoms. For example, a patient with congestive heart failure may have shortness of breath, fatigue, and swelling. The cardiac vascular nurse would choose NANDA-I diagnoses related to those symptoms, such as decreased CO.
    - **Planning:** Set measurable goals and outcomes for the patient and identify nursing interventions aimed to meet those goals.
    - **Intervention:** Implement the care plan.
        - The nurse's role in the implementation phase may include both oversight of and action on interventions.
    - **Evaluation:** Determine if the goals and outcomes from the planning stage have been achieved.
        - Care and outcomes should be continuously monitored, and the care plan should be modified per the patient response.
- **Concept mapping** is a way of organizing and planning the course of the patient's care. It is a visual tool that addresses each element of the ADPIE and provides a path to outcomes assessment.
- **Discharge planning** is the process of planning for the patient's exit from the health care facility.
    - It begins when a patient is admitted to an inpatient, rehab, procedural, or surgical setting.

- It considers the patient's ability to care for themselves independently, medical equipment or care needed in the home, referrals, available social support, and available community resources.
- It includes discharge teaching relevant to the patient's care plan.

- A key responsibility of the cardiac vascular nurse is patient education, including health promotion and lifestyle changes; this information should be included in the care plan. (See Chapter 9 for more information on patient education.)

- **Nursing diagnoses** should be prioritized with consideration for Maslow's hierarchy of needs. (Most nursing diagnoses will fall in the first two levels of the hierarchy.) The needs, in order of importance, are as follows:
  - physiological needs: food, water, rest, health
  - safety: security of body, security of resources
  - love and belonging: friendship, intimacy, family
  - esteem: feelings of accomplishment
  - self-actualization: achieving one's full potential

- Cardiac vascular nursing requires critical thinking and prioritization to meet a patient's needs based on the severity of the patient's symptoms or the potential for harm.
  - Planning includes triaging the patient's clinical presentation of diagnoses from those with the most potential to cause harm to those with the least potential to cause harm.
  - The top priority is to manage or prevent the occurrence of life-threatening symptoms.
  - The following sources of potential harm should be addressed as high priorities:
    - symptomatic dysrhythmias
    - decreased O_2 levels
    - lack of palpable or Doppler pulses
    - acute changes in the patient's pain level
    - acute changes in the patient's blood glucose level
    - changes from baseline in critical labs

Quick Review Question

1. The nurse is reviewing the care plan for a patient with congestive HF who is currently on BiPAP for fluid volume overload. The patient's labs return with a potassium of 2.9 mEq/L. The patient's morning medications are due, and the nurse is also being called by another patient who requires insulin before eating breakfast. What is the nurse's priority?

Coordinating Care Across the Continuum

- The cardiac vascular nurse is a member of an interdisciplinary health care team, which includes health care providers from different fields who work together to provide care for the patient.
- The members of a patient's health care team largely depend on the client's chief complaint, diagnosis, and treatment goals. Generally, the team will comprise the following members:
    - physician: may be an internist, family practitioner, or cardiologist (depends on the organization); provides a medical diagnosis and contributes to the plan of care
    - CV nurse: contributes to the plan of care for the patient, the management of the patient's disease, and discharge planning
    - technicians/aides: act under the delegated authority of the physician and the nurse; other technicians that may participate in the care of the cardiac patient include echocardiography technicians, radiological technicians, or ultrasound technicians
    - case manager: responsible for coordinating care throughout the patient's stay and beyond; a key player in the discharge planning process
    - social worker: may participate on the care team if patient support is needed (e.g., counseling, meal services) after inpatient care
- The goal of **care coordination** is to achieve safe, effective care through the deliberate organization of patient care activities within the interdisciplinary health care team. Examples of care coordination include the following:
    - sharing knowledge within the health care team
    - managing care transitions
    - aligning resources with patients' medical, emotional, and social needs
    - setting patients up with community resources

As the member of the health care team who spends the most one-on-one time with the patient, the cardiac vascular nurse is a key component of successful care coordination. Care coordination can significantly impact the efficacy and economics of health care:

- Patients who receive high-quality care coordination have better health outcomes as they are less likely to miss follow-up appointments and less likely to be rehospitalized.
- Care coordination ensures that resources are being efficiently allocated and can minimize the cost of care for the patient and health care provider.
- Care coordination ensures that the standard of care is met for every patient, which is necessary for some insurance reimbursements.

Quick Review Question

2. A patient who requires an ongoing milrinone infusion is being discharged. What are some considerations and services that must be in place before the patient leaves the facility?

Creating a Safe and Therapeutic Environment

Cardiac vascular nurses are responsible for creating a safe, therapeutic environment that minimizes the risk of physical and emotional harm to the patient. **Patient safety** is the responsibility of each member of the interdisciplinary team. The following considerations for patient safety are the specific responsibilities of the CV nurse:

- Preventing **medication errors:** These errors are more common in emergency situations or resuscitation efforts, which can occur regularly in cardiac care units. Drills and practice in these situations will increase nurses' confidence and efficiency in administering emergency drugs.
- Preventing **falls:** Patients receiving cardiac care often have high risks of falling. Communication with the patient, provision of call lights, and hourly rounding are good ways to mitigate the risk of patient falls.
- **Communicating effectively:** The CV nurse is responsible for clearly and promptly communicating information about changes in the patient's condition to other members of the health care team.
- **Following protocols:** CV nurses should know the protocols for their units and follow them.

Environment of care refers to the environment in which care is provided to patients. Nurses are part of the interdisciplinary team responsible for maintaining safety within the environment of care:

- **Inpatient care settings** are those in which a patient remains hospitalized for at least one day; these types of settings often house patients with complex medical issues who have a high risk of complications.
- **Procedural care environments** are where patients receive same-day procedures and are then discharged to their homes. Nurses are responsible for providing clear, accurate, and comprehensive discharge instructions to the patients in order to prevent post-procedure complications.
- **Surgical care** settings are those in which patients receive operative procedures that require them to remain as inpatients.
    - Safety concerns for CV nurses in a surgical setting include wrong-site surgeries, infection prevention, DVT prevention, and reactions to anesthetic agents.
- **Rehabilitation environments** are often designed to more closely resemble the home environment, which can present unique safety concerns.
    - Rehabilitation environments often house patients who are considered high-risk for falls, infection, and pressure ulcers.

- The cardiac vascular nurse is responsible for identifying the severity and nature of the safety risks for each patient and initiating appropriate interventions within the plan of care to mitigate the risks.

The **therapeutic environment** refers to the physical, psychological, and social environments in which patients receive care. Different patients require different therapeutic considerations, and the nurse is responsible for determining the patient's needs. The CV nurse's goal is to create a therapeutic environment that is physically and emotionally healing. This environment should meet the following criteria:

- support and practice excellence in treating the patient
- have positive, measurable patient outcomes
- have positive staff effectiveness
- anticipate and support the patient's psychosocial and spiritual needs
- anticipate the family's needs

Quick Review Question

3. The nurse is caring for a patient who is admitted to the telemetry unit. The patient discloses that he has fallen several times at home before admission. What safety interventions should the nurse include in this patient's care plan?

Risk-Reduction Measures

While numerous risk-reduction measures exist to prevent cardiac and vascular diseases, the cardiac vascular nurse must also employ measures and interventions to help prevent complications that arise from or are exacerbated by cardiovascular disease and its related risk factors (e.g., obesity). For example, prophylactic measures to prevent thromboembolisms, such as venous thromboembolisms (VTE) and pulmonary embolisms, from occurring include the following:

- **Early mobilization:** Repositioning should occur at least every two hours if the patient is bedridden, with ambulation taking place four to six times daily if possible—this intervention alone may be adequate for low-risk patients.

- **Mechanical prophylaxis:** Knee-high, properly fitted and positioned graduated antiembolism compression stockings and/or intermittent pneumatic compression devices should be used. In order to improve circulation and prevent stasis, mechanical prophylaxis should be used around the clock until the patient's mobility and circulation are normal. (Note: these must be fitted correctly in order to be effective.) Mechanical prophylaxis alone may be adequate for patients with moderate risk.

- **Leg exercises:** Patients should flex and extend their hips, knees, and ankles every 2 to 4 hours, if they are able to do so. If their mobility is limited, patients may use venous foot pumps.

- **Hydration:** Unless fluid intake is limited, 2 to 3 liters of fluid daily are recommended.

- **Anticoagulation:** Low-molecular-weight heparin (LMWH; e.g., enoxaparin, dalteparin), unfractionated heparin, direct oral anticoagulants (e.g., rivaroxaban, apixaban, dabigatran), aspirin, or a vitamin K antagonist (e.g., warfarin) should be administered. This risk-reduction measure is recommended for patients who are at high risk as well as some patients who are at moderate risk.

Quick Review Question

4. If a patient is generally in good health but has a moderate risk for VTE due to a BMI of 35, what type of VTE prophylaxis is likely indicated if the patient is undergoing a minor surgical procedure?

Interventions

Patients who have experienced cardiac arrest and are in a comatose state require interventions to improve their neurological outcomes and reduce mortality. **Targeted temperature management (TTM)** is an intervention that is used for such patients. American Heart Association guidelines for the consideration of TTM include the following:

- out-of-hospital pulseless ventricular tachycardia
- out-of-hospital ventricular fibrillation
- inpatient cardiac arrest
- nonshockable rhythm

Guidelines from the **International Liaison Committee on Resuscitation** include out of-hospital cardiac arrest with shockable or unshockable rhythm, or in-hospital cardiac arrest with an initial rhythm. During TTM, patients are sedated and paralyzed with a secure airway and ventilation. Phases of TTM are as follows:

- **Induction:** This phase involves cooling the body to achieve a target core body temperature of between 32°C to 34°C; cold saline IV, ice packs, cooling blankets, or intravascular core cooling systems can be used.

- **Maintenance:** This describes the phase during which the core body temperature is monitored, ideally with a pulmonary artery catheter or an esophageal probe. Bladder probes are less accurate and have a 20-minute lag time. Hypothermia is maintained for 24 hours.

- **Rewarming:** During this phase, the core body temperature is slowly increased by 0.2°C to 0.5°C per hour until the temperature exceeds 36°C, usually up to about 8 hours.

Complications with targeted temperature management may include coronary artery vasoconstriction, cold-induced diuresis, electrolyte imbalance (i.e., hyperkalemia during rewarming), and/or hemodynamic instability.

Quick Review Question

5. If a patient's temperature was lowered to 33°C, and the patient is rewarmed at 0.4°C per hour, how many hours will it take for the patient's temperature to reach 36.2°C?

Changes in Patient Condition

The CV nurse is responsible for monitoring patients for acute changes in condition and communicating these changes to the appropriate member of the health care team. The CV nurse must know how to recognize changes in the patient's condition—no matter how minute—and react accordingly. Failure to do so can result in harm of the patient. Communication of changes in a patient's condition will depend on the acuity and level of concern related to the change in condition:

- Improvement in patient condition requires that the plan of care be updated; the provider should be notified so that the care and discharge plans can be reevaluated.
- A decline in the patient's status requires rapid and precise communication to the provider using the SBAR method (see Chapter 6).
- CV nurses should continually assess patients based on their needs; such assessments may include the following:
    - ongoing assessment of patient condition
    - reassessment after intervention
    - continuous cardiac monitoring and telemetry
- The following are examples of changes in patient condition that require immediate communication:
    - ECG changes (changes from the baseline measurement, such as STEMI/NSTEMI)
    - respiratory distress or arrest
    - cardiac arrest
    - acute changes in mental status
    - new onset of chest pain
    - diaphoresis and nausea
    - vital sign changes of 20% from baseline

Quick Review Question

6. A cardiac vascular nurse is caring for a patient on continuous cardiac monitoring in the CV unit. He notices that the patient's heart rhythm has changed to SVT with a rate of 210 bpm. The patient's current medication has had no effect. What action should the nurse take next?

Outcomes Evaluations

An **outcome** is a change in a patient's status. Outcomes are used to evaluate the effect of an intervention or nursing practice on a patient:

- Outcomes should be developed based on the care plan, the patient's needs, and the health care team's goals for the patient.

- Outcomes should be **SMART:**
    - **S**pecific
    - **M**easurable
    - **A**ttainable
    - **R**ealistic
    - **T**ime-restricted
- Common patient outcomes include the following:
    - objective data (e.g., blood pressure, blood sugar)
    - symptoms (e.g., dizziness, pain)
    - functional status (e.g., ADLs, employment)
    - lifestyle factors (e.g., diet, exercise)
- If the patient cannot maintain the interventions required for an outcome, the nurse should modify the outcome so that the patient can sustain it.
- In an inpatient setting, plans of care are evaluated twice or more per day. The care plan is updated at every shift, when outcomes are met, or when goals change.
- Medical and nursing professional associations, such as those listed below, have prepared evidence-based guidelines for the care of certain patient populations:
    - American Heart Association (AHA)
    - American Association of Cardiovascular and Pulmonary Rehabilitation (AACVPR)
    - The Society for Vascular Nursing (SVN)
    - The Joint National Committee on Prevention, Detection, Evaluation, and Treatment of High Blood Pressure (JNC)
    - the National Heart, Lung, and Blood Institute (NHLBI)
    - the National Institutes of Health (NIH)

Situation	- A patient comes to the hospital with high blood pressure. He is a smoker and does not eat well or exercise.
Nursing diagnosis	- decreased cardiac output r/t hypertension
Outcomes/SMART goals	- The patient's SBP and DP will be maintained within a range of 110/75 to 130/90 per protocol and physician's orders. - The patient will verbalize the importance of smoking cessation by day 2. - The patient will verbalize the importance of following up with a cardiologist in 1 week. - The patient will demonstrate the ability to select a lunch that complies with a cardiac diet by day 3.

	· The patient will verbalize how exercise affects the body by day 3.
Nursing interventions	· The nurse will assess the patient's blood pressure at least hourly or per unit protocol, and administer ordered medication and titrate drips as needed to maintain range. · The nurse will educate the patient on hypertension and its effects on the body by day 2. · The nurse will assist the patient in selecting appropriate foods for a cardiac diet by day 3. · The nurse will assist the patient in obtaining smoking cessation materials by day 2.

Figure 5.1. Example of a Care Plan with Outcomes

Quick Review Question

7. A cardiac vascular nurse is caring for a patient with the nursing diagnosis of acute pain related to myocardial ischemia. What are some possible outcomes the nurse could include in the care plan for this patient?

Answer Key

1. The nurse should focus on the patient who requires BiPAP, as this patient has a higher potential for serious harm. The nurse should review the patient's medications for any that would be potassium wasting [e.g., furosemide (Lasix)], which would be an expected treatment for this patient population. Unless contraindicated, morning medications should be administered followed by a call to the physician for further orders on holding diuretics and/or potassium replacement therapy.

2. Care coordination outside the facility must be in place. An assessment of the patient's ongoing access to care and medications will identify any needed interventions before the patient goes home. The nurse should ensure that future visits with the primary care physician and follow-up with cardiology are arranged. The patient will need home infusion equipment at discharge and to have an appointment scheduled with the visiting infusion nurse. The patient and family should be given resources and contacts to ensure that they know what to do in case of any complications.

3. The nurse should consider the patient a high-fall risk and update the plan of care to reflect the risk for falls. Appropriate safety interventions include initiating fall precautions, notifying the health care team, clearing the room of any obstacles, and discussing fall risk education with the patient.

4. A BMI of 30 to 40 puts a patient at moderate risk for VTE. Since this patient is otherwise in good health and should be able to ambulate early, it is likely that only mechanical prophylaxis, such as compression stockings and/or an intermittent pneumatic compression device, will be needed.

5. The temperature difference (36.2°C to 33°C) is 3.2°C. With a warming rate of 0.4°C, the time required $(\frac{3.2}{0.4})$ is 8 hours to warm the patient to 36.2°C.

6. The nurse should contact the cardiologist and prepare to intervene appropriately based on the patient's condition, which may include a 12-lead ECG, administration of adenosine, or direct current cardioversion.

7. Possible outcomes for this diagnosis include the patient reporting a decrease in chest pain at less than $\frac{3}{10}$ on the pain scale; serial troponins drawn every 6 hours a total of three times, with abnormal values reported to the cardiologist; and systolic BP that remains between 110 and 130 for the duration of the patient's stay.

Chapter 6 – The Professional Role of the Cardiac-Vascular Nurse

Communication

Components of Communication

Therapeutic communication is a set of communication techniques that address the physical, mental, and emotional well-being of patients:

- The therapeutic communication that is used should be tailored to the situation or context.
- The cardiac vascular nurse should consider the patient's age, language, any barriers to communication, and the nature of the information being communicated.

Best practices for therapeutic communication are described in Table 6.1.

Table 6.1. The Dos and Don'ts of Patient Communication	
Do . . .	Do not . . .
<ul><li>make eye contact with the patient.</li><li>introduce yourself and use the patient's name.</li><li>speak directly to the patient when possible.</li><li>ask open-ended questions.</li><li>speak slowly and clearly.</li><li>show empathy for the patient.</li><li>be silent when appropriate to allow patients time to think and process emotions.</li></ul>	<ul><li>use medical jargon.</li><li>threaten or intimidate the patient.</li><li>lie or provide false hope.</li><li>interrupt the patient.</li><li>show frustration or anger.</li><li>make judgmental statements.</li></ul>

- Some of the following techniques are used for therapeutic communication:
    - **Active listening** includes facing the client, being attentive to what they are saying, and maintaining eye contact (if it is culturally appropriate to do so).
    - **Sharing** observations may open the conversation up to how the patient is feeling.
    - **Empathy**, or trying to understand and accurately perceive the patient's feelings and experiences, can make the patient more comfortable.

- o **Using touch**, such as a gentle hand on the shoulder or arm, when appropriate or welcome, can offer comfort.
- o **Silence** allows the patient a moment to absorb or process information given.
- o **Summarizing and paraphrasing** information back to a patient helps ensure or confirm understanding.
- o **Asking relevant questions** that pertain to the situation helps the nurse gather information for decision-making.
- Communication includes both verbal and nonverbal components:
  - o **Verbal communication** is the use of language to convey information. Characteristics of verbal communication include tone, volume, and word choice.
  - o **Nonverbal communication** includes behavior, gestures, posture, and other non-language elements of communication that transmit information or meaning.

Quick Review Question

1. What elements of therapeutic communication should the nurse use when sharing news that may be troubling to a patient?

Barriers to Communication

Barriers to communication can prevent the effective transmission of information between the nurse and the patient; they include the following:

- language differences
- sensory impairments
- cognitive impairments
- time constraints
- personality conflicts

Language barriers can occur when a nurse does not speak the patient's primary language or speaks it as a second language:

- When an interpreter is required, the organization should provide professional interpretation services for the patient; it is not appropriate for staff to act as interpreters.
- Sensory impairments include hearing or vision loss either as a result of heredity, disease, or injury.
- Patients with sensory impairments should be offered interpretation services when needed.
- Whenever possible, the nurse should ask patients about their preferred methods of communication.

Cognitive impairments can often result from trauma or injury, particularly stroke. In these cases patients may not be able to speak due to motor impairments, or they may have neurological impairments that prevent them from processing communication:

- The nurse should determine the method of communication that works best for the patient.
- Nurses should be aware of changes in a patient's cognitive status.

Time constraints are common in all care settings and can be the result of understaffing, high-acuity patient loads, or unanticipated emergencies:

- When the nurse is speaking with patients and their families under time constraints, the nurse should share this issue with the patient. Being clear with patients will prevent misunderstandings.
- Personality conflicts can occur between two people with different communication or work styles. These issues are often outside the control of the patient or the nurse.
    - If the conflict is infringing on the quality of patient care, arrangements should be made to mitigate the issue whenever possible (e.g., reassigning nurses).

> **Helpful Hint**
> When treating patients who are blind or have low vision, describe what actions are being taken throughout assessment and treatment so that the client understands what is occurring.

Quick Review Question

2. A patient is admitted to the cardiac vascular ward and the nurse realizes that the patient is a native speaker of Spanish who understands some English. What should the nurse do?

Interview Techniques

- **Patient interviewing** is a skill cardiac vascular nurses must develop so that they can gather the information needed to perform a comprehensive assessment and create a plan of care. General interviewing techniques include the following:
    - **Active listening:** This means concentrating on the patient and responding appropriately to what they say.
    - **Adaptive questioning:** This is the use of guided questions that get progressively more specific, while allowing the patient to provide information in an uninterrupted narrative.
    - **Echoing:** Repeating words used by the patient in the form of a question can elicit more information.
    - **Open-ended questioning:** Yes-no questions do not actively elicit information; patients should be encouraged to expand on their answers.
    - **Empathy:** Showing concern and understanding when the patient is speaking can make the patient feel comfortable.
    - **Validation:** Patients need to know that their emotions and experiences are real and valid.

- o **Reassurance:** The patient needs to know that their concerns are being heard.
- **Motivational interviewing** is used to elicit a patient's personal reasons for changing behavior patterns in order to promote health.
  - o Nurses can use motivational interviewing to guide the plan of care and education given to the patient.

Quick Review Question

3. How does motivational interviewing contribute to the overall plan of care for the cardiac vascular patient?

Documenting Communication

- Documentation of communication should occur whenever information is passed from the patient to the nurse or from the nurse to the patient. Types of communication that should be documented include the following:
  - o patient contribution to assessment details (subjective)
  - o notification of change in condition from patient
  - o updates in care plan from nurse to patient
  - o concerns or questions expressed by the patient
  - o education provided to the patient by the nurse
  - o confirmation of patient understanding of information given

Quick Review Question

4. A patient calls the nurse to his room to explain that his chest pain has increased and he now feels nauseous. What should the nurse document after this interaction?

Professional Communication

- Professional communication includes the following:
  - o comprehensive handoff communication between nurses
  - o professional interdisciplinary communication
  - o conflict resolution in a variety of circumstances
- **SBAR** (**S**ituation, **B**ackground, **A**ssessment, and **R**ecommendations) handoff is a reporting tool used during shift change, when a patient is being admitted, or when an acute change in the patient's condition needs to be communicated to the care team:
  - o **Situation:** nurse's name, patient's name and location, any current problems
  - o **Background:** diagnosis, history, and current care plan
  - o **Assessment:** relevant vital signs and diagnostic testing

- ○ **Recommendation:** recommendations for further testing, changes to care plan, or transfers
- **Interdisciplinary communication** is communication among disciplines (e.g., other medical staff, nursing staff, consultative services, ancillary services, support staff). Such communication should have the following characteristics:
  - ○ be mutually respectful
  - ○ be timely
  - ○ be patient-focused
- **Conflict resolution** should be used in circumstances in which conflict within the interdisciplinary team is interrupting patient care. Conflict resolution strategies include the following:
  - ○ **Accommodating:** The goal of accommodating is to preserve harmony and relationships within the care team. It can be used to promote goodwill but should be used sparingly.
  - ○ **Compromising:** Compromising involves concessions on both sides in order to preserve the interdisciplinary relationship; it may be used as a temporary solution to a complex issue.
  - ○ **Collaborating:** Collaborating is true problem solving, in which the goal is to come to a mutual solution that is acceptable for all parties.
  - ○ **Avoiding:** Avoiding is generally not the best approach in the context of patient care. It can be a temporary solution but should not be the final strategy used to resolve a particular conflict.
  - ○ **Competing:** Generally viewed as a negative way to manage conflict, competing is a strategy in which one party "wins." It may be useful when quick, decisive action is necessary.

Quick Review Question

5. A nurse in the cardiac vascular intensive care unit is preparing to hand off a patient recovering from a CABG. What information should the nurse be prepared to provide?

The Work Environment

Leadership

Nurses are expected to be leaders in the care setting. There are several leadership styles, but those commonly found in the nursing profession include transactional, transformational, and authoritarian leadership:

- **Transactional leadership** is an approach in which leaders promote compliance from subordinates through the use of rewards and punishments:
  - ○ This leadership style is typically effective for the short term but does not create a positive long-term work environment.

- **Democratic leadership** is a style that allows members of the group to participate in decision-making:
  - This leadership style works well in settings that have already established shared governance practices, such as Magnet hospitals.
- **Laissez-faire leadership** is characterized by a hands-off approach in which staff is allowed to make decisions without input from leadership.
  - This type of leadership generally leads to low productivity among group members and is not ideal in nursing settings.
- **Transformational leadership** promotes change in individuals and systems:
  - Valuable and positive interaction with team members results in the transformation of followers into leaders.
  - It is often considered an ideal leadership approach for nursing leaders.
- **Authoritarian leadership**, also known as **autocratic leadership**, includes little input from staff, with the majority of decisions made by the leader:
  - Authoritarian leadership does not follow a model of shared governance and does not provide opportunities for input or advice from team members, resulting in low morale.

Cardiac vascular nurses can assume the role of preceptor, mentor, clinical resource, or change agent:

- **Preceptors** are registered nurses who act in the dual role of nurse and educator for a newly hired or newly graduated nurse.
  - Preceptors are generally subject matter experts and leaders within the nursing unit.
- **Mentors** are experienced nurses whose roles include guidance, education, and the support of nursing practice and career decisions for new nurses.
  - Mentors are usually assigned on a volunteer basis and are matched with mentees based on personality and similarity in career goals or paths.
- **Clinical resource nurses** are recognized as subject matter experts and are available to nurses within a unit.
  - Some organizations may employ clinical resource nurses as nurse educators or clinical nurse specialists, with a focus on acting as resources for other nursing staff; other organizations may use this role as a resource for patients.
- **Change agents** are recognized nurse leaders within units who encourage and enable change.
  - Change is usually brought about as a result of an evidence-based practice/process improvement project.

> **Helpful Hint**
>
> Evidence-based practice refers to scientifically tested methods and processes that have yielded consistent outcomes.

Quick Review Question

6. The charge nurse on a unit is known to reward nurses who comply with directives by allowing them to have preference in daily assignments. What type of leadership does this charge nurse display?

Working as a Team

Healthy nursing work environments are built upon professional relationships, civility, team building, and shared governance:

- An absence of positive relationships, mutual respect, and good communication can result in a negative or toxic work environment.
- Nurses have a responsibility to contribute to a positive work environment by working toward the following:
    - professional relationships
    - workplace civility
    - team building
    - diversity
    - shared governance
    - the appropriate delegation of tasks
- **Professional relationships** with the care team and interdisciplinary team result from good communication and mutual respect:
- **Workplace civility** is achieved through professionalism, respect, courtesy, and a general awareness of the feelings of others.
- **Team building** contributes to overall organizational effectiveness and civility within the work environment. Team building is usually prompted by nurse leaders or nurse managers.
- A **healthy work environment** is one that is accepting and welcoming of all diverse individuals, including those of different races, genders, ethnic groups, ages, religions, and sexual orientations.
- **Shared governance** provides the opportunity for team members to work together to make decisions that affect practice and the work environment:
    - Unit or clinical nursing practice councils are one way for team members to participate in shared governance.
    - Shared governance follows the constructs of a professional practice model.
- **Delegation of tasks** is governed by local organizational policies, state nurse practice acts, and professional association practice guidelines:
    - State nurse practice acts outline specific scopes of practice for all licensed personnel working in health care settings. Registered nurses in the clinical setting may delegate tasks to the following licensed personnel:

- - - LPNs/LVNs
    - medical assistants
    - nursing assistants
    - technicians
  - Delegation does not take away the nurse's responsibility for completion of the task and its outcome.
  - The nurse should have in mind the scope of practice as well as the skills and abilities of the individual to whom they are delegating tasks.

Quick Review Question

7. What can a CV nurse do in order to contribute to a work environment that promotes shared governance?

Quality Improvement and Risk Management

Quality and process improvements are the assessments and critiques of processes and systems within a health care organization:

- **Quality improvement** uses data to monitor the outcomes of care processes and to improve the quality and safety of health care systems:
  - Cardiac vascular nurses are responsible for participating in quality improvement initiatives.
  - Cardiac vascular nurses who believe processes are not efficient or conducive to safe, high-quality patient care should make recommendations to the quality management team.
- **Risk management** is the assessment and mitigation of risk in a health care setting:
  - The role of a risk manager is to work to prevent situations that can result in losses or liabilities stemming from the care of patients.
  - Risk managers investigate adverse events, sentinel events, or any patient complaint or concern that could lead to litigation.
- Risk managers get case referrals from many sources:
  - medical or nursing quality councils
  - internal patient-safety reporting systems
  - nurse or provider referrals
  - reports of adverse or sentinel events
  - patient referrals through patient-relations channels
- Quality improvement and risk-management practices are often governed by regulatory or accrediting agencies such as the Centers for Medicare and Medicaid Services and The Joint Commission.

Quick Review Question

8. A cardiac vascular nurse identifies a process that could be improved to be more efficient. What can the nurse do with that information?

Legal and Ethical Considerations

Ethical Issues

The American Nurses Association (ANA) established the **Nursing Code of Ethics**. The code of ethics has nine provisions that span the following ethical constructs:

- compassionate and respectful care
- commitment to the patient holistically
- patient advocacy
- responsibility in practice
- promotion of patient and self-health
- promotion of ethical practice
- participation in research
- collaboration with the health care team
- professional practice

The **core ethical principles** include autonomy, beneficence, nonmaleficence, justice, and veracity:

- **autonomy:** acknowledging that patients are unique individuals with the right to have their own opinions, values, beliefs, and perspectives
- **beneficence:** acting with the intent of doing the right thing or the most good
    - The nurse has an obligation to act in the best interest of the patient, regardless of other competing interests.
- nonmaleficence: doing no harm
    - This principle addresses the nurse's responsibility to keep the patient from harm in the care setting.
- **justice:** the provision of equitable access to care, including providing care to all patients regardless of socioeconomic status, demographic category, or insurance coverage
- **veracity:** the practice of complete truthfulness with patients and families

The **patient's bill of rights** may vary among medical organizations and professional nursing organizations; however, the core bill of rights originates from the Centers for Medicare and Medicaid, and includes the following:

- the right to make decisions regarding care

- the right to accept or refuse treatment
- the right to formulate or establish advance directives
- the right to accurate, easy-to-understand information about the health plan
- the right to choose providers
- the right to access emergency services
- the right to confidentiality
- the right to respect and nondiscrimination
- the right to a fair review of any complaint made with regard to health plan or care

Ethical dilemmas are circumstances that require health care providers to make medical decisions using ethical principles such as those found in the Code of Ethics. Ethical dilemmas found in the setting of cardiac vascular nursing include the following:

- advance directive actions
- decisional capacity determination
- refusals of care

In situations where the cardiac vascular nurse is faced with an ethical dilemma, the nurse should remember the following:

- Patients have a right and responsibility to be an active participant in their care, and they should be treated with dignity and respect regardless of their choices.
- The role of the nurse is to be a patient advocate.
- The nurse has an obligation to clearly communicate such issues to the health care team and objectively document them in the medical record.

Quick Review Question

9. A patient admitted to the inpatient ward does not want to be resuscitated in the event her heart stops beating again. The patient worries that her spouse will try to reverse the decision if the patient is unable to communicate. What should the nurse do?

Regulatory Issues

Regulatory considerations for the cardiac vascular nurse include knowing and understanding the scope of practice and eligibility for board certification:

- Both the ANA and the state where the nurse practices dictate the scope of practice:
  - It is the obligation of the cardiac vascular nurse to know the scope of practice and to practice within the limits of that scope.
  - Individual organizations may have more restrictive scopes of practice; nurses employed by such organizations must operate under the scope of the organization, as long as it does not violate the state or ANA scope.

- Nurses are eligible for board certification if they meet the following criteria:
  - have practiced nursing for at least two years
  - hold an active, unencumbered nursing license
  - have completed 30 hours of continuing education in cardiac vascular nursing within the last three years
  - have a minimum of 2,000 hours of clinical practice in cardiac vascular nursing within the last three years

Quick Review Question

10. Where can cardiac vascular nurses find information regarding the scopes of practice under which they are regulated?

Legal Issues

The following legal issues may present in the context of cardiac vascular nursing:

- intentional and unintentional torts
- negligence
- privacy violations
- the application of advance directives

Intentional torts are actions that result in harm to the patient. The harm is not necessarily intentional, but the act that resulted in harm is:

- A typical example of an intentional tort is the act of forcing unwanted medical care on a patient.

An **unintentional tort** is the result of unintended harm or injury to someone in a situation where a care provider should have known harm would result. Unintentional torts are most often characterized as negligence in the context of nursing:

- An example of negligence would be a significant delay in care, such as giving a medication several hours later than scheduled, resulting in harm or injury to a patient.

The **Health Insurance Portability and Accountability Act (HIPAA)** requires that individual health care providers and health care organizations make every attempt to safeguard the **protected health information (PHI)** of the patient:

- PHI is defined as any information that concerns the past, present, or future mental or physical health of the patient, along with the treatments of such health conditions and the methods of payment for health services rendered.
- Organizations are required to take measures to protect all PHI on electronic platforms or in electronic formats.
- HIPAA is based on the minimum necessary requirement; in other words, the minimum amount of PHI needed to accomplish a task should be shared.

- Sharing of PHI with patient's family, friends, or others is only possible with the patient's consent.
- Sharing of PHI is permissible under HIPAA in the following contexts:
  - activities involving reimbursement or payment for care premiums, determining coverage or provision of benefits, etc.
  - health care operations, such as quality improvement activities
  - competency assurance
  - audits of medical records for legal or competency reviews
  - insurance use
  - business planning, development, or management
- PHI may also be released for the following reasons:
  - public health reporting
  - fraud reporting
  - abuse and neglect reporting
  - organ and tissue donation
  - law enforcement proceedings
  - crime reporting
  - military and veterans' health and national security

Advance directives are written statements of individuals' wishes with regard to medical treatment decisions such as resuscitation, intubation, and other interventions; they are made to ensure that the wishes of the individual are carried out in the event the person is unable to express those wishes at the time of care:

- They are used to provide answers to difficult questions or decisions needing to be made in the context of end-of-life care.
  - States and organizations may have policies that guide the establishment and use of advance directives.
- Advance directives must be valid, up to date, and documented before they can be honored in the clinical setting. In order to honor an advance directive, the physician must see the paperwork, validate the paperwork, and place an order that indicates the advance directive status of the patient.
- Advance directives generally dictate the level of lifesaving measures to be taken in certain circumstances:
  - **Do not resuscitate (DNR)** typically indicates that no heroic measures should be taken to sustain the patient's life.
  - **Do not intubate (DNI)** indicates that the patient does not wish to be intubated if the need presents.

- o **Allow natural death (AND)** indicates the patient does not want any intervention that may sustain life or prevent a natural progression to death.
- Any combination of DNR, DNI, and AND may be requested, as can other directives present in the documentation if applicable to the patient's circumstance.
- DNR, DNI, and AND all allow for palliative care and comfort measures.

Living wills are used in situations where a patient may have a terminal illness or is acutely in a vegetative state.

> **Helpful Hint**
>
> Advance directives may also address organ donation and specify which organs a patient is choosing to donate and/or specific recipients.

- Living wills allow an individual to state which treatments they would like in the event they are unable to express this information at the time of illness/treatment needs.
- The document must be present and valid in order to be applied to care in the clinical setting.

Durable power of attorney (also called **medical power of attorney** or **health care proxy**) may be appointed to make health care decisions for a patient who does not have the capacity to do so.

> **Helpful Hint**
>
> Patients who are alert and competent cannot have their medical decisions overridden by their health care proxies.

- The range of decisions the surrogate can make may be general or very specific.
- A durable power of attorney must be present and valid in order to be used for decisions in care.

In the absence of legal documentation to guide such decisions, a multidisciplinary approach should be taken to inform patients and families of options for these decisions.

Quick Review Question

11. A patient's family member calls the unit to ask for an update on the patient's condition. What should the nurse do before providing the information?

Answer Key

1. When delivering troubling news, the nurse should use communication skills such as active listening, empathy, touch (when appropriate), and silence to assist the patient with processing the information.

2. The nurse should arrange for an interpreter to complete the admission assessment and to communicate any pertinent information between the patient and the care team. It would not be appropriate to try to communicate with the patient in a language other than Spanish.

3. Information gathered from a motivational interview can be used to assist a patient with making behavioral and lifestyle changes that can have positive impacts on their disease progression.

4. The nurse should document that the patient called to notify the nurse of a change in condition. The documentation should include the date, time, and nature of the change; any resulting assessment findings, such as the nature and quality of the pain, the nature of the nausea, and any other pertinent findings. The nurse should also document any intervention or action taken as a result of the change in condition.

5. The nurse should be prepared to provide an SBAR report that describes the situation, background, assessment, and recommendations. For this patient, the SBAR report may include the following:

- situation: patient's name, location, and attending physician
- background: diagnosis, date of surgery, relevant medical history
- assessment: code status, vital signs, recent abnormal assessments, recent medications or procedures
- recommendation: any recommended changes to the care plan

6. This nurse is displaying a transactional leadership approach by using a rewards-based system.

7. The nurse can join a unit-level or hospital-level nursing practice council to participate in practice and policy discussions and change.

8. The nurse can bring that information, and any recommended solution, to the quality management team for consideration for a process improvement project. The nurse can play a role in supporting and implementing that change.

9. The cardiac vascular nurse is responsible for understanding the patient's advance directive preferences and communicating and documenting those preferences in the medical record. In the event that the advance directive must be used, the nurse must act as an advocate for the patient's end-of-life decisions. The nurse should inform the physician of the patient's preference for the advance directive and should document the discussion in the medical record.

10. The cardiac vascular nurse should review the ANA scope of practice, the scope of practice of the state in which they work, and the organizational scope of practice, if established.

11. The nurse should first determine if the patient has given permission to disclose medical information to family members, and, if so, which family members specifically. If the patient has given permission, the nurse must confirm the identity of the patient on the phone through the use of a HIPAA password or other method.

Chapter 7 - Cardiovascular Technologies and Procedures

Cardiac Monitoring

An **event recorder** is a battery-operated portable device used to monitor a patient's heart rhythm:

- **Loop recorders** are implanted devices that continuously monitor and record heart rhythms.
- **Symptom event monitors** are handheld or worn on the patient's wrist.
    - If the patient detects an abnormal rhythm, the patient places the device on the chest and presses a button so the device will start recording.
- A **Holter monitor** is a portable cardiac monitor that a patient wears for a short time, usually 24 – 48 hours.
    - The patient does not have to press a button to activate recording.
- An **insertable cardiac monitor (ICM)** is a cardiac monitor inserted under the skin by a cardiologist or an electrophysiologist; such monitors can last up to five years.
- **Mobile cardiac telemetry (MCT)** is the continuous monitoring of heart rhythms by means of a small sensor and monitor that a patient wears on the chest.

Quick Review Question

1. For the third time in a month, a patient has been admitted to the hospital with complaints of chest pain, palpitations, and dizziness. No ECG abnormalities were found during the patient's hospital stay. What intervention does the nurse expect?

Care for Extremities

Sequential compression devices (SCD) are wrapped around the calf areas of both legs and alternately inflate and deflate:

- The compression device improves blood flow by preventing "pooling" of the blood in the legs and helps prevent DVT in patients with limited mobility.
- The nurse should ensure that the correct size is used.
    - SCDs that are too tight may cause pressure necrosis, and those that are too large will be ineffective.

- **Thromboembolic deterrent (TED)** stockings are compression stockings worn by post-op or non-ambulatory patients to prevent DVT:
  - The nurse should assess for skin breakdown and pedal pulses when the TED stockings are in place.
  - In order to give the patient relief from the pressure against the skin, the nurse should remove the TEDs at night, or for any part of the day during which the patient is comfortable; if removed at night, TEDs should be applied before the patient gets out of bed in the morning.
- An **Unna boot** is a compression dressing made from gauze infused with zinc, glycerin, or calamine:
  - Unna boots are used in the treatment of venous leg ulcers and lymphedema.
  - The dressing is contraindicated in patients with arterial insufficiency.

Quick Review Question

2. Before placing an SCD or a TED stocking on a patient, what priority action should the nurse complete?

Cardiac Catheter Procedures

Catheter Procedure Pre-Op and Post-Op

In **cardiac catheter procedures**, a catheter is inserted into a large blood vessel to diagnose and treat damage in the arteries, heart muscles, and valves:

- The CV nurse assists with procedures, administers medication, monitors the patient's vital signs, and documents the patient's condition before, during, and after the procedure.

Pre-procedure nursing considerations include the following:

- Make sure that the patient has had NPO beginning at midnight before the procedure.
- Ask the patient about current medications, including antiplatelets, anticoagulants, and insulin:
  - Warfarin should be stopped and replaced with LMWH 48 hours before the procedure.
  - Aspirin may be given before the procedure.
- Ensure that baseline labs are drawn; these should include CBC, CMP, PT/INR, PTT, and type and cross (blood typing and cross-matching).

Post-procedure complications include the following:

- retroperitoneal bleeding
- cardiac ischemic pain
- excessive bleeding

- dysrhythmia
- hematoma
- neurovascular insufficiency (signs include pale limbs, an extremity that feels cool to the touch, and weak or absent pulses)
- When educating patients, the following information should be shared:
  - The affected leg (for catheterization through femoral artery) should be kept straight immediately after the procedure.
  - It is normal for the insertion site to show bruising or discoloration; a small lump may also be present.
  - The patient should refrain from strenuous physical activity and heavy lifting for approximately 3 – 4 days.
  - Patients should drink plenty of fluids to flush out the contrast dye.

> **Helpful Hint**
> Signs of retroperitoneal bleeding include hypotension; bradycardia; ecchymosis on the flank (Grey Turner's sign); and abdominal, back, or flank pain.

Compression Devices

- A **femoral compression device** (see Figure 7.1.) is used to prevent further bleeding after the removal of femoral sheaths, venous sheaths, and intra-aortic balloon pumps (IABPs):
  - A plastic dome is used to apply pressure at the insertion site.
  - The nurse inflates the dome to prevent bleeding and deflates the device once hemostasis has been achieved.

Figure 7.1. Femoral Compression Device

- **Radial compression devices** are used to achieve hemostasis and prevent arterial damage after a transradial (i.e., transradial cardiac catheterization) procedure.
  - The device wraps around the patient's wrist to apply pressure at the insertion site.

- - While the device is in place, the nurse should place a pulse oximeter probe on the affected hand.

Figure 7.2. Radial Compression Device

- Nursing considerations include the following:
  - The nurse should monitor vital signs and peripheral pulses while the device is in place.
  - Numbness, tingling, cyanosis, or diminished pulse in the extremity may indicate that the pressure on the device should be reduced.

Angioplasty

Percutaneous transluminal angioplasty (PTA) is used to widen arteries in patients with peripheral artery disease or stenosis in the carotid, renal, or coronary arteries. **Percutaneous coronary intervention (PCI)** (also called **coronary angioplasty**) is performed to revascularize the coronary arteries of the heart. PCI is commonly performed for the following conditions:

- unstable angina or angina that does not respond to medication
- acute coronary syndrome
- patients who are not candidates for a coronary artery bypass graft (CABG)

During an angioplasty, a balloon is placed in the stenotic artery via a catheter and inflated:

- The inflated balloon applies pressure to the plaque occluding the artery and increases blood flow.
- A stent may also be placed to keep the artery open.

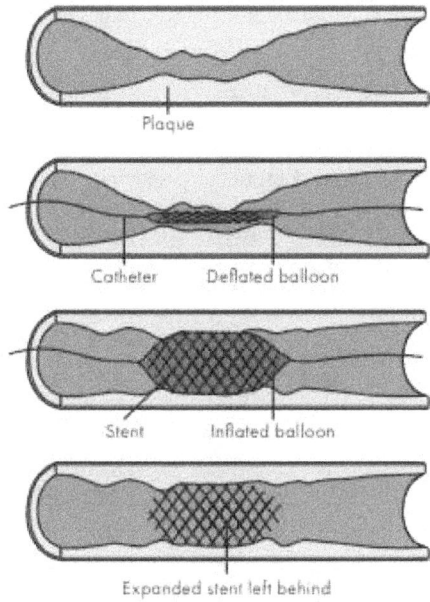

Figure 7.3. Angioplasty with Stent

Atherectomy

During an **atherectomy**, plaque is removed from atherosclerotic arteries:

- The artery is accessed with a specialized catheter that cuts the plaque into small pieces that can be removed.
- Some types of atherectomies will cut the plaque into pieces small enough to be left in the vasculature.

Catheter Ablation

Catheter ablation is performed to correct dysrhythmias, including atrial flutter, A-fib, SVT, and V-tach:

- An ablation is performed if the patient is not tolerating antidysrhythmic medications or is at a high risk for cardiac arrest or V-fib.
- In the heart's electrical conduction systems, the tissue that is causing the dysrhythmia is ablated using heat (radiofrequency ablation) or cold (cryoablation).
- The procedure is performed percutaneously via bilateral groin access.

Intra-Aortic Balloon Pump (IABP)

Intra-aortic balloon pump (IABP) therapy is used in patients with cardiogenic shock to increase coronary artery perfusion and raise blood pressure:

- The intra-aortic balloon is inserted into the ascending aortic arch via the femoral artery.

- The balloon inflates during diastole and forces blood flow back into the coronary arteries.

- During systole, the balloon deflates, which decreases afterload and increases CO.

- Contraindications for IABP include coagulopathies, aortic regurgitation, and dissecting/ruptured aortic aneurysm.

> **Helpful Hint**
>
> IABPs should only be paused briefly, as thrombus formation can occur quickly.

Figure 7.4. Intra-Aortic Balloon Pump (IABP) Therapy

Quick Review Question

3. The nurse is caring for a patient who just returned from the cardiac catheterization lab. While assessing the patient on initial return, the nurse notes swelling at the groin site. At the 15-minute reassessment, the nurse notes increased swelling from the initial assessment and notifies the charge nurse and performing physician. What device could the nurse anticipate using as an intervention for this patient?

Surgical Interventions

Coronary Artery Bypass Graft (CABG)

A **coronary artery bypass graft (CABG)** revascularizes ischemic heart tissue by diverting blood through the left internal thoracic artery or by grafting a section of the great saphenous vein to the aorta:

- CABG is performed in patients with cardiac ischemia who cannot be treated with PCI.
- Post-procedure complications include the following:
    - excessive bleeding or anemia
    - dysrhythmias (particularly A-fib): common postoperatively and may require medication or cardioversion; patient may be given prophylactic amiodarone
    - cardiac conditions, particularly perioperative MI and vasodilatory shock
    - post-pericardiotomy syndrome, which may present with fever, pericarditis, pericardial effusion, or tamponade
    - neurological conditions, including stroke, post-cardiotomy delirium, and peripheral neuropathy

> **Helpful Hint**
>
> Around 30 percent of patients will require a blood transfusion after CABG.

Figure 7.5. Coronary Artery Bypass Graft (CABG)

Chapter 7 - Cardiovascular Technologies and Procedures

Patient Education

- The patient should be enrolled in cardiac rehabilitation.
- The patient will require instruction on the prescribed medication regimen, which will likely include a statin, a beta blocker, and an ACE inhibitor.
- The patient should be instructed to avoid heavy lifting or other strenuous activity for approximately eight weeks after surgery.

Arterial Bypass Graft

During an **arterial bypass graft**, surgeons use harvested veins or synthetic grafts to reroute blood flow around obstructed arteries. The procedure is performed in patients with peripheral artery disease or aortoiliac disease. Bypass sites are named for the arteries being joined by the graft. The following are common sites for bypass:

- aortobifemoral bypass (aortic to each femoral artery)
- axillobifemoral bypass (axillary to each femoral artery)
- fem-pop (femoral to popliteal artery)
- fem-fem (femoral to femoral)

When taking baseline vitals, pay special attention to peripheral pulses, and regularly assess for adequate distal pulses and tissue perfusion in extremities. Post-procedure complications include the following:

  - swelling of the extremities (patients may require vascular boot)
  - compartment syndrome (signs include intense pain and urinalysis consistent with rhabdomyolysis)
  - mesenteric ischemia

> **Helpful Hint**
>
> **Post-pericardiotomy syndrome** is caused by an immune response to pericardial damage that leads to inflammation.

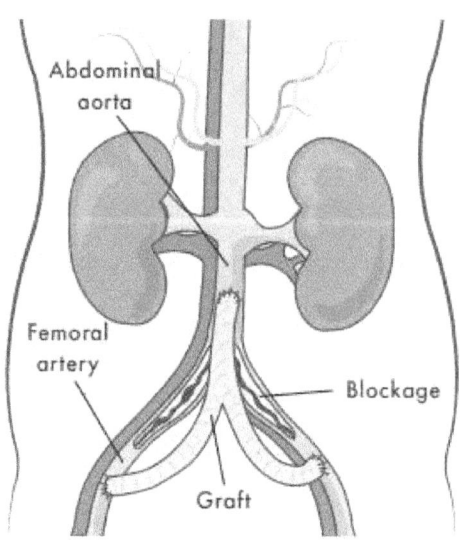

Figure 7.6. Aortobifemoral Bypass

Aneurysm Repair

Aortic and thoracic aneurysms can be surgically repaired if the risk of dissection is considered sufficiently high. Surgical repairs are the only treatment for a dissection that has already occurred:

- The majority of aneurysm repairs require surgery to open the aneurysm and place a graft.
- In some cases, the surgeon may perform an endovascular aneurysm repair (EVAR), a less invasive procedure in which a catheter is used to place an endovascular stent graft across the aneurysm.

Post-procedure complications include the following:

- cardiac complications (e.g., MI, dysrhythmias)
- pulmonary complications (e.g., pulmonary embolism)
- small-bowel obstruction
- lower-limb ischemia

Patient Education

- Instruct patients on ways to prevent the aneurysm from rupturing, including smoking cessation, lowering BP, and lowering cholesterol.
- Patients require CTs at 3- or 6-month intervals to monitor the growth of aneurysms.

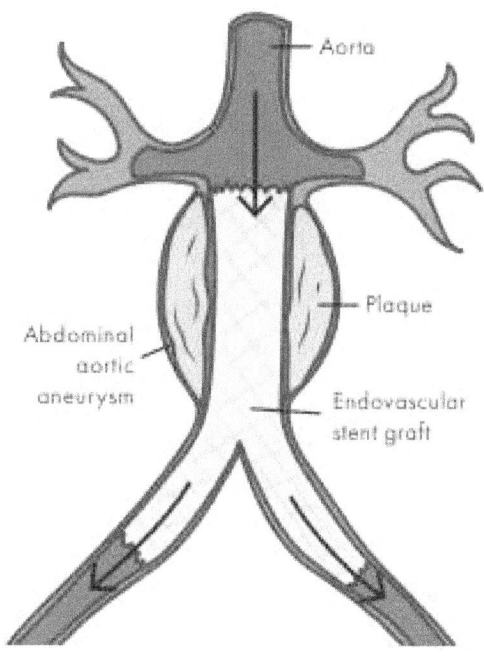

Figure 7.7. Endovascular Aneurysm Repair (EVAR)

Carotid Endarterectomy

A **carotid endarterectomy** is a surgical procedure to remove plaque from carotid arteries in patients with carotid stenosis:

- The vascular surgeon surgically opens the affected carotid artery and removes the plaque from the vessel; the artery is then closed via suturing.

- Monitor for post-procedure complications:

    o Ensure that the patient has frequent neurological assessments (at least every hour).

    o Assess cranial nerves, including the hypoglossal, facial, and vagal nerves, for impairment.

    o Monitor vital signs, especially blood pressure (important because of baroreceptors close to the carotid artery).

    o Monitor patient for headache unrelieved by analgesics; the headache may indicate intracranial bleeding.

    o Monitor patient for dysrhythmias.

> **Helpful Hint**
>
> Maintaining normotensive BP is a nursing priority for patients with aortic aneurysm. Elevated BP increases pressure on the aortic walls and may cause dissection or rupture.

Patient Education

- Instruct patients to not do any strenuous activities for the first few days after discharge and to incrementally increase their activities when they are cleared to do so.

- Discuss expected post-surgery changes in sensations along the patient's earlobe, jaw line, and incision site; such changes can include short- to long-term loss of feeling in those areas.

- Instruct the patient to monitor for fever, neck swelling, and/or signs of infection at the incision site; the patient should contact their health care provider in such instances.

- Ensure that the patient understands the warning signs of a stroke and instruct the patient to seek immediate medical care should any of those symptoms present themselves.

Heart Valve Repair and Replacement

Damaged valves can be repaired or replaced. Replacement valves may be mechanical or **bioprosthetic** (bovine, porcine, or human):

- **Mechanical heart valves (MHV)** are implanted surgically.

- **Bioprosthetic heart valves (BHV)** can be implanted surgically or via transcatheter procedure.

- Surgical valve repair and replacement requires cardiopulmonary bypass.

- Post-procedure complications:

    o retroperitoneal bleeding

- dysrhythmias
- thromboembolism
- bacterial endocarditis

Patient Education

- Patients with MHVs will require lifelong anticoagulation medication to prevent prosthetic valvular thrombosis.
- All patients with heart valve repair or replacement require prophylactic antibiotics before dental and surgical procedures to prevent infective endocarditis.

Heart (Cardiac) Transplantation

- In an **orthotropic heart transplant**, the recipient's heart is removed and replaced with the donor heart.
- In a **heterotopic heart transplant**, the donor heart is placed alongside the recipient's heart, which remains in place.
- Heart transplantation is the last resort for patients with end-stage heart failure.
  - Candidates for heart transplantation usually have a life expectancy of 1 year without the surgery.
  - Very rarely, a heart transplant may be done on a patient with refractory V-tach in the absence of heart failure.

Nursing care for heart transplant patients is specialized, complex, and intense. The patient will be closely monitored and treated for the following:

- organ rejection
- infection
- graft dysfunction
- other serious complications

Signs and symptoms of organ rejection include the following:

- fever, even low-grade
- weakness
- palpitations
- shortness of breath
- weight gain
- elevated WBC count

Surgical Thrombectomy

- Thrombus or emboli that result in acute arterial occlusion may be removed during a surgical thrombectomy to restore blood perfusion to tissues.
- During the procedure, the surgeon opens the blood vessel to remove the thrombus or embolus and then closes the vessel; a stent may also be placed.
- While open surgery is the most common form of thrombectomy, some patients may be candidates for the less invasive mechanical thrombectomy; this involves inserting a catheter into the groin and up to the location of the clot, and inserting a stent retriever to physically remove the clot.
- Post-procedure complications:
  - thromboembolism
  - compartment syndrome

Quick Review Question

4. A patient presents to the ED with chest pain and the ECG shown below. What priority intervention should the nurse expect?

Devices

Pacemaker

A **pacemaker** is a device that uses electrical stimulation to regulate the heart's electrical conduction system and maintain a normal heart rhythm. The following conditions commonly require a pacemaker:

- sinus node dysfunction
- AV block, third- or second-degree
- chronic or transient bifascicular block
- post MI
- neurocardiogenic syncope and hypersensitive carotid sinus syndrome
- post cardiac surgery

> **Helpful Hint**
>
> Implantable cardiac devices, including pacemakers and ICDs, may lead to localized or systemic infections, including endocarditis.

Pacing can be permanent or temporary:

- **Permanent pacemakers** are implanted subcutaneously, and the leads are then run through the subclavian vein into the heart.
    - The device is battery-operated and allows the physician to continuously monitor the patient's rhythm.
- **Temporary pacemakers** can include transvenous leads or transcutaneous adhesive pads attached to the chest.
    - Temporary pacemakers are controlled by an external pulse generator.
- Pacing can be single chamber (atrium or ventricle) or dual chamber.
- The pacemaker will have a set rate (number of times it fires per minute):
    - Rate-modulated pacemakers use a physiological sensor to match the patient's heart rate to his activity level.
    - The electrical activity of the pacemaker appears on the ECG as a **pacing spike**, a sharp vertical line that may appear below or above the isoelectric line.
- Pacemakers are classified with a 5-letter code. Because the last 2 letters are omitted if they are "O," many pacemakers are referred to by using a 3-letter code, as described in Table 7.1.

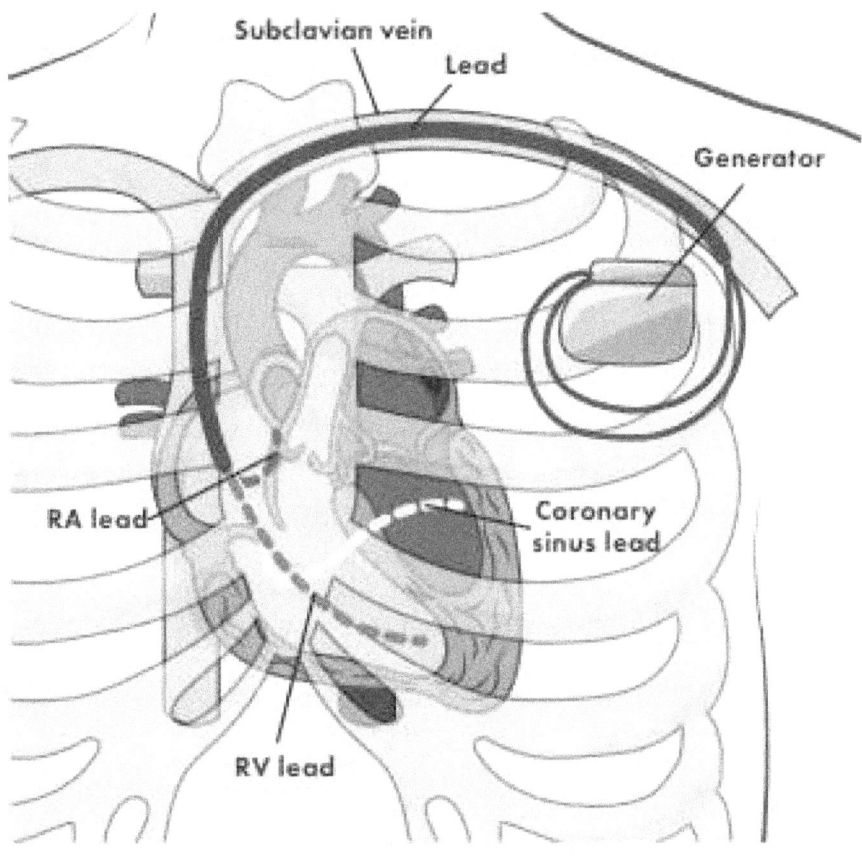

Figure 7.8. Lead Placement in Permanent Pacemaker

Figure 7.9. Pacing Spikes

Table 7.1. NASPE/BPEG Codes for Pacemakers

I: Chamber(s) Paced	II: Chamber(s) Sensed	III: Response to Sensing	IV: Rate Modulation	V: Multisite Pacing
O = none	O = none	O = none	O = none	O = none
A = atrium	A = atrium	T = triggered	R = rate modulation	A = atrium
V = ventricle	V = ventricle	I = inhibited		V = ventricle
D = dual (A+V)	D = dual (A+V)	D = dua; (T+I)		D = dual (A+V)

Table 7.2. Common Pacemaker Errors

Error	Description	Corrective Measures
Failure to pace (output failure)	• Absence of needed pacing stimulus. • See Figure 7.10.	• Ensure device is turned on. • Check battery. • Check leads. • Ask patient about possible magnetic interference with pacemaker.
Failure to capture	• Device provides pacing stimulus when needed, but depolarization is not triggered (seen on ECG as pacing spike with no	• Increase mA voltage.

Table 7.2. Common Pacemaker Errors		
Error	Description	Corrective Measures
	corresponding QRS complex). • See Figure 7.11.	
Oversensing	• Device does not provide pacing stimulus when needed because it detects noncardiac electrical activity (physiologic or nonphysiologic).	• Reset sensitivity of device.
Undersensing	• Device provides pacing stimulus when not needed because it cannot sense native cardiac activity.	• Reset sensitivity of device.

Figure 7.10. Failure to Pace (Output Failure)

Figure 7.11. Failure to Capture

- Pacemaker malfunction procedures:
    - Notify the physician.
    - Assess the pacemaker for mechanical issues. (See Table 7.2.)
    - Be prepared to provide temporary TCP.

Helpful Hint

Do not use the patient's carotid pulse to confirm mechanical capture, as the electrical impulses can be mistaken for the pulse.

Patient Education

- Signs of pacemaker malfunction include chest pain, palpitations, dizziness, syncope, and weakness.
- Patients should avoid being near strong magnets, as they can reset the device settings.
- Patients should be educated on device battery life (typically 5 – 10 years) and device interrogation schedule.
- Patients may need long-term anticoagulant therapy to prevent stroke.

Implantable Cardioverter Defibrillator (ICD)

- An implantable **cardioverter defibrillator (ICD)** continuously monitors heart rhythms and emits an electric shock that terminates emergent dysrhythmias such as V-tach and V-fib, preventing cardiac arrest.
- A **transvenous ICD (TV-ICD)** is placed like a pacemaker. The device is implanted subcutaneously, and the leads run through the left subclavian vein and superior vena cava into the right atrium and ventricle.
- A **subcutaneous ICD (S-ICD)** is also implanted subcutaneously but does not include leads placed in the vasculature; instead, the lead is placed subcutaneously along the rib cage.
- Nursing considerations and patient education for ICD patients are similar to those for patients receiving a permanent pacemaker.

Figure 7.12. Implantable Cardioverter Defibrillator (ICD)

Left Ventricular Assist Device (LVAD)

- A **left ventricular assist device (LVAD)** provides support for weakened left ventricles in patients with end-stage heart failure.
- This device is sometimes used as "bridge" treatment while a patient waits for heart transplantation.
- A mechanical pump is placed in the left ventricle:
  - The pump moves blood from the left ventricle to the ascending aortic branch, from which it can be further circulated to the rest of the body.
- The LVAD is battery operated, and patients can remain on the device for months to years.
- Nursing considerations:
  - Monitor MAP closely, with the goal ranging from 60 – 90 mm Hg.
  - Monitor the patient's electrolytes to prevent dysrhythmias.
  - Monitor the patient for signs of pump thrombosis, which include shortness of breath, tachycardia, and hypotension.
  - Ensure that spare batteries are accessible.

Figure 7.13. Left Ventricular Assist Device (LVAD)

Patient Education

- The patient should be taught how to change batteries and to perform daily self-tests in order to ensure that the device is functioning properly.
- The patient should learn about the medications that may be prescribed, such as anticoagulants to prevent thrombosis and antihypertensives to control blood pressure.

Quick Review Question

5. A patient presents to the clinic with complaints of a temperature of 101.3°F (38.5°C), night sweats, pain in the knees, cough, and bloody sputum. The patient recently had a permanent pacemaker implanted. What condition should the nurse suspect?

Cardioversion and Defibrillation

Cardioversion

- During **cardioversion**, electrical current or medications are used to reset the heart to a normal sinus rhythm.
- Cardioversion is indicated for the following conditions:
  - narrow or wide QRS complex tachycardias (per ACLS guidelines)
  - SVT
  - V-tach with a pulse
  - A-fib
  - atrial flutter
- Synchronized electrical cardioversion uses electrical current supplied by external electrode pads placed on the anterior chest; current is supplied during the R wave of the QRS complex.
- Electrical cardioversion can be monophasic (unidirectional current) or biphasic (bidirectional current):
  - Monophasic devices deliver current at a more consistent magnitude and are more effective at lower energies.
- The energy supplied during electrical cardioversion depends on the type of device and the underlying rhythm.
- General guidelines for biphasic devices are as follows:
  - narrow QRS, regular: 50 – 100 J
  - narrow QRS, irregular: 120 – 200 J
  - wide QRS, regular: 100 J
  - A-fib: 75 J

- Pharmacologic cardioversion uses antidysrhythmic medications, such as adenosine:
  - Adenosine should be administered via rapid IV push at 6 mg for the first dose, followed by 12 mg if needed for the second dose.

Defibrillation

- During defibrillation, also known as **unsynchronized cardioversion**, electrical current is used to reset the heart to a normal sinus rhythm.

- The electrical current is supplied randomly during the cardiac cycle, disrupting the heart's electrical rhythm and allowing the SA node's normal sinus rhythm to restart.

- Defibrillation is an emergent treatment for patients with the following conditions:
  - pulseless V-tach
  - V-fib

> **Helpful Hint**
>
> Paddles should be placed away from implanted pacemakers and ICDs (most guidelines recommend a distance of about 1 inch).

- Common defibrillation doses start with 200 J, followed by 300 J for the second shock, with a maximum of 360 J.

Quick Review Question

6. A patient presents to the ED with chest pain, dyspnea, and diaphoresis. The nurse finds a narrow complex tachycardia with a heart rate of 210 bpm, blood pressure of 70/42 mm Hg, and a respiratory rate of 18. What priority intervention should the nurse anticipate?

Answer Key

1. The patient may need to have long-term cardiac monitoring since the patient's ECG has not shown any abnormalities during the hospital stay. The nurse should anticipate that the patient will receive an ICM, such as a loop recorder, in order to continuously monitor the heart rhythm so that the patient can be discharged home.

2. The nurse should make sure that there is no skin breakdown on the legs where the SCD or TED stocking is placed. Further restriction of an area of skin breakdown can worsen ulceration and necrosis. The nurse should also use the correct-sized device or stocking for the patient's leg to ensure efficacy.

3. The nurse should anticipate using a femoral compression device on this patient. Because the patient is demonstrating signs of a developing hematoma at the insertion site, a femoral compression device applied can stop the hematoma from worsening and help produce hemostasis for the patient.

4. The patient is experiencing a STEMI and needs immediate transport to the catheterization lab for PCI for reperfusion.

5. The patient is at increased risk for infective endocarditis because of the recent pacemaker implantation and is showing signs and symptoms of this infection (low-grade fever, arthralgias, night sweats, cough, and hemoptysis).

6. The patient is experiencing an unstable SVT (with BP of 70/42 mm Hg) and requires immediate synchronized cardioversion.

Chapter 8 – Cardiovascular Pharmacology

Administering Medications

There are seven "rights" to medication administration:
- **Right Patient:**
    - Verify that the medication is for the patient who is about to receive it.
    - Use two patient identifiers (usually name and date of birth as these demographics are patient-specific).
    - Check the ID band to make sure it matches the patient's reported name and DOB.
    - Make sure the drug matches the patient's diagnosis.
    - Ensure that the medication was ordered for the right patient.
- **Right Drug:**
    - Check that the medication to be delivered matches the order.
    - Have another nurse check the order if necessary; some high-risk medications require two nurses to check the order.
- **Right Route:**
    - Assess if the patient can take the drug via the route ordered.
    - Administer the drug via the route ordered.
- **Right Dose:**
    - Clarify the dose written by the provider and administer only that dose.
    - Verify drug calculations.
- **Right Time:**
    - Determine how often to administer the medication, based on its duration of action.
    - Give the medication at the appropriate time so that the dosing schedule is undisrupted.
- **Right Response:**
    - Monitor for the anticipated response of the drug.
- **Right Documentation:**
    - If it is not documented, it is not done.

Quick Review Question

1. During shift change, the incoming nurse asks about the time of the last administration of PRN pain medication. How will the currently assigned nurse verify the administration of the last dose of pain medication?

Angiotensin-Converting Enzyme (ACE) Inhibitors

Mechanism of Action

- lowers systemic vascular resistance (SVR) by blocking the angiotensin-converting enzyme (ACE) from converting angiotensin I to angiotensin II (a potent vasoconstrictor)
- lowers levels of aldosterone, reducing retention of water and sodium
- lowers blood pressure

Therapeutic Uses

- hypertension (first-line)
- congestive heart failure (recommended when left ventricular ejection fraction 40%)
- medical management following MI (reduces remodeling)
- diabetic nephropathy

Possible Adverse Reactions

- persistent dry cough (due to buildup of bradykinin)
- hypotension
- worsening renal function
- hyperkalemia
- angioedema
- neutropenia

Contraindications

- aortic and renal artery stenosis
- acute kidney injury
- hyperkalemia
- pregnancy
- persistent dry cough on ACE inhibitor (switch to ARB)
- angioedema (considered an allergy to this drug class)

Common ACE Inhibitors (suffix –*pril*)

- lisinopril
- ramipril
- enalapril
- benazepril

Quick Review Question

2. The nurse is preparing to administer lisinopril 10 mg. The patient has a blood pressure of 138/95 mm Hg and a heart rate of 88 bpm. Labs show K+ 5.5 and Cr 1.7. What action should the nurse take?

Adrenergic Group - Alpha$_1$-Adrenergic Agonists

Mechanism of Action

- stimulate vascular smooth muscle, causing vasoconstriction and increased SVR and BP

Therapeutic Uses

- hypotension
- shock

Helpful Hint

Since 2012, Lisinopril (Prinivil, Zestril) has been one of the three most commonly prescribed medications in the United States (along with levothyroxine and atorvastatin [Lipitor]).

Possible Adverse Reactions

- bradycardia
- hypertension
- headache
- vision deficits
- erythema multiforme

Contraindications

- CAD
- hypertension
- tachycardia
- acute renal failure
- thyrotoxicosis
- pheochromocytoma

Common Drugs

- methoxamine (Vasoxyl)
- midodrine (ProAmatine)
- phenylephrine (Neo-Synephrine)

Quick Review Question

3. A patient presents with cardiogenic shock secondary to aortic stenosis. What medication is likely to be ordered for this patient?

Adrenergic Group Alpha$_1$-Adrenergic Blockers

Mechanism of Action

- block alpha1-adrenergic receptor sites in vascular smooth muscle resulting in vasodilation and decreased tone of vasculature

Therapeutic Uses

- hypertension (fourth-line)
- BPH (second-line)

Possible Adverse Reactions

- orthostatic hypotension (especially after first dose)
- tachycardia
- dysrhythmias
- dizziness
- nausea
- diaphoresis
- weakness and fatigue

Contraindications

- hypotension
- heart failure
- renal failure
- pregnancy
- erectile dysfunction medications

Common Drugs (suffix –*zosin*)

- doxazosin
- prazosin
- terazosin

Quick Review Question

4. The nurse has orders to give a patient terazosin 1 mg PO at bedtime for treatment of BPH. Knowing the effects of terazosin, what should the nurse assess to ensure safe administration?

Alpha$_2$ -Adrenergic Agonists

Mechanism of Action

- bind to alpha$_2$-adrenergic receptors in the brain, which reduces the action of the sympathetic nervous system
- results in decreased heart rate, speed of cardiac contraction, and BP

Therapeutic Uses

- hypertension (fourth-line)
- ADHD (third-line)

Possible Adverse Reactions

- hypotension
- bradycardia
- heart failure
- drowsiness or fatigue
- constipation

Contraindications

- CAD
- renal failure

Common Drugs

- clonidine (Catapres)
- guanabenz (Wytensin)
- guanfacine (Tenex)

Quick Review Question

5. A possible adverse reaction of alpha$_2$-adrenergic agonists is bradycardia. Which other class of cardiovascular medications should be used with caution with alpha$_2$-adrenergic agonists?

Alpha$_2$-Adrenergic Blockers

Mechanism of Action

- block alpha$_2$-adrengeric receptors, which will disable the sympathetic response of peripheral blood vessels and result in decreased SVR and lowered BP

Therapeutic Uses

- hypertension (especially due to pheochromocytoma)
- hypertensive crisis (emergency-level reaction to anesthesia)

Possible Adverse Reactions

- orthostatic hypotension (especially after first dose)
- tachycardia
- dysrhythmias
- dizziness
- nausea
- peptic ulcer disease
- priapism

Contraindications

- recent MI
- renal failure
- CAD
- angina
- breastfeeding

Common Drugs

- phentolamine (Regitine)

Quick Review Question

6. Why are alpha$_2$-adrenergic blockers contraindicated in patients with a recent MI?

Beta-Adrenergic Antagonists (Beta-Blockers)

Mechanism of Action

- block beta-adrenergic receptors in the heart (beta$_1$) and blood vessels (beta$_2$), resulting in lowered BP and HR and decreased cardiac output
- block beta$_1$-adrenergic receptors in the kidneys that promote the secretion of renin, reducing renin production and SVR

Therapeutic Uses

- post-MI (first-line)
- hypertension (second-line)
- chronic angina
- cardiac dysrhythmias (A-fib, SVT)
- prophylactic treatment of migraines
- anxiety (off-label use)

Possible Adverse Reactions

- bradycardia
- heart block
- hypotension
- exacerbation of asthma (beta$_2$ blockade effect)
- fatigue
- memory loss and confusion
- masking of hypoglycemia

Contraindications

- bradycardia
- sick sinus syndrome without pacemaker
- second- or third-degree AV block (including Mobitz II)
- junctional rhythm
- dual BBB
- asthma (only beta$_1$-selective beta blockers should be used)
- COPD (only beta$_1$-selective beta blockers should be used)

Common Drugs (suffix –*olol*)

- metoprolol
- atenolol
- bisoprolol
- propranolol

Quick Review Question

7. For which dysrhythmias are beta blockers contraindicated?

Sympathomimetics

Mechanism of Action

- alpha- and beta-adrenergic agonists that activate $alpha_1$, $alpha_2$, $beta_1$, and/or $beta_2$ receptors
- result in vasoconstriction, increased force of cardiac contraction, or increased rate of cardiac conduction (depending on the affected receptors)
- dopamine: at lower doses acts on dopaminergic receptors to stimulate renal vasodilation and perfusion
- include endogenous catecholamines (e.g., epinephrine) and drugs that mimic endogenous catecholamines (e.g., dobutamine)

Therapeutic Uses

- hypotension
- heart failure
- cardiogenic shock
- cardiac arrest/asystole/PEA
- acute bronchospasm
- anaphylaxis

Possible Adverse Reactions

- hypertension
- tachydysrhythmias
- headache
- nausea and vomiting

Contraindications

- V-fib

Common Drugs

- epinephrine (Adrenalin)
- norepinephrine (Levophed)
- dobutamine (Dobutrex)
- dopamine (Intropin)

Quick Review Question

8. The nurse is caring for a patient who is being administered Levophed to maintain a mean arterial pressure (MAP) greater than 60 mm Hg. The infusion is currently at the maximum dose, and the patient has a MAP of 55 mm Hg. What does the nurse anticipate the physician will order for this patient?

Angiotensin II Receptor Antagonists (ARBs)

Mechanism of Action

- block angiotensin II receptor site, causing vasodilation and lowered BP
- have a similar mechanism of action to ACE inhibitors but cause fewer adverse effects (e.g., do not affect bradykinin levels)

Therapeutic Uses

- hypertension (second-line if intolerant to ACE inhibitors)
- heart failure (recommended when left ventricular ejection fraction 40%)
- medical management following MI (second-line if intolerant to ACE inhibitors)
- diabetic nephropathy

Possible Adverse Reactions

- hyperkalemia
- acute kidney injury
- dizziness
- syncope
- headache
- angioedema (considered an allergy to the medication)

Contraindications

- hypotension
- acute renal failure
- pregnancy
- angioedema (considered an allergy to the medication)

Common Drugs (–artan)

- losartan
- irbesartan
- valsartan

> **Helpful Hint**
>
> NSAIDs, ARBs, and ACE inhibitors can cause or worsen prerenal disease and acute tubular necrosis.

Quick Review Question

9. The nurse is completing medication reconciliation with a patient in the clinic. The patient states that he was previously taking lisinopril for high blood pressure but that the cardiologist recently switched his prescription to losartan. What is a likely reason that the patient's medication was switched?

Anticoagulants

Mechanism of Action

- increase clotting time via various mechanisms that disrupt the production of clotting factors
- warfarin: disrupts the hepatic production of vitamin K clotting factors (II, VII, IX, X, proteins C and S)
- heparin: binds to the enzyme antithrombin III, catalyzing the inactivation of thrombin and other clotting factors
- low molecular weight heparins (enoxaparin): bind to the enzyme antithrombin III and accelerate activity, inhibiting thrombin and factor Xa
- direct Xa inhibitors (apixaban, rivaroxaban, edoxaban): inhibit action of factor Xa

Therapeutic Uses

- known thrombosis (e.g., PE or DVT)
- prophylaxis of thrombosis (e.g., post A-fib, cardiac post-op procedures)
- antiphospholipid syndrome
- hypercoagulable states (protein C and S deficiencies)
- adjunct therapy in mechanical valve replacements, MI, and stroke

Possible Adverse Reactions

- hemorrhage
- nausea and vomiting
- headache
- thrombocytopenia (HIT)
- direct Xa inhibitors: false elevation in INR levels

Contraindications

- active hemorrhage or suspected acute blood loss
- epidural or spinal anesthesia
- valvular disorders
- use with caution in patients >65 years of age who are at high risk for falls
- use with caution in patients with heart failure or fever
- pregnancy [only low molecular weight heparin (LMWH) or heparin can be used safely]

Helpful Hint

Heparin is neutralized with protamine sulfate. Warfarin is neutralized with Vitamin K.

Helpful Hint

Heparin-induced thrombocytopenia (HIT) causes platelet activation, significantly increasing the risk of thrombosis (usually 5 – 10 days after exposure to heparin.) If HIT is suspected, heparin should be discontinued immediately, and the patient should be placed on a different anticoagulant.

Common Drugs

- warfarin
- apixaban (Eliquis)
- rivaroxaban (Xarelto)
- enoxaparin (Lovenox)
- heparin

Quick Review Question

10. During morning rounds, the nurse receives orders to discontinue enoxaparin (Lovenox) injections and transition the patient to apixaban (Eliquis). It is 11:00 a.m., and the patient received the morning enoxaparin injection at 8:00 a.m. What is the appropriate time for the first dose of apixaban?

Antidysrhythmics

Mechanism of Action

- suppress cardiac dysrhythmias and restore normal cardiac conduction

Table 8.1. Classes of Antidysrhythmics

Class	Mechanism	Common Medications	Therapeutic Uses
Class IA	fast sodium-channel blockers	disopyramide	treats ventricular dysrhythmias
		procainamide	
Class IB	fast sodium-channel blockers	lidocaine	
		mexiletine	
Class IC	fast sodium-channel blockers	flecainide	chemical conversion of A-fib, prophylactic treatment of paroxysmal A-fib and atrial flutter, maintenance therapy for SVT, treats ventricular dysrhythmias
Class II	l beta blockers (discussed in detail above)		
Class III	l potassium-channel blockers	amiodarone	treats V-fib, A-fib, atrial flutter
Class IV	slow calcium-channel blockers	verapamil	treats A-fib and atrial flutter; can lower blood pressure
		diltiazem	treats A-fib and atrial flutter; can lower blood pressure
Class V	variable mechanisms	adenosine	restarts the heart; commonly used to treat SVT
		digoxin	treats A-fib, heart failure
		magnesium sulfate	treats V-tach, torsades de pointes, eclampsia, hypomagnesemia, and cerebral edema

Possible Adverse Reactions

- bradycardia
- subsequent lethal ventricular dysrhythmias
- hypotension
- cardiac arrest
- lidocaine: decreased seizure threshold

Contraindications

- hypotension
- heart block
- respiratory depression
- cautious use in patients with bilateral BBB if pacemaker is not present
- use caution in patients with heart failure

Quick Review Question

11. A patient presents to the ED complaining of shortness of breath and syncope. Once the patient is placed on telemetry, the nurse observes the following rhythm:

Which antidysrhythmic medication should the nurse anticipate being ordered by the physician?

Antiplatelets

Mechanism of Action

- decrease platelet aggregation and inhibit thrombus production via various mechanisms
- ADP receptor inhibitors: inhibit ADP receptor sites on platelets
- aspirin: prevents activation of platelets
- glycoprotein IIB/IIIA inhibitors: inhibit receptors on platelets that bind to fibrinogen

Therapeutic Uses

- PCI/stent placement for ACS
- treatment and prophylaxis for ischemic stroke
- unstable angina

Possible Adverse Reactions

- increased bleeding risks (may need to be held before major invasive procedures)
- headache
- nausea or other GI distress
- rash
- thrombocytopenia
- ticagrelor (Brilinta): mild, transient shortness of breath that typically resolves within a week
- aspirin: GI bleeding especially with dual antiplatelet therapy

Contraindications

- hypersensitivity
- active bleeding
- recent surgery (must be held for at least 4 hours post-op)

Common Drugs

- clopidogrel (Plavix)
- ticagrelor (Brilinta)
- prasugrel (Effient)
- aspirin

Quick Review Question

12. In preparation for major surgery, the nurse instructs a patient to stop taking clopidogrel (Plavix). The patient becomes concerned regarding coronary artery stents he had placed 18 months prior and asks if it is safe to stop taking clopidogrel. How should the nurse respond?

Diuretics

Therapeutic Uses

- hypertension
- heart failure

- edema
- osmotic diuretics: intracranial pressure (ICP)

Possible Adverse Reactions

- electrolyte imbalances including hypokalemia, hyponatremia, and hyperuricemia
- metabolic alkalosis
- acute kidney injury related to over-diuresis
- dehydration
- hypotension

Contraindications

- hypotension
- acute renal failure
- dehydration
- use with caution in patients with dysrhythmias

Table 8.2. Types of Diuretics		
Type of Diuretic	**Mechanism of Action**	**Common Medications**
Loop diuretics	<ul><li>prevent reabsorption of sodium, potassium, and chloride in the ascending loop of Henle and the distal renal tubule</li><li>result in excretion of water, sodium, chloride, and large amounts of potassium</li></ul>	furosemide (Lasix) bumetanide (Bumex) torsemide (Demadex)
Thiazide diuretics	<ul><li>prevent reabsorption of sodium and chloride primarily in the distal convoluted renal tubule</li></ul>	chlorothiazide hydrochlorothiazide

Table 8.2. Types of Diuretics

Type of Diuretic	Mechanism of Action	Common Medications
	• result in increased excretion of water, sodium, chloride, and moderate amounts of potassium	
Potassium-sparing diuretics	• block aldosterone-specific mineralocorticoid receptors in the distal convoluted renal tubule • result in excretion of water and sodium; retain potassium	spironolactone triamterene
Osmotic diuretics	• elevate glomerular filtrate osmolarity active in the loop of Henle that can be used to reduce fluid volume and ICP • result in increased excretion of water and small amounts of sodium	mannitol

Quick Review Question

13. A patient on a continuous furosemide (Lasix) drip starts to have bilateral lower extremity muscle cramps and non-sustained V-tach. What could potentially be causing these issues?

Inotropic Agents - Cardiac Glycosides

Mechanism of Action

- increase intracellular calcium by inhibiting Na-K ATPase
- cause increased myocardial contraction, decreased heart rate, and slowed cardiac conduction
- increase cardiac output and renal perfusion (inotrope)

Therapeutic Uses

- atrial dysrhythmias (e.g., A-fib, third-line)
- PSVT conversion
- heart failure

Possible Adverse Reactions

- heart block
- bradycardia
- dizziness
- headache
- nausea and vomiting

Contraindications

- V-fib
- acute MI
- hypertrophic cardiomyopathy

Common Drugs

- digoxin (Lanoxin)

> **Helpful Hint**
>
> Digoxin toxicity presents with dysrhythmias, confusion, weakness, and/or GI symptoms (e.g., nausea, vomiting); it is treated with digoxin immune fab (Digibind).

Quick Review Question

14. The nurse is caring for a patient who has been admitted with an acute kidney injury, Cr 3.4 mg/dL. The patient has been taking digoxin as part of his treatment regimen for A-fib. The nurse understands digoxin is excreted by the kidneys. What is the nurse's best practice before administering a dose of digoxin?

Inotropic Agents - Phosphodiesterase Inhibitors

Mechanism of Action

- increase calcium concentrations in cardiac muscle cells by inhibiting cAMP phosphodiesterase
- cause increased myocardial contraction, resulting in decreased cardiac preload and afterload

Therapeutic Uses

- heart failure

Possible Adverse Reactions

- hypotension
- ventricular dysrhythmias
- headache
- worsening heart failure over long term

Contraindications

- aortic or pulmonic valve disease (severe)
- ventricular dysrhythmias
- acute MI

Common Drugs

- milrinone (Primacor)

Quick Review Question

15. What is the difference in the mechanism of action between milrinone (Primacor) and dobutamine (Dobutrex)?

Other Vasodilators - Nitrates

Mechanism of Action

- vasodilators; relax vascular smooth muscle
- result in decreased venous return, which leads to decreased cardiac output
- cause decreased afterload and reduce work effort of LV

Therapeutic Uses

- treatment and prophylaxis of angina (outpatient setting)
- MI [MONA (morphine, oxygen, nitroglycerin, aspirin) treatment in ED]
- hypertension (critical care setting)

Possible Adverse Reactions

- hypotension
- tachycardia
- headache
- nausea

Contraindications

- phosphodiesterase inhibitors taken within 48 hours
- right ventricular infarction
- hypotension
- intracranial hemorrhage
- pregnancy

Common Drugs (often contain the roots *nitro* or *nitra*)

- nitroglycerin
- isosorbide dinitrate
- isosorbide mononitrate
- nitroprusside
- minoxidil

Quick Review Question

16. A patient reports a headache after starting a nitro drip for chest pain. The patient asks the nurse why the medication helped his chest pain but caused a headache. How should the nurse respond?

Other Vasodilators - Calcium Channel Blockers

Mechanism of Action

- Dihydropyridines hinder the movement of calcium into vascular smooth muscle and cardiac muscle, resulting in lower concentrations of intracellular calcium
- Non-dihydropyridines cause coronary vasodilation from smooth muscle relaxation, slowed cardiac conduction, decreased heart rate, decreased myocardial contraction, and prolonged AV node refractory period (class IV antidysrhythmic)

Therapeutic Uses

- hypertension
- Prinzmetal angina
- artery vasospasm
- non-dihydropyridines: cardiac dysrhythmias

Possible Adverse Reactions

- hypotension
- bradycardia
- dizziness
- light-headedness

Contraindications

- second- or third-degree heart block
- hypotension (SBP 90 mm Hg)
- use with caution in patients with ventricular dysfunction

Common Drugs

- amlodipine (dihydropyridine)
- nicardipine (dihydropyridine)
- diltiazem (non-dihydropyridine)
- verapamil (non-dihydropyridine)

Quick Review Question

17. What hemodynamic response should the nurse expect to observe in a patient after the administration of diltiazem IV push?

Antihypertensive Vasodilators

Mechanism of Action

- act primarily on the arterioles in the peripheral vessels to cause vasodilation and relax smooth muscle

Therapeutic Uses

- hypertension (third line outpatient, can be first-line IV in emergency situations)
- increase or sustain renal perfusion

Possible Adverse Reactions

- reflex tachycardia
- angina
- headache
- fatigue

Contraindications

- hypotension
- tachycardia
- acute MI
- acute hypertrophic cardiomyopathy
- mitral valvular rheumatic heart disease
- pregnancy

Common Drugs

- hydralazine

Quick Review Question

18. What is the pathophysiology that produces the adverse reaction of reflex tachycardia in patients who have been given antihypertensive vasodilators?

Thrombolytics (Fibrinolytic Agents)

Mechanism of Action

- promote the destruction of fibrin clots (thrombus) by activating the conversion of plasminogen to plasmin
- can be administered systemically via IV but are most effective if administered directly into the area of the clot

Therapeutic Uses

- MI when coronary angiography is unavailable (most effective if given within 6 hours of MI)
- acute CVA (most effective if given within 3 hours of CVA; time frame may extend up to 4.5 hours)
- massive pulmonary embolism
- restore blood flow in central venous catheters (1 – 2 mg doses; dwell time of 30 min – 2 hours)

Possible Adverse Reactions

- bleeding
- intracranial hemorrhage
- cardiac arrhythmias

Contraindications

- hypertension (SBP >180)
- active bleeding
- recent stroke history
- recent intracranial surgery
- hepatic dysfunction in patients >65

Common Drugs (suffix –*plase*)

- tPA or alteplase
- tenecteplase (TNKase)

Quick Review Question

19. A patient is receiving tPA for the treatment of acute pulmonary embolism, and the nurse is observing the patient. What types of adverse effects related to tPA could present during this time?

Drug Interactions

Drugs have many interactions that may decrease or increase their desired effects; some of these are discussed below.

Angiotensin-Converting Enzyme (ACE) Inhibitors

For people taking ACE inhibitors, consuming foods that contain high levels of potassium (e.g., bananas, tomatoes, avocados) may result in hyperkalemia and cardiac arrhythmias. Black licorice and salt substitutes containing potassium may also increase the risk of hyperkalemia. Potassium-sparing diuretics increase the risk of hyperkalemia, while furosemide and hydrochlorothiazide may cause excessive hypotension with the first dose of an ACE inhibitor. Nonsteroidal anti-inflammatory drugs (NSAIDs) reduce the effects of ACE inhibitors and increase the risk of renal damage.

Angiotensin II Receptor Blockers (ARBs)

Potassium-sparing diuretics; ACE inhibitors; potassium-rich foods (e.g., bananas, spinach, oranges); and salt substitutes increase the risk of hyperkalemia for patients taking ARBs. ACE inhibitors and NSAIDs increase the risk of renal damage for people taking ARBs. Loop diuretics may cause severe hypotension with the first dose of an ARB. Angiotensin II receptor blockers may also increase lithium levels in the body, increasing the risk of toxicity.

Antiarrhythmics

For people taking antiarrhythmics (e.g., amiodarone, dronedarone), grapefruit and other inhibitors of CYP3A4 (a liver enzyme that metabolizes drugs) can interfere with the drug's effectiveness and increase the blood levels of a drug. This can result in toxicity and heart rhythm abnormalities.

Antihypertensives

Generally, decongestants that contain pseudoephedrine or phenylephrine result in vasoconstriction, which counteracts the vasodilatory effects of antihypertensives. NSAIDs and high-sodium diets may also counteract the effects of antihypertensives.

Atenolol

For patients on atenolol, taking verapamil (a calcium channel blocker) may lead to heart block or bradycardia. Fruit juices (e.g., apple juice and orange juice) may decrease drug levels. Alcohol may increase the risk of hypotension.

Beta Blockers

For patients taking beta blockers, alcohol in general can increase the risk of hypotension while caffeine may reduce the drug's effectiveness. Amiodarone, calcium channel blockers, monoamine oxidase inhibitors, and clonidine may increase the occurrence of bradycardia. Selective serotonin reuptake inhibitors (some of which are inhibitors of CYP2D6—another type of enzyme in the body that metabolizes drugs) may increase drug levels.

Calcium Channel Blockers

Grapefruit and other CYP3A4 inhibitors can interfere with drug effectiveness and increase the blood levels of a drug, resulting in toxicity. Grapefruit can also cause hypotension.

Digoxin

High-fiber foods and antacids may interfere with drug absorption. Diuretics that cause potassium loss can increase the risk of digoxin toxicity. Proton pump inhibitors increase the risk of toxicity.

Nitroglycerin

Beta blockers, calcium channel blockers, antihypertensives, vasodilators, benzodiazepines, and aspirin may increase the drug's effects. The effects of heparin may be decreased with nitroglycerin use. The hawthorn herb can increase the blood levels of nitroglycerin.

Warfarin

Foods containing high levels of vitamin K (e.g., leafy greens, broccoli, seaweed) as well as St. John's wort and green tea, may reduce the effectiveness of warfarin and increase the risk of blood clotting. Cranberry juice may increase the risk of severe bleeding. Metronidazole and fluroquinolones increase the risk of bleeding.

Quick Review Questions

20. Grapefruit may increase drug levels for which types of cardiovascular drugs?

21. With which blood thinner should cranberry juice be avoided?

22. Which types of drugs can inhibit the vasodilatory effects of antihypertensives?

Answer Key

1. The nurses will open the medication administration record and verify the documented time of the last administration.

2. The nurse should consider the potential to aggravate the current elevated K+ and Cr levels. The nurse should hold the dose and contact the physician to consider the safest option for the patient.

3. Phenylephrine is the first-line medication used to increase BP in patients with aortic stenosis.

4. The nurse should obtain the patient's blood pressure before administering the medication. If the patient is hypotensive, terazosin should be avoided.

5. Beta blockers can potentially cause bradycardia, so the combined effects of the two medications may cause harm if not monitored.

6. The mechanism of action and resulting effects of lowered blood pressure and heart rate can cause hemodynamic instability in patients with recent MI.

7. Contraindications to beta blockers include junctional rhythm, Mobitz II, and bilateral BBB. Administering beta blockers to these patients will increase the likelihood of dangerously low heart rates and possible hemodynamic compromise.

8. The nurse should anticipate an order for fluids (colloids or crystalloids). The vasopressor will constrict the blood vessels and increase SVR but will not add volume to the body. Additional fluids will need to be introduced into circulation.

9. The patient was likely experiencing side effects when taking an ACE inhibitor (e.g., a persistent dry cough), so his doctor prescribed an ARB.

10. Due to the duration of action of enoxaparin, the nurse should administer the first dose of apixaban approximately 12 hours following the enoxaparin injection.

11. The patient's ECG shows V-tach. The nurse can anticipate that the physician will order amiodarone. The IV administration and preceding bolus dosing can help chemically convert the patient or maintain normal sinus rhythm if the patient is cardioverted.

12. The nurse should inform the patient of the significant bleeding risk related to the antiplatelet action of clopidogrel. To minimize this risk, clopidogrel should be held at least 3 – 5 days before the procedure. Since the patient's coronary artery stents were placed more than 12 months ago, holding the medication will not compromise the patency of the stents.

13. Furosemide is a loop diuretic and removes potassium as well as magnesium from the body. It is possible that these serum levels could be low in the patient, causing the muscle cramps and non-sustained VT. Frequent lab monitoring is necessary to keep these electrolytes replaced and within normal serum levels.

14. The nurse should search the patient's lab work for a digoxin level. An acute kidney injury evidenced by elevated creatinine could indicate a decrease in glomerular filtration rate and subsequent decrease in digoxin excretion. The nurse needs to know if the patient has a toxic digoxin level before administering more digoxin.

15. Dobutamine creates vasodilation, which reduces afterload by lowering systemic vascular resistance. Milrinone creates more forward cardiac flow by stimulating cardiac receptors.

16. Nitroglycerin works as a vasodilator to open coronary arteries and increase blood flow. The increased blood flow to the heart decreases chest pain, but the vasodilation is systemic, causing venous pooling, and can increase the amount of blood in the brain, resulting in headache.

17. The nurse should anticipate a slower heart rate and lower blood pressure as a result of the negative dromotropic, chronotropic, and inotropic effects.

18. As antihypertensive vasodilators cause vasodilation, the systemic blood pressure is reduced; subsequently, the decreased force in the arterioles activates baroreceptors, which elevate the heart rate as a compensatory mechanism.

19. The nurse should assess the patient for any signs consistent with internal bleeding. These signs include neurological changes that may indicate intracranial hemorrhage, hematuria, bright red blood per rectum, epistaxis, or an acute drop in hemoglobin.

20. Grapefruit and other CYP3A4 inhibitors can increase drug levels of calcium channel blockers and antiarrhythmics, such as amiodarone and dronedarone.

21. Cranberry juice inhibits the CYP2C9 enzyme, which metabolizes warfarin in the liver, leading to increased warfarin levels and the risk of severe bleeding.

22. Decongestants containing pseudoephedrine or phenylephrine, and NSAIDs can cause vasoconstriction, which can counter the vasodilatory effects of antihypertensives.

Chapter 9 – Patient and Community Education

The Learning Process

Characteristics of Adult Learners

Adult learners have several distinct traits that cardiac vascular nurses should consider while developing patient education plans:

- Adult learners are **independent** and **self-directed**; nurses should actively engage them in the learning process and encourage them to help develop their health plans.
- Adult learners are **results-oriented** and **practical**; nurses should give them information that they can apply immediately.
- Adult learners may be **resistant to change** and will require justification for new behaviors.
- Adults may **learn more slowly** than younger learners; however, they may be more skilled at integrating new knowledge with previous experience.

Psychologist Benjamin Bloom described three domains of learning:

- The **cognitive domain** includes collecting, synthesizing, and applying knowledge.
- The **affective** domain involves emotions and attitudes, including the ability to be aware of emotions and to respond to them.
- The **psychomotor domain** relates to motor skills, including the ability to perform complex skills and create new movement patterns.

The "knowledge, skills, and attitude" discussed in nursing education align with the three learning domains: **knowledge** is cognitive learning, **skills** are psychomotor learning, and **attitude** is affective learning. Patient education plans should address all three learning domains. For example, a patient who is learning about smoking cessation may need to be taught about the negative health impacts of smoking (cognitive domain), how to manage negative emotions related to quitting (affective domain), and how to correctly apply a nicotine patch (psychomotor domain).

A person's **learning style** is their preferred method of receiving new information:

- **Visual** learners do best with pictures, diagrams, and modeling.
- **Auditory** learners should be taught using spoken language, mnemonic devices, and music.
- **Kinesthetic** (i.e., physical) learners should be taught using bodily motion.

- **Social** learners learn best when interacting with other people.
- **Solitary** learners prefer to learn on their own.

Quick Review Question

1. A nurse is teaching a patient how to take her own blood pressure. While the patient is trying to apply the cuff, the nurse asks the patient to state her target blood pressure range. The patient becomes visibly frustrated and claims not to know. How can the nurse's teaching style meet this patient's needs?

Health Literacy

Health literacy is the degree to which an individual has the ability to obtain, process, and understand the basic health information needed to make personal health decisions. A patient's health literacy depends on many factors:

- communication skills and ability
- cultural considerations
- knowledge of health topics
- situation or context of the information delivery

Health literacy has a critical impact on the delivery of health care and educational initiatives, and it is measured as one of the components of the National Assessment of Adult Literacy. The assessment categorizes people's health literacy as follows:

- below basic
- basic
- intermediate
- proficient

Only a small percentage of adults in the United States have proficient health literacy, meaning they have the knowledge and skills to effectively manage their health. The US Department of Education's National Center for Education Statistics reports that the following populations are vulnerable to poor health literacy:

- people >65 years of age
- minorities
- people with mental illness
- immigrants
- people with low incomes

Health care providers who are communicating with patients through speaking or writing should consider the patient's level of health literacy. There are a number of health literacy assessments:

- the Rapid Estimate of Adult Literacy in Medicine (REALM)
- the Test of Functional Health Literacy in Adults (TOFHLA)

- the Newest Vital Sign (NVS) screening tool

Nurses should use available tools to measure the reading levels of printed materials. The following interventions can be used for patients with low health literacy:

- asking patients questions to assess their current knowledge
- using plain language and short sentences
- limiting important points to three or fewer
- using teach-backs to confirm the patient's understanding (see "Patient Education Strategies")
- using visual materials, such as videos or models
- discussing issues in terms of short time spans (10 years)
- being consistent when discussing numeric values (e.g., units, risk, dosage)
- simplifying procedures and regimens as much as possible

Quick Review Question

2. A nurse is meeting with a clinic patient who was recently diagnosed with hypertension and hyperlipidemia. During the interview, the nurse discovers that the patient is confused by the medication labels and so has not been taking the medications. What can the nurse do to help this patient adhere to the medication regimen?

Conditions for Learning

Patients' willingness and ability to learn depend on their motivation, readiness, and functional status:

- **Motivation** is the driving force behind people's actions.
- The cardiac vascular nurse should assess patients' sources of motivation in the context of managing their health in order to better educate, encourage, and advocate for them.
- **Intrinsic motivation** is the desire to achieve a goal, seek challenges, or complete a task that is driven by enjoyment and personal satisfaction (e.g., exercising because it is enjoyable); patients with an internal locus of control will attribute their success or failure to themselves.
- **Extrinsic motivation** is the desire to accomplish a goal that is driven by external rewards or punishment (e.g., exercising to prevent cardiovascular disease); patients with an external locus of control will attribute their success (or failure) to outside forces.
- Patients' readiness to learn can be shaped by many factors:
    - openness to new information
    - emotional response to illness (e.g., denial, anxiety)
    - religious and cultural beliefs
    - social support systems

> **Helpful Hint**
>
> Patient health literacy improves as patients become more involved in their own care.

Assessing patients' readiness to learn will allow the cardiac vascular nurse to deliver educational information to patients when they will be most receptive. Patients' **functional statuses**—their abilities to perform basic cognitive and physical tasks—will affect their abilities to learn:

- Patients with physical impairments may lack the strength, coordination, or sensory abilities to learn new skills.
- Cognitive impairments may disrupt patients' abilities to process new knowledge and maintain emotional stability.

Functional status can be measured by assessing patients' abilities to perform daily activities:

- **activities of daily living (ADLs):** personal care activities such as toileting, bathing, dressing, and eating
- **instrumental activities of daily living (IADLs):** activities necessary for independent living, such as shopping and doing housework

The cardiac vascular nurse must assess the functional status of a patient before developing an education plan for that patient; doing so ensures that the plan aligns with the patient's abilities and capacities to learn.

Quick Review Question

3. A nursing student asks a cardiac vascular nurse why she became a nurse. The nurse replies that she truly enjoys helping people and finds the medical field fascinating. What type of motivation does the nurse have?

Patient Education Strategies

The following strategies are used for teaching:

- **Lectures** (groups or one-on-one) are effective for conveying cognitive knowledge, particularly to auditory learners.
- **Group discussions** in which patients can ask questions are effective for social learners and can help with affective learning (e.g., changing attitudes).
- **Role-playing** is a good way to teach affective skills (e.g., responding to peer pressure).
- **Demonstrations** or modeling are useful for teaching psychomotor skills.
- **Instructional materials**, such as films or pamphlets, may be used as part of a larger education plan; however, they may be ineffective if patients are disengaged or the material does not match patients' needs and learning abilities.

The following strategies are used to assess patient understanding:

- During a **teach-back**, patients use their own words to state what they have learned.
  - This strategy is often used at discharge but can be used while teaching as an ongoing measure of patient understanding.
- **Oral or written tests** may be used to measure patient understanding, but many patients find these intimidating.

Some specific strategies to engage patients and families in the learning process include the following:

- Link new information to current behavior; new learning is better received when it focuses on what the patient already knows.
- Be clear, explicit, and specific when speaking with patients.
- Involve other health providers (e.g., dieticians) to engage patients and reinforce learning.

Use technology to engage patients and connect them to providers and support communities:

- **Webinars** or **live events** are often available in the community and are geared toward specific patient populations (e.g., parents).
- Patients can often find support groups for specific conditions on **social media**; nurses should caution patients to join such groups for support—<u>not</u> medical advice.
- Nurses should instruct patients on how to use **patient care interfaces** if they are available; these allow patients to send secure messages to providers and receive timely replies to questions.

Quick Review Question

4. A 50-year-old patient with cardiovascular disease attends a group class on self-management of hypertension. The nurse notices that the patient is not participating in the group session. What can the nurse do to better meet the patient's needs?

Education Plans

Components of an Education Plan

The cardiac vascular nurse should develop an education plan tailored to the learning needs of each patient. Patient education plans should be comprehensive and adaptable to patients' changing needs. Education plans should address the following topics:

- procedures
- risk factor modification
- disease management
- health promotion

Procedural education should be included for patients who are going to—or have already undergone—a procedure from which they will have to recover; such education should include the following:

- details about the procedure
- what the patient can expect after the procedure
- the self-care responsibilities of the patients after the procedure

Risk factor modification education should be included when a patient needs to make lifestyle changes, such as smoking cessation or following a restricted diet, to promote healthy outcomes.

Disease management education should focus on the role of patients in managing their chronic conditions; topics may include the following:

- knowledge of the disease process
- management of disease symptoms
- diet and exercise recommendations
- medication administration
- management of medication side effects

Health promotion education includes ways that patients can prevent deterioration in their health, including diet, exercise, and stress management.

Quick Review Question

5. The cardiac vascular nurse is providing patient education after a patient returns from a percutaneous transluminal coronary angioplasty (PTCA) procedure. The patient appears anxious. What should the nurse include in the teaching plan?

Developing Teaching Objectives

Objectives or **expected outcomes** are short-term outcomes that support long-term goals. Every education plan should have measurable objectives that allow the cardiovascular nurse to identify a patient's ongoing needs and gauge the success of the education plan. Objectives can address cognitive, affective, or psychomotor knowledge and skills. Both the nurse and the patient should understand how the objective will be measured (e.g., teach-back, verbalization of understanding, compliance with the care plan).

Measurable objectives in patient education must address the ultimate goals of the educational activity or plan; possible goals fall into several broad categories:

- increasing the patient's knowledge and skills
- increasing adherence to or effectiveness of treatment
- increasing self-efficacy and self-management
- reducing physical morbidity and the risk of mortality
- reducing stress and anxiety
- enhancing self-esteem and decision-making capacity
- improving quality of life

Objectives should explicitly state the following:

- what the patient will do
- how it will be measured
- when it should be accomplished

Examples of specific measurable objectives include the following:

- The patient will be able to demonstrate how to take his blood pressure prior to discharge.
- The patient will be able to verbalize how much weight gain to report to his provider one day before discharge.
- The patient will be able to identify three signs and symptoms of heart failure to monitor for and report to his provider by the end of the nurse's shift.

Quick Review Question

6. A cardiac vascular nurse is preparing an education plan for a patient recently diagnosed with congestive heart failure who will need to measure her weight daily at home. One of the nurse's teaching objectives is for the patient to be able to use a scale accurately by the time of discharge. Which elements should the nurse include in the education plan to help the patient meet this objective?

Factors That Influence Care

Patient and Family Support

There are numerous factors that influence the care of the cardiac vascular patient:

- family dynamics
- cultural considerations
- religious considerations
- socioeconomic factors
- diverse health practices

The cardiac vascular nurse should ask patients and families directly about such factors when possible, ideally during the admission assessment:

- **Family dynamics** may facilitate or impede patient care; it is important to determine the patient's preferences with regard to family involvement with care.
- **Cultural considerations** should be taken into account if the patient or patient's family shares specific cultural practices that are important to the patient.
- **Religious considerations** should be taken into account if the patient or the family indicates that certain interventions should be avoided.

> **Helpful Hint**
>
> Never ask family members to monitor or care for patients who are agitated, delirious, violent, or suicidal. This places an undue burden on the family. If they choose to provide support, the nurse must ensure that appropriate monitoring or restraints are in place.

Chapter 9 – Patient and Community Education

- **Socioeconomic factors** should be considered when making plans for discharge.
    - Socioeconomic status may affect patients' abilities to meet discharge requirements, such as physical therapy or rehabilitation; some patients may be unable to miss work for follow-up care.
- **Diverse health practices** should be considered if the patient discloses them; such practices include preferences for alternative therapies or the desire to avoid certain interventions.

Quick Review Question

7. The spouse of a patient who is approaching the end of life shares that the couple would like a priest to come to the bedside to give last rites. The nurse does not share the same religion as the patient and family. What should the nurse do?

Support Systems

Ancillary services and support systems may be available to assist directly or indirectly with the care of the cardiac vascular patient. The cardiac vascular nurse's responsibility is to understand the scope of responsibility and roles of these care support systems:

- Volunteers
    - Volunteers can be used as ancillary support in the event the nurse needs supplies or basic support.
    - Volunteers do not routinely provide patient care.
- Transportation
    - Transportation services include moving patients within the care facility as well as transporting patients outside the facility.
    - Transportation services should be chosen based on the acuity of the patient.
    - The nurse should travel with the patient within the facility when the patient requires monitoring during transport.
- Support groups
    - Support groups are usually available to patients with similar diagnoses or disease processes in order to help them cope with illness or to support required behavioral changes.
- Medication assistance
    - Financial assistance for medication may be available to patients, depending on socioeconomic status and the level of need.
    - The nurse should engage appropriate resources in order to get such support for patients.

> **Helpful Hint**
>
> **Pastoral counseling** integrates a faith-based perspective and spiritual guidance with psychology. It is offered by a trained minister or other clergyperson.

178   Chapter 9 – Patient and Community Education

- Community support
  - The cardiac vascular nurse can provide information on community resources that can help patients and their families with basic needs related to their illness or disease process.
  - Such resources include support groups, rehab services, meal services, and others.

Quick Review Question

8. A cardiac vascular nurse is caring for three patients with moderate acuity. One of the patients is scheduled to undergo a stress test in 30 minutes in the cardiac clinic. How can the nurse arrange for the patient to be transported to the appointment?

Coping Strategies and Defense Mechanisms

The cardiac vascular nurse may encounter patients and families experiencing the diagnosis of a chronic or terminal illness; such circumstances will elicit varied reactions and coping strategies from patients and families. Coping strategies, which are psychological efforts to manage stress and negative emotions, include the following:

- **Active coping** is characterized by solving problems, seeking support, seeking professional consultation, and planning activities.
- **Passive coping** is characterized by a feeling of helplessness in the face of stress or change; it generally involves withdrawal and wishful thinking.
- **Avoidance** is considered maladaptive and involves changing behavior to avoid thinking about or feeling sad about uncomfortable things.
- **Denial** gives the patient time to adjust to a distressing situation; it is acceptable for a short time but can interfere with treatment if it continues.

When confronted with a terminal illness, patients may choose to suspend aggressive interventions and opt for palliative care or hospice:

- **Palliative care** is an approach to care that improves the quality of life for patients and families experiencing terminal or life-threatening illness; it focuses on the prevention and relief of suffering through assessment and early identification of pain and other physical and mental health concerns related to the illness.
- **Hospice** is an approach to care for patients nearing the end of life; interventions include palliative care but are extended to the patient in a place of comfort—most often the patient's home—in the presence of family.

Quick Review Question

9. A patient has just been diagnosed with moderate cardiovascular disease. The patient's spouse begins seeking medical advice from specialists and has hired a nutritionist for the family. How is the spouse coping with the new information regarding the patient?

Outpatient Monitoring

Remote Telemetry

Remote telemetry uses wireless technology to monitor a patient's cardiovascular status at a distance. A patient's heart can be monitored continuously, and health care providers can be alerted in real time if abnormalities occur that require interventions. Various devices can be used for remote telemetry:

- wearable sensors (e.g., smart watches with EKG applications)
- pocket-sized EKG devices (e.g., KardiaMobile)
- Holter monitors and other short-term event recorders for temporary monitoring
- implanted devices (e.g., pacemakers and implantable cardioverter defibrillators with telemetry)
- tiny implantable devices [e.g., the Reveal LINQ insertable cardiac monitor (ICM)], which allow long-term cardiac monitoring.

Issues to consider with telemetry include compliance with the Health Insurance Portability and Accountability Act of 1996 (HIPAA). If data are to be transmitted over the internet, then reliable service in the home is necessary. Patients should be educated about maintenance issues and how to manage alerts, including false alerts. Patients should learn how the device works; how to use the device; and any steps they need to take, such as placing the LINQ receiver/transmitter close to their bed to ensure proper recording during the night.

Quick Review Question

10. If a patient has a LINQ ICM (Medtronic) in place that records data during the night, what is the BEST placement for the monitor base?

Point-of-Care Testing

Point-of-care testing is an important component of outpatient monitoring. In most cases, patients should be taught to carry out their own testing and to keep a record of the results, although some patients may be unable to do so because of physical or mental impairments. Types of point-of-care testing often used for outpatient monitoring include the following:

- Blood glucose monitors: for diabetes management and medication dosing; require fingersticks
- Coagulation testing: measures PT and INR to monitor anticoagulation management and reduce the need for frequent visits to laboratories for testing; requires fingersticks
- Urinalysis testing: to assess urine for glucose, protein, and white blood cells to monitor for kidney disease, diabetes, and urinary tract infections; uses test strips
- Spirometry: measures lung function for those with respiratory disorders
- Cholesterol/lipid tests: measure lipid levels; require fingerstick

- Infectious disease kits: use nasal swabs to rapidly identify infectious conditions, such as strep throat, influenza, and COVID-19
- Hemoglobin monitors: used in the management of anemia; require fingerstick

Quick Review Question

11. What type of testing is MOST commonly required for the various infectious disease point-of-care testing kits?

Population Health Risk Management

Risk Management

Cardiac risk factors may lead to the development of cardiovascular diseases. Modifiable risk factors (discussed in more depth in Chapter 2) can be controlled by the patient with healthy lifestyle changes and decisions. Examples of modifiable risk factors include the following:

- smoking
- diet
- exercise
- cholesterol levels
- hypertension
- diabetes

Non-modifiable risk factors are those which cannot be controlled by the patient and include the following:

- Race
  - Non-Hispanic people of African descent have higher rates of cardiovascular disease (particularly hypertension) and higher age-adjusted mortality rates.
  - Native Americans/Alaskan Natives also die from cardiovascular disease at much younger ages than other populations.
- Biological sex
  - Heart disease (including MI, heart failure, and other cardiovascular conditions) is the leading cause of death for both men and women.
  - The onset of cardiovascular diseases in women occurs on average about 10 years later than in men.
- Age
  - People aged 65 or older have a greater risk of dying from cardiovascular disease.

- Family history
    - Cardiac risk increases in patients with first-degree family members who developed cardiovascular disease early in life.
    - A patient's risk of cardiovascular disease is usually calculated as a 10-year risk or a lifetime risk:
        - A 10-year risk >20% is classified as high-risk.
        - A 10-year risk 5% is classified as low-risk.
    - High-risk patients are treated aggressively, even if they have not had a cardiac event.
    - Low-risk patients are monitored and educated on disease prevention.
    - Treatment guidelines vary for patients at intermediate risk.
    - The American College of Cardiology (ACC) website includes a calculator for estimating cardiac risk based on specific patient characteristics (https://tools.acc.org/ASCVD-Risk-Estimator-Plus/); calculators based on the Framingham Heart Study are also available.

The level of prevention is based on the level of cardiovascular disease:

- **Primary prevention** aims to prevent the occurrence of disease (e.g., smoking cessation, maintaining a healthy diet).
- **Secondary prevention** is the early identification of disease (often before symptoms appear) to alter the disease process (e.g., management of hypertension before a cardiac event occurs).
- **Tertiary prevention** is the treatment of the disease to mitigate further harm (e.g., cardiac rehabilitation after an MI).

> **Helpful Hint**
>
> Patients with chronic kidney disease have elevated risks of CAD and worse outcomes after MI, CABG, and PCI.

Quick Review Question

12. A cardiac vascular nurse is planning to discharge a 68-year-old patient with obesity who is newly diagnosed with PVD. The patient states, "Since I have the nicotine patch, I can still occasionally smoke if I remove it." What modifiable and non-modifiable risk factors should the nurse review with the patient?

Health Agencies and Community Resources

The cardiac vascular nurse should be knowledgeable about community resources that are available to patients. The nurse may also partner with providers of community resources to ensure that the most up-to-date information is available and provided to patients:

- **Cardiac rehabilitation programs** are available for qualified patients who need intensive outpatient follow-up for behavior modification and disease management. Cardiac rehabilitation has three phases:
    - **Phase I** occurs in the hospital and includes referrals, assessment of exercise capability, and education.

- Phase II occurs in an outpatient setting and includes education about lifestyle changes along with monitored exercise.
- Phase III also occurs in an outpatient setting. Patient education continues, and exercise is supervised but not monitored.

Anticoagulation clinics provide management and monitoring to patients who are receiving anticoagulation therapy to reduce the risks of complications (e.g., bleeding or thromboembolic events) and hospitalizations, and to allow patients to be safely maintained in the community. These clinics typically provide interdisciplinary coordination of care with nurses, pharmacists, and physicians. The prothrombin time (PT) and international normalized ratio (INR) are routinely tested to ensure that the current anticoagulation dosage is sufficient to achieve the target range, without being excessive and increasing risks for bleeding.

Many anticoagulation clinics focus on serving patients who are receiving antivitamin K antagonists (e.g., warfarin); some also provide services for other types of anticoagulation, such as direct oral anticoagulants (e.g., apixaban, rivaroxaban). Initially, visits to this type of clinic are usually weekly, becoming less frequent over time. Services include the following:

- Medication management: ensuring appropriate dosage and helping patients to transition from one type of anticoagulant to another; reviewing prescriptions and over-the-counter drugs to identify potential adverse interactions
- Laboratory assessment and point-of-care testing: monitoring PT and INR to assess the need for change in dosage for those on warfarin and routine laboratory assessment as indicated for other anticoagulants
- Education: teaching the patient and family about adherence, drug interactions, adverse effects, surgical and dental procedural management, and dietary modifications

Other community resources available to patients typically include the following:

- **Mobile clinics** are available in rural or other areas that have limited access to cardiac care.
- **Home health services** are available to qualified patients with medical necessities for home health visits.
- **Telehealth services** can increase access to care for patients in underserved areas; they may also be used with patients who require frequent monitoring (e.g., patients with heart failure).
- **Faith community nurses** are specialty practitioners who integrate spiritual care with medical treatment. They are usually attached to a specific church or religious organization and provide services such as screenings, referrals, and education.
- **Navigators** are cardiac vascular nurses who assist patients with the transition from the hospital to the home. These nurses also assist patients with self-care related to their disease processes.

Quick Review Question

13. If a patient has just started treatment with warfarin, how frequently should the patient go to an anticoagulation clinic for testing?

Health Promotion and Disease Prevention Strategies

The US Office of Disease Prevention and Health Promotion creates 10-year objectives—**Healthy People initiatives**—for improving the health of Americans. **Healthy People 2030** aims to reduce death from heart disease and stroke by focusing on the following:

- increasing the number of adults who survive heart attacks and are referred to rehabilitation programs
- increasing the number of adult stroke survivors who take part in rehabilitation services
- reducing the number of stroke-related deaths
- reducing the number of deaths related to coronary heart disease
- improving the cardiovascular health of adults
- reducing the number of hospitalizations due to heart failure in adults
- increasing the number of patients who receive IV reperfusion therapy within three hours of stroke onset

The list of cardiac vascular and stroke objectives for Healthy People 2030 can be found at https://odphp.health.gov/healthypeople/objectives-and-data/find-objectives.

Healthy People 2030 also provides an up-to-date repository of evidence-based practice in the care of the cardiac vascular patient. These resources can be accessed at https://odphp.health.gov/healthypeople/tools-action/browse-evidence-based-resources.

Many communities and health care organizations arrange educational activities in order to increase community knowledge and understanding of cardiovascular diseases. For example, **health fairs** are events that provide education and health care products to community members; they are often held at offices, churches, or schools and may include partnerships with local health care providers. Health fairs may also offer screenings to identify health risks in asymptomatic patients; screenings may include blood pressure, weight, BMI, cholesterol, and A1C.

> **Helpful Hint**
>
> Be sure to review the Healthy People 2030 objectives before taking the exam.

Quick Review Question

14. One of the Healthy People 2030 objectives is to decrease the number of coronary heart disease-related deaths. As of 2022, the figure for this currently stands at nearly 87.6 deaths per 100,000 people. What is the target number of coronary heart disease-related deaths per 100,000 people for the Healthy People 2030 objective?

Answer Key

1. Psychomotor skills require concentration. When the nurse asked the patient about a BP target while the patient was trying to apply the cuff, the nurse disturbed the patient's focus on this skill. The nurse should help the patient learn to apply the cuff, and once that skill has been mastered, the nurse can ask questions within the cognitive domain.

2. The nurse should develop an education plan to help the patient better understand how to manage the medications. The nurse might use models or visual aids to teach the patient how to read the medication labels, or the nurse could suggest that the patient use aids such as pillboxes or calendar alerts. The nurse might also work with the patient and provider to simplify the medication regimen and align it with the patient's current schedule.

3. The nurse is intrinsically motivated—she is doing something that is personally rewarding.

4. The nurse should determine why the patient is not engaging in the group discussion and then develop a new education strategy. For example, if the patient is uncomfortable in social settings, the nurse could suggest a webinar. If the patient lacks the foundational knowledge necessary to actively participate in a group discussion, the nurse could provide one-on-one teaching. The nurse should also consider the possibility that the patient's functional status prevents active participation and provide the necessary accommodations.

5. To reduce the patient's anxiety, the nurse should explain that he is being monitored after the procedure. The nurse should say something like, "We will be checking your vital signs and heart rhythm frequently to assess for any changes." The nurse should not give the patient false reassurance or provide results of the procedure.

6. The nurse should demonstrate how to use the scale the patient will have at home and ask for a return demonstration. The nurse should ensure that the patient understands what information is needed each day and where to find that information on the scale. If necessary, the patient should also be given a point of contact for questions or for troubleshooting equipment.

7. The nurse should facilitate the presence of the requested clergy at the bedside if possible. The nurse's personal beliefs should not influence the care of the patient.

8. The nurse should understand the role of and availability of ancillary services, and what can and cannot be delegated to them. In this situation it would be appropriate to arrange for transport services within the hospital to bring the patient to the appointment so that the nurse can stay with the other two patients.

9. The patient's spouse is actively coping with the diagnosis by seeking appropriate information and support.

10. The monitor base for the LINQ ICM (Medtronic) should be within 2 m (6.5 ft) of the bed so that it can adequately receive data.

11. Nasal swabs are generally required for infectious conditions, such as strep throat, influenza, respiratory syncytial virus, COVID-19, and multi-pathogen respiratory panels.

12. The nurse should educate the patient on several risk factors for a cardiac event. The patient's age is non-modifiable, but other risks, including weight and smoking, are modifiable and can contribute to the management of PVD. The patient's education plan should include information on smoking cessation, a healthy diet, and exercise, as well as how to effectively manage PVD.

13. After initially beginning treatment with warfarin, patients should undergo testing at the anticoagulation clinic for PT and INR weekly or biweekly so that the levels can be carefully monitored and their dosages can be adjusted as needed.

14. According to the Healthy People 2030 objective to reduce the number of coronary heart disease-related deaths, the target is to reduce this number to 71.1 per 100,000 people. Note that the status of this objective is currently considered to be improving since the Healthy People 2020 objective; however, the goal remains to further decrease the number of such deaths.

Practice Test

Directions: Read the question, and then choose the most correct answer.

1. The nurse is assessing a patient who was hit in the chest by the steering wheel during a car accident. The patient has a blood pressure of 88/40 mm Hg, a heart rate of 140 bpm, and has labored breathing at 30/min. Which injury is the patient MOST likely experiencing?
    A. myocardial contusion
    B. aortic dissection
    C. cardiac tamponade
    D. pulmonary embolism

2. A patient who just had an ICD placed is concerned about upcoming travel plans and going through airport security screenings with the device. The cardiac vascular nurse should tell him that he must do which one of the following?
    A. cancel his travel plans since he cannot fly for a period for 6 months after the procedure
    B. inform airport security before going through the metal detectors that he has an ICD
    C. take a strong magnet with him so he can deactivate the ICD before flying
    D. travel how he normally does without any modifications

3. A patient presents to the ED with severe chest pain. The nurse knows which one of the following would be a contraindication to administering nitrates?
    A. presence of ST elevation on the ECG
    B. recent phosphodiesterase use
    C. anterior wall infarction
    D. use of beta blockers

4. Why would dopamine (Intropin) be ordered for a patient with heart failure?
    A. because the drug will lower the patient's heart rate
    B. because the drug opens blocked arteries
    C. because the drug prevents plaque from building up
    D. because the drug increases the amount of oxygen delivered to the heart

5. According to the National Heart, Lung, and Blood Institute (NHLBI), which of the following can be a trigger for a heart attack?
    A. stress
    B. abrupt smoking cessation
    C. moderate exercise
    D. caffeine1

6. Which of the following is a Healthy People 2030 objective?
    A. reduce the proportion of adults who get a referral to a rehab program after having survived a heart attack
    B. reduce the proportion of stroke survivors who go on to take part in rehabilitation services
    C. reduce the number of people who die from strokes
    D. raise the proportion of patients suffering a stroke who get IV reperfusion therapy within 4 hours of the onset of symptoms

7. Which of the following can BEST help reduce hospital readmission rates?
    A. having the patient complete a discharge survey to address concerns
    B. ensuring collaborative care
    C. providing the patient with comprehensive information regarding diagnosis
    D. keeping patients with chronic illnesses in the hospital for an additional day

8. A patient on digoxin is being discharged from the hospital and asks the nurse if she can continue using an herbal remedy of St. John's Wort. What should the nurse know about the interaction between these two medications?
    A. that it is not significant, and the patient can continue taking both
    B. that it is not significant, but the patient should stop all medications prescribed by any other physicians
    C. that it is significant due to St. John's Wort's clotting factors
    D. that it is significant because St. John's Wort can cause toxic effects when combined with digoxin

9. After a patient has been diagnosed with A-fib, the cardiac vascular nurse knows that the patient understands his risk factors when he states he is at greater risk for which of the following?
    A. arthralgia
    B. influenza
    C. DIC
    D. stroke

10. A patient diagnosed with heart failure needs to be started on a new medication. The patient speaks only Spanish and does not understand English. What should the cardiac vascular nurse do before administering the new medication?
    A. ask a family member who speaks both fluent English and Spanish to translate information regarding the reason for the medication and side effects
    B. find a hospital employee who speaks fluent English and Spanish to translate the information
    C. use a language line to translate the conversation with an interpreter
    D. wait until shift change to administer the new medication so that the patient can be assigned a Spanish-speaking nurse to explain the plan of care

11. The nurse is reviewing the history of a patient with heart failure. Which of the following coexisting health problems will cause an increase in the patient's afterload?
    A. diabetes
    B. endocrine disorders
    C. hypertension
    D. Marfan syndrome

12. The registered CV nurse can delegate tasks to all of the following staff members EXCEPT which one of the following?
    A. a licensed practical nurse (LPN)
    B. a patient care tech
    C. a respiratory therapist
    D. a medical assistant

13. When serving a population with varied health literacy, at which grade level should printed materials should be prepared?
    A. first to second
    B. third to fourth
    C. fourth to fifth
    D. sixth the seventh

14. A patient's ECG shows torsades de pointes, and magnesium sulfate is ordered STAT. The nursing priority is to do which one of the following?
    A. monitor the patient for bradycardia and respiratory depression
    B. prepare the patient for synchronized cardioversion
    C. monitor the patient for tachycardia and hyperventilation
    D. prepare the patient for a Swan-Ganz catheter

15. The nurse reviews a 12-lead ECG from a patient who is complaining of crushing chest pain. The ECG reveals ST elevation in leads II, III, and aVF. Which area of the heart is being affected?
    A. anterior
    B. lateral
    C. inferior
    D. posterior

16. The cardiac vascular nurse is educating a patient following a PTA procedure. The patient appears anxious. Which one of the following is an appropriate response from the nurse?
    A. "Your procedure went well, so you have nothing to worry about."
    B. "Would you like some medication for your anxiety?"
    C. "We will be monitoring your vital signs and heart rhythm frequently to assess for any changes."
    D. "The physician will be in soon to discuss the rest of your treatment plan."

17. A 75-year-old patient complains of fatigue, weakness, and visual disturbances. The cardiac vascular nurse reviews the patient's medication history and finds that she has been taking digoxin (Lanoxin), a potassium supplement, and amlodipine. What is the patient MOST likely experiencing?
    A. ineffective dosing of digoxin
    B. digoxin toxicity
    C. hypercalcemia
    D. hypotension

18. When providing a hospitalized cardiac patient with a therapeutic environment, what should the nurse consider?
    A. assigning the same nurse to the patient each day
    B. restricting friends and family visitation hours
    C. administering all medications within an appropriate time frame
    D. ensuring the patient's psychosocial and spiritual needs are met

19. Which of the following is an example of a SMART goal for a cardiac patient?
    A. "I will walk for 10 minutes, 3 times a day, for 5 days this week."
    B. "I will increase my physical activity this week."
    C. "I will begin a moderate walking program by the end of the month."
    D. "I will record a log of each time I exercise this week."

20. Advance directives are applicable in which one of the following patient situations?
    A. an alert and oriented patient who is being admitted for heart failure
    B. a patient who is post-cardiac arrest and remains unconscious with a poor prognosis
    C. a stable patient who is being extubated after open heart surgery
    D. any patient who is discharged to a long-term care facility

21. A patient arrives to the ED with midsternal chest pain radiating down the left arm and left jaw. He slumps to the floor and is unresponsive, pulseless, and apneic. High-quality compressions are started, and the patient's ECG shows the following rhythm. What is the priority nursing intervention?

    A. administer a fluid bolus of 1 L normal saline
    B. defibrillate with 200 J
    C. administer 1 mg epinephrine IV
    D. insert an advanced airway

22. The cardiac vascular nurse enters a patient's room and finds her to be unresponsive. The nurse is aware that the patient has a DNR order in place. Which one of the following would be the MOST appropriate action for the nurse to take?
    A. begin chest compressions immediately
    B. apply the AED pads and deliver an unsynchronized shock
    C. administer oxygen via a non-rebreather mask and notify the physician
    D. prepare equipment for the physician to intubate

23. The nurse assists a patient in creating a measurable goal during the shift. Which one of the following is an appropriate goal?
    A. The patient will take all scheduled pain medications.
    B. The patient will have a pain level of 5 or less on a scale of 1 – 10 by the end of the shift.
    C. The patient will be pain-free by the end of the shift.
    D. The patient will take less pain medication than during the previous shift.

24. A patient in the ED is diagnosed with a right ventricular infarction with hypotension. The nurse should prepare to administer which one of the following to treat the hypotension?
    A. NS fluid boluses 1 to 2 L
    B. dopamine (Intropin) at 10 mcg/kg/min
    C. D5W fluid boluses titrate 3 L
    D. furosemide drip at 20 mg/hr

25. The cardiac vascular nurse is caring for a patient with STEMI. Which home medication would the nurse report to the physician as being contraindicated with an ordered dose of nitroglycerin?
    A. phosphodiesterase inhibitors
    B. antihypertensives
    C. statins
    D. beta blockers

26. Having tables set up in a shopping center to provide free blood pressure checks is an example of which type of health promotion effort?
    A. primary
    B. secondary
    C. tertiary
    D. quaternary

27. The nurse is evaluating a patient's home medication list and discovers that the patient has been taking his warfarin dose twice daily instead of once daily. Which one of the following orders would the nurse expect?
    A. PT/INR lab draw
    B. aPTT lab draw every 4 hours
    C. 2 units of packed FFP
    D. administer vitamin K

28. The nurse is evaluating a patient with pericarditis. Which one of the following heart sounds would the nurse MOST likely hear?
    A. friction rub
    B. crackles
    C. wheezing
    D. S3 gallop

29. The nurse is evaluating a patient's lipid panel results and notes elevated LDL and triglyceride levels. Which one of the following dietary recommendations should the nurse make to this patient?
    A. avoid saturated fats
    B. increase water intake
    C. reduce sodium intake
    D. increase fiber consumption

30. The cardiac vascular nurse is giving discharge instructions to a patient diagnosed with pericarditis. What is the BEST technique the nurse can use to demonstrate active listening?
    A. sit facing the patient while making eye contact
    B. speak clearly, loudly, and slowly
    C. ask the patient open-ended questions to ensure understanding
    D. move around the room while talking to the patient so that they do not feel anxious

31. A student nurse tells the cardiac vascular nurse that he found a printout of a patient's lab report left on the table in the cafeteria. Which information listed on the paper is NOT considered personally identifiable information?
   A. patient Social Security number
   B. patient first and last name
   C. patient date of birth
   D. patient medical record number

32. A patient with stage 4 congestive heart failure agrees to palliative care. A family member is concerned that the patient will no longer receive appropriate care. What is the BEST way for the nurse to explain what palliative care is?
   A. Palliative care is for patients who have no other treatment options.
   B. Palliative care is focused on relieving the symptoms to help improve quality of life.
   C. Palliative care only begins once it is certain that the person will not survive for much longer.
   D. Palliative care only lasts for approximately 3 months.

33. The cardiac vascular nurse is discharging a 75-year-old patient. Which one of the following support systems would be the MOST appropriate to help transport the patient to his car via wheelchair?
   A. the patient's wife
   B. a ride-sharing service
   C. a hospital volunteer
   D. the patient's daughter, who is an off-duty nurse

34. A nurse from the surgical unit is floated to the cardiac care unit. What is the BEST patient assignment to give to the float nurse?
   A. The float nurse should receive the easiest assignment on the unit.
   B. The float nurse should be assigned postsurgical patients.
   C. The float nurse should receive the same assignment as any nurse on the unit.
   D. The float nurse should refuse any assignment, as a surgical nurse cannot care for cardiac patients.

35. The nurse is caring for a patient with DVT. Which one of the following should be included in the plan of care?
   A. bed rest with the affected extremity elevated
   B. bed rest with the bed in reverse Trendelenburg
   C. walking slowly in the hall with assistance in order to prevent pneumonia
   D. sitting up in the chair for all meals and during visitation time

36. The nurse is evaluating patients for risk of heparin-induced thrombocytopenia (HIT). Which patient is at the greatest risk for HIT, based on the nurse's assessment?
   A. a male patient who just completed a 1-week course of heparin
   B. a male patient taking enoxaparin for management of unstable angina
   C. a female patient receiving heparin for postsurgical thromboprophylaxis
   D. a female patient taking enoxaparin to prevent clots following a mild MI

37. Which of the following is MOST likely to be found in a patient with left-sided heart failure?
    A. JVD
    B. crackles
    C. hepatomegaly
    D. ascites

38. The cardiac vascular nurse is assessing a patient who is complaining of chest pain. A 12-lead ECG shows ST elevation in diffuse leads, and the nurse hears a friction rub on auscultation of the heart. The patient states that the chest pain feels better when she is sitting up and leaning forward. What is the MOST likely diagnosis for this patient?
    A. V-fib
    B. coronary thrombosis
    C. pericarditis
    D. congestive heart failure

39. Which of the following is a modifiable risk factor that would place a patient at greater risk for cardiovascular disease?
    A. male gender
    B. being more than 65 years old
    C. smoking one pack of cigarettes a day
    D. regular exercise

40. When evaluating a patient with mitral stenosis, the cardiac vascular nurse knows that the patient is at higher risk for which cardiac dysrhythmia?
    A. A-fib
    B. V-fib
    C. SVT
    D. bradycardia

41. The nurse is evaluating the ECG rhythm of a patient with a first-degree heart block. Which one of the following would be consistent with this diagnosis?
    A. widened QRS complex
    B. heart rate >150 bpm
    C. inverted P waves
    D. PR interval >0.20

42. A patient is being evaluated for a DVT. Which of the following risk factors would place the patient at greater risk for developing clot formation?
    A. a plane trip from Florida to California
    B. recent travel on a cruise ship
    C. the start of training to run a marathon
    D. employment in a high-stress job

Practice Test

43. A patient diagnosed with an AAA states, "I just had a physical last month with blood work and imaging tests, and nothing was wrong with me! You guys don't know what you're talking about!" What is the BEST response by the cardiac vascular nurse?
    A. "I understand you feel upset. What concerns you about your diagnosis the most?"
    B. "Your other physician was wrong. I can assure you that our results are correct."
    C. "You shouldn't worry because the aneurysm isn't large enough to require surgery."
    D. "Calm down. Let's discuss this rationally."

44. The cardiac vascular nurse and physician are at bedside obtaining consent for a procedure. The nurse is asked to sign as a witness to the consent. The nurse knows this means that she is responsible for which one of the following?
    A. ensuring that the patient understands the risks and benefits of the procedure
    B. making certain that the patient understands all of the medications she will receive before, during, and after the procedure
    C. observing that the correct patient signs the consent form
    D. explaining how the procedure is performed

45. A patient asks about a holistic treatment plan for her CAD that is based on spirituality rather than taking pharmaceuticals. To what or whom might the cardiac vascular nurse refer the patient?
    A. a religious-based hospital organization
    B. the chaplain
    C. a faith community nurse
    D. a physician who follows the same religion as the patient

46. Which one of the following options will NOT help teach a patient with hyperlipidemia how to reduce cholesterol levels?
    A. maintaining an exercise program
    B. eating a diet low in HDL and LDL cholesterol
    C. quitting cigarette smoking
    D. taking statin medications

47. Which one of following activities could the cardiac vascular nurse participate in to promote population health?
    A. organizing team-building activities for Nurse Appreciation Week
    B. running in a corporate 5k race
    C. volunteering at a free community blood pressure screening event
    D. participating in a research study

48. A patient presents to the ED with chest pain, dyspnea, and diaphoresis. The nurse finds a narrow complex tachycardia with a heart rate of 210 bpm, blood pressure of 122/72 mm Hg, and a respiratory rate of 18. The nurse should first prepare to do which one of the following?
    A. administer adenosine 6 mg IV
    B. perform synchronized cardioversion at 100 J
    C. perform defibrillation at 300 J
    D. perform vagal maneuvers

49. Which one of the following substances is contraindicated for an 80-year-old patient with acute heart failure?
    A. dopamine
    B. adrenaline
    C. digoxin
    D. dobutamine

50. EKG monitoring devices that use finger electrodes, such as KardiaMobile, typically produce which one of the following?
    A. a single-lead EKG
    B. a double-lead EKG
    C. a three-lead EKG
    D. a six-lead EKG

51. A patient has an organized rhythm with a rate of 45 bpm and tall peaked T waves. The nurse should suspect which one of the following?
    A. hypokalemia
    B. hyperkalemia
    C. hyponatremia
    D. hypernatremia

52. A patient who was initially admitted for cardiac observation is told he needs more tests done and will need to stay a few days longer. The patient is competent, but he refuses to stay and that states the hospital is just trying to make money off of him by doing extra tests. What is the BEST action for the nurse to take?
    A. have the business office discuss a payment plan with the patient
    B. tell the patient he cannot leave because the tests are mandatory
    C. call the physician to have the patient involuntarily committed
    D. provide the patient with as much information as possible so he can make an informed decision regarding his care

53. Which one of the following statements made by the cardiac vascular nurse is an example of motivational interviewing during smoking cessation counseling?
    A. "Smoking has been linked to cardiovascular disease and depression, so it is important that you stop immediately to prevent further damage to your heart."
    B. "Did you know that over 450,000 people die from smoking every year in the United States?"
    C. "What encourages you to stop smoking?"
    D. "I will contact the physician to write you a prescription-strength medication that will help you to quit smoking."

54. The cardiac vascular nurse is caring for a patient from a different culture than her own. Which one of the following statements is appropriate for her to make in terms of providing culturally competent care?
    A. "Do you have any special cultural needs we can provide for you during your stay?"
    B. "We may not be able to accommodate all of your needs because we care for many different patients with different cultural needs."
    C. "Would you like me to call the chaplain to pray with you?"
    D. "We can only allow one visitor at a time, so your extended family will have to switch out with one another to visit with you."

55. Which one of the following individualized learning activities would be MOST appropriate for a 25-year-old male patient admitted to the cardiac unit?
    A. attending a group classroom meeting
    B. role-playing
    C. an interactive, online educational game
    D. reading written information

56. The cardiac vascular nurse does not feel a pedal pulse in a patient's right foot. What is the next appropriate intervention?
    A. take the patient for a STAT CT to rule out a pulmonary embolus
    B. order a lower-extremity ultrasound to obtain blood flow measurements
    C. call the physician to report that the patient does not have a pedal pulse
    D. use a Doppler to confirm if pulses are present

57. The American Heart Association recommends that patients who are diagnosed with hypertension reduce their sodium intake. What is the current recommended ideal limit of daily sodium intake?
    A. 1,000 mg
    B. 1,500 mg
    C. 2,500 mg
    D. 3,000 mg

58. A competent 74-year-old patient has given power of attorney (POA) to his son. Upon admission to the cardiac unit, the patient is told that he will need an implanted defibrillator due to his persistent third-degree heart block. The son agrees, but the patient refuses the surgery and wants to rescind the paperwork that designates his son as the POA. What is the MOST appropriate action for the nurse to take?
    A. to tell the patient he can revoke his son as POA and the hospital will follow his wishes regarding care
    B. to tell the patient that because his son is the POA, the son's decisions are final
    C. to tell the patient that the POA is legally binding and no changes can be made
    D. to tell the patient he needs to work out a compromise with his son and decide on a treatment plan

59. A patient with PVD is having a Doppler ultrasound of the lower extremities to rule out occlusion. Which explanation by the CV nurse BEST describes the purpose of this diagnostic test?
    A. "Having a Doppler ultrasound will help identify if you have cardiovascular disease."
    B. "You are having a Doppler ultrasound because it is faster and cheaper than other diagnostic tests used to diagnose PVD."
    C. "The Doppler ultrasound helps rule out an aneurysm."
    D. "A Doppler ultrasound will measure blood flow and visualize any blocked arteries."

60. Which of the following is NOT considered a predisposing factor to clot formation?
    A. hypercoagulability
    B. venous stasis
    C. endothelial damage
    D. the presence of a heart murmur

61. The nurse is evaluating a patient's ECG rhythm after administering a dose of adenosine. Which of the following is an expected finding indicating treatment was effective?
    A. a flat line, followed by a normal sinus rhythm
    B. bradycardia
    C. a narrow-complex rhythm with a rate of 185 bpm
    D. an irregular, chaotic rhythm

62. A pediatric patient is being resuscitated in a trauma bay, and his father wants to be in the room. What should the nurse do?
    A. Tell the father that he may not be in the trauma room during resuscitation.
    B. Allow the father in the trauma room with a knowledgeable staff member for support.
    C. Ask the father to stand just outside the trauma room.
    D. Call the legal department for advice.

63. A patient has a Zio XT Patch (iRhythm) applied to the left chest for cardiac monitoring. The patient should be advised to avoid which one of the following?
    A. security screening at the airport
    B. proximity to electronic devices
    C. all types of exercise
    D. submerging the device

64. The cardiac vascular nurse is caring for a patient with acute heart failure. Which one of the following is the BEST way to evaluate fluid and electrolyte balance in this patient?
    A. record the patient's weight every morning
    B. draw labs every 4 hours to monitor for changes
    C. insert a Foley catheter
    D. reduce dietary sodium intake

65. If using the iSTAT 1 (Abbott) point-of-care blood analyzer to assess a patient's troponin I level, the results are usually available within which time frame?
    A. 60 seconds
    B. 2 minutes
    C. 5 minutes
    D. 10 minutes

66. Which one of the following is considered objective data that would require reporting to the physician for a patient change in status?
    A. a patient's complaint of dizziness
    B. increased blood pressure of 200/98 mm Hg
    C. troponin of 0.02 ng/ml
    D. a family member who tells the nurse that the patient seems more depressed

67. A patient being discharged with a LifeVest is shown by the nurse how to wear the vest and the monitor. The nurse asks the patient to demonstrate putting the LifeVest on and to explain what he is doing. Which type of education is the nurse providing?
    A. procedural
    B. adherence
    C. memorization
    D. teach-back

68. A patient admitted with SSS needs to have an implanted pacemaker. Which one of the following is required in order for the patient to sign informed consent?
    A. that the patient is alert, oriented, and deemed competent to make her own medical decisions
    B. that the patient's insurance has been verified, and a complete history and physical are completed
    C. that the patient has been informed of only the benefits of the procedure
    D. that the patient expresses that he does not want the procedure done, so a family member signs the consent form for her

69. Which laboratory finding indicates that a 62-year-old male patient is at risk for ventricular dysrhythmia?
    A. magnesium 0.8 mEq/L
    B. potassium 4.2 mmol/L
    C. creatinine 1.3 mg/dL
    D. total calcium 2.8 mmol/L

70. The triage nurse is assessing a patient with complaints of dyspnea. The nurse should suspect heart failure when the patient states which one of the following?
    A. "I have been taking a beta blocker for many years."
    B. "I was diagnosed with a pulmonary embolism last year."
    C. "I get chest pain when I walk to the mailbox."
    D. "When I walk upstairs to my bedroom I have to stop and rest halfway up."

71. A patient's cardiac monitor shows the following rhythm. He is awake and alert but is pale and confused. His blood pressure reads 64/40 mm Hg. What is the priority nursing intervention for this patient?

    A. defibrillate at 200 J
    B. prepare for TCP
    C. administer epinephrine 1 mg
    D. begin CPR

72. What is the primary purpose of wellness counseling?
    A. to monitor treatment adherence
    B. to prevent disease complications
    C. to prescribe specific interventions
    D. to encourage healthy choices

73. Which of the following is NOT an appropriate way for the nurse to protect a patient's PHI?
    A. logging out of the computer each time the nurse is finished using it
    B. placing any documents with PHI that are no longer needed in the shred bin
    C. asking the HIPAA compliance officer of the hospital if the nurse has concerns about patient privacy
    D. giving a newly hired RN the nurse's password so he can assist with a medication passes and then changing the password at the end of the shift

74. Which observation in a patient with AAA indicates the need for immediate treatment?
    A. complaints of yellow-tinted vision
    B. hemoptysis
    C. urinary output of 75 mL/hr per urinary catheter
    D. complaints of sudden and severe back pain and dyspnea

75. A patient on the cardiac care unit goes into sudden cardiac arrest. All of these actions are within the new graduate CV nurse's scope of practice EXCEPT which one?
    A. administering epinephrine
    B. preparing the patient for defibrillation
    C. intubating the patient
    D. inserting an IV

76. A patient's troponin level comes back elevated. The patient is informed that he is having an acute MI and will need a cardiac catheterization. The patient states, "I exercise every day and I eat well, there is no possible way I'm having a heart attack." This statement is an example of which type of defense mechanism?
    A. passive coping
    B. avoiding
    C. active coping
    D. denial

77. The cardiac vascular nurse is assessing a patient before administering a scheduled dose of digoxin. What should the nurse assess first?
    A. apical pulse
    B. chest X-ray results
    C. blood glucose level
    D. blood pressure

78. The nurse is admitting a young female patient to the cardiac care unit. Which one of the following is an open-ended interview question the nurse could ask?
    A. "Do you have any pain right now?"
    B. "Are you feeling any better after your last dose of pain medication?"
    C. "Is there any chance you could be pregnant?"
    D. "What is your main goal during your hospital stay?"

79. The cardiac vascular nurse receives an order to administer 4 mg of morphine to a patient who is having an acute MI. Which of the following is true about this medication?
    A. Morphine has a short half-life.
    B. Morphine decreases the oxygen demand of the heart.
    C. Morphine is contraindicated in an acute MI.
    D. Morphine reduces ST elevation.

80. When assessing a patient, which one of the following would be considered part of the initial survey?
    A. vital signs
    B. skin color
    C. lab results
    D. chief complaint

81. The cardiac vascular nurse is caring for a patient who begins to experience sharp, severe chest pain that is radiating to the left arm. The nurse notifies the physician, performs an ECG, and administers a nitroglycerin tablet sublingually. What is the MOST appropriate way to document the situation?
    A. "Patient c/o chest pain, acute MI suspected. Physician notified. See EMAR for medications given."
    B. "Patient began having chest pain. Tech performed ECG. Medication administered STAT. Patient currently has no complaints."
    C. "Patient c/o sharp, severe chest pain radiating to left arm. Physician notified and received order to obtain ECG and administer 0.4 mg nitroglycerin tablet sublingually. Will continue to monitor patient for changes and medication side effects."
    D. No documentation is needed since the physician was notified.

82. When assessing a patient's risk stratification for a scheduled cardiac surgery, which one of the following would place the patient at the highest risk?
    A. creatinine level of 1.3 mg/dL
    B. allergy to latex
    C. history of asthma
    D. MI within the last 6 months

83. A patient is scheduled for a contrast CT chest angiography. Which one of the following is a priority to assess before the exam?
    A. allergies
    B. past medical history
    C. history of claustrophobia
    D. chief complaint

84. The nurse is assessing a patient who is suspected of having cardiac tamponade. Which assessment technique would help confirm this diagnosis?
    A. assessing for pedal edema
    B. performing a vagal maneuver
    C. percussion of the cardiac border
    D. auscultating heart sounds

85. The nurse knows that cardiovascular changes that occur with increasing age include which one of the following?
    A. decreased blood pressure
    B. increased drug metabolism
    C. decreased CO
    D. increased CO

86. The cardiac vascular nurse is caring for a 2-year-old pediatric patient who experiences a sudden change in rhythm. The nurse notes that the heart rate has dropped from 130 bpm to 50 bpm. What is the priority intervention that the nurse should take?
    A. begin chest compressions
    B. prepare to transcutaneous pace
    C. provide bag-valve mask ventilations with 100% oxygen
    D. administer atropine 0.02 mg/kg

87. The cardiac vascular nurse is evaluating an infant who has been experiencing cyanotic episodes. With which one of the following congenital heart defects is this presentation consistent?
    A. patent ductus arteriosus
    B. tetralogy of Fallot
    C. atrial septal defect
    D. ventricular septal defect

88. A patient being treated for a DVT is scheduled for an IVC filter placement. The nurse knows that the patient understands the purpose of the IVC filter when she states which one of the following?
    A. "I will need to have the IVC filter surgically replaced approximately every 6 months."
    B. "Having an IVC filter will help dissolve the clot in my leg."
    C. "I won't be able to eat high-protein meals while the IVC filter is in place."
    D. "The IVC filter will prevent blood clots from dislodging through the bloodstream to the lungs."

89. A patient is being discharged after an ICD placement. Patient education provided by the nurse to the patient regarding wound care would include which one of the following?
    A. written instructions for how to perform wet to dry dressing changes
    B. how to be aware of the signs and symptoms of infection of the incision site
    C. the importance of engaging in upper body exercise to improve circulation
    D. the importance of handwashing after completing a dressing change

90. A patient goes into SVT and has a sustained heart rate of 225. After attempting vagal maneuvers and administering 2 doses of adenosine, the cardiologist tells the nurse to prepare for synchronized cardioversion. What should the nurse tell the patient about the procedure?
    A. "You will be awake during the procedure, and you should not feel any pain at all."
    B. "This procedure is optional. Your heart rate will likely return to normal soon without it."
    C. "You will be given medication before the procedure to sedate you so that you will not feel pain."
    D. "This procedure will have to be repeated several times over the course of a few visits to in order to be effective."

91. The cardiac vascular nurse is caring for a patient who suddenly develops a second-degree, type 2 heart block. The patient states that he feels okay, but his heart rate is 45 bpm. There is no physician on the unit. What should the nurse do first to expedite care and ensure interdisciplinary collaboration?
    A. monitor the patient for any further changes in rhythm or symptoms since the patient is asymptomatic
    B. call a code blue
    C. use the telehealth cart to communicate with the physician remotely
    D. educate the patient on the symptoms of worsening heart blocks

92. A patient having a left ventricular assist device (LVAD) placed should receive which instruction before the procedure?
    A. "You will receive anticoagulation therapy during your hospital stay and at home to prevent clots, and your lab values will be closely monitored."
    B. "Most patients can typically be discharged home the same day as the procedure."
    C. "You will not have to take your medications after the device is placed."
    D. "You may still go into cardiac arrest with an LVAD, but standard resuscitation techniques such as chest compressions and defibrillation will improve your chance of survival."

93. A cardiac vascular nurse is working on a project that aligns with a Healthy People 2030 objective. What is an example of a Healthy People 2030 objective the nurse can use to implement health promotion strategies in the community?
    A. increasing the frequency of bystanders who use an AED when confronted with cardiac arrests in public places
    B. increasing hospitalizations for adults with heart failure
    C. reducing cholesterol treatment for adult patients
    D. reducing the use of aspirin for secondary prevention of atherosclerotic cardiovascular disease

94. A patient with heart failure is being discharged after a lengthy hospital stay. Which one of the following discharge instructions should the cardiac vascular nurse provide?
    A. "You should weigh yourself daily and report a weight gain of 2 lbs. or more in 24 hours, or more than 5 lbs. per week."
    B. "You should make sure that you do not eat any sodium because it causes fluid retention."
    C. "If you begin to experience difficulty breathing, you should use your nebulizer to give yourself a breathing treatment."
    D. "If you notice your feet swelling, you should put on compression socks."

95. A patient with diabetes and admitted for an MI has an HgbA1C result of 9.0. Which one of the following is important for the nurse to consider when developing a care plan for this patient?
    A. The patient has a normal HgbA1C value and should be encouraged to continue her current lifestyle.
    B. The patient has a low HgbA1C value and will need to take folic acid and vitamin C daily.
    C. The patient has an elevated HgbA1C value and should be given information about lifestyle modifications.
    D. The patient should have a fasting blood glucose level to confirm the HgbA1C result.

96. Which activity is part of the planning phase of the nursing process?
    A. auscultating heart sounds
    B. evaluating lab results
    C. checking a patient's blood pressure
    D. setting a goal to reduce pain

97. Which one of the following anticoagulants would the nurse expect to administer to a patient who is having an MI?
    A. aspirin
    B. heparin
    C. nitrates
    D. clopidogrel

98. The nurse is evaluating a patient's ECG rhythm strip and notices a prolonged QT interval. Which one of the following laboratory findings would the nurse expect to correlate to this?
    A. hypomagnesemia
    B. hypocalcemia
    C. hyperkalemia
    D. hyponatremia

99. The nurse is evaluating a patient's past medical history. Which one of the following would the nurse consider a risk factor for developing an aneurysm?
    A. Addison's disease
    B. diabetes
    C. skin cancer
    D. Marfan syndrome

100. The cardiac vascular nurse is assessing a 55-year-old female with a chief complaint of chest pressure. Her blood pressure is 105/70 mm Hg, her heart rate is 80 bpm, and her pulse oximetry reads 98%. Her breathing is even and unlabored at a rate of 16 breaths per minute. What is the priority intervention for this patient?
    A. obtain a 12-lead ECG
    B. complete a full health history examination
    C. review hospital policies and procedures for admission
    D. obtain expert consultation

101. The nurse is evaluating the vital signs of a patient with an AAA. Which of the following vital signs would be MOST concerning?
    A. oxygen saturation of 94%
    B. temperature of 38°C (100.4°F)
    C. blood pressure of 190/80 mm Hg
    D. heart rate of 100 bpm

102. The cardiac vascular nurse is performing an initial admission health history for a cardiac patient. The patient tells her that she has felt down lately, has less energy, and has had difficulty falling asleep. Which type of screening should the nurse perform?
    A. depression
    B. diabetes
    C. dementia
    D. drug abuse

103. The nurse is reviewing lab results of a patient admitted to the cardiac unit. Which of the following laboratory values is MOST concerning?
    A. Hgb 11.9
    B. WBC 5.2
    C. INR 2.0
    D. troponin 0.10

104. The nurse notes a patient who was previously in a sinus rhythm and is now in a second-degree, type II heart block. How should the nurse initially respond to this change?
    A. prepare to administer atropine
    B. obtain orders for sedation to prepare for synchronized cardioversion
    C. place pacing pads on the patient
    D. continue to monitor the patient

105. The cardiac vascular nurse is helping a patient develop a home exercise plan. Which one of the following statements by the patient shows that he understands appropriate short-term goals?
    A. "I will cut out all processed foods from my diet."
    B. "I will start wearing a nicotine patch to help me quit smoking."
    C. "Every time I go grocery shopping, I will check my blood pressure at the kiosk in the pharmacy."
    D. "I will use an exercise log to record 15-minute daily walks at least 4 times a week."

106. The cardiac vascular nurse provides sodium reduction education to a patient with hypertension. The nurse knows that his teaching was effective if the patient says she will eat which one of the following meals?
    A. canned vegetable soup with crackers
    B. a sandwich made of deli meat and cheese and whole wheat bread
    C. baked chicken with sweet potatoes and a side salad
    D. leftover pepperoni pizza with fresh fruit

107. The cardiac vascular nurse is evaluating a patient's adherence to treatment for hypertension. Which one of the following indicates that he has followed his treatment plan?
    A. He tells the nurse that he feels much better since his last visit.
    B. He has not refilled his medications.
    C. He complains of intermittent chest pain.
    D. He has a normal blood pressure.

108. The cardiac vascular nurse gets a phone call from a patient's husband asking how his wife is doing. What should the nurse do before giving the caller any information?
    A. ask him to verify the patient's full name, birth date, and room number
    B. ask him for the security code or HIPAA password
    C. give him vague information about the patient's status and tell him to come in person for updates on care
    D. tell him that no information can be released over the phone for privacy reasons

109. A patient is advised to attend cardiac rehabilitation. The nurse should explain that which one of the following is a reason that patients can benefit from this?
    A. because it is covered by all insurance plans
    B. because it provides a support system for patients during their recovery
    C. because it is required so that the cardiologist can continue providing follow-up care
    D. because it ensures that the patient does not have any further heart attacks

110. The cardiac vascular nurse's husband has labs drawn at the hospital where she works. The nurse wants to check on the results and knows that the BEST practice is to do which one of the following?
    A. access the chart to read the report since she is an employee of this hospital
    B. ask the physician to provide her with the results
    C. have her husband sign a release form to get the results
    D. ask her friend who is working to access the chart to read the results

111. The CV nurse is caring for a patient diagnosed with endocarditis. Which of the following laboratory values would the nurse expect to be elevated?
    A. sedimentation rate
    B. lactic acid
    C. troponin
    D. BNP

112. Which one of the following cardiovascular changes would be considered normal for a patient who is pregnant?
    A. tachycardia
    B. decreased cardiac output
    C. reduced blood volume
    D. hypertension

113. The cardiac vascular nurse is having a busy shift and is behind on tasks. Which task is the MOST appropriate for the nurse to assign to the patient care technician?
    A. assisting a patient to the bathroom
    B. taking a patient's vital signs
    C. hanging a normal saline IV bag
    D. inserting a Foley catheter to a patient with strict intake and output orders

114. The CV nurse is caring for a patient diagnosed with heart failure. Which of the following would be the priority nursing diagnosis related to heart failure?
    A. ineffective breathing pattern
    B. activity intolerance
    C. impaired urinary elimination
    D. risk for ineffective renal perfusion

115. A patient has been administered a fibrinolytic for an acute STEMI. What is an expected finding by the cardiac vascular nurse that would indicate that the treatment has been effective?
    A. The patient's troponin levels increase.
    B. There is no longer ST elevation present on the ECG.
    C. A new BBB is present.
    D. The patient's pain level has decreased.

116. Which of the following is an expected outcome for a patient on day 3 of admission for an MI?
    A. decreased pain
    B. increased mobility
    C. improved breathing pattern
    D. reduced urinary output

117. If planning a health fair, how long before the event date should vendors, sponsors, and other parties be invited to participate?
    A. 15 to 30 days
    B. 30 to 60 days
    C. 60 to 90 days
    D. 90 to 120 days

118. The cardiac vascular nurse is caring for a patient following synchronized cardioversion. Which one of the following evaluations is a priority?
    A. post-cardioversion ECG rhythm
    B. ensure airway patency
    C. IV placement
    D. pulse strength

119. The nurse is caring for a low-vision, 85-year-old patient admitted to the cardiac care unit. How should she modify the room to create a safer environment?
    A. have a sitter stay with the patient at bedside
    B. place all furniture away from the patient's bed
    C. place the patient's glasses next to the call light on the bedside table within reach
    D. disconnect the television to reduce excess stimulation

120. A patient is discharged from the cardiac unit after being started on an ACE inhibitor that is to be continued at home. Which one of the following common side effects should the nurse tell the patient to expect to experience while taking an ACE inhibitor?
    A. polyuria
    B. cough
    C. tachycardia
    D. nausea

121. The nurse is evaluating vital signs of a patient admitted with heart failure. She notes the oxygenation saturation is 88%, which is a change from the last documented reading of 98%. What is the nurse's priority intervention?
    A. to ask the patient to bear down
    B. to perform bag-valve mask ventilations
    C. to apply oxygen
    D. to prepare the patient for intubation

206   Practice Test

122. The cardiac vascular nurse inadvertently administers an incorrect dosage of a medication. She immediately notifies the physician and the patient and monitors for any side effects. The patient was not harmed, but the nurse worries she will be sued for negligence. Why is this unlikely?
    A. The nurse immediately notified the physician, which reduces the risk of litigation.
    B. The patient was not harmed.
    C. The patient was notified promptly.
    D. The nurse properly documented the incident and charted frequent assessments after the event.

123. A patient with cardiogenic shock is expected to have which one of the following?
    A. hypertension; dyspnea
    B. decreased urine output; warm, pink skin
    C. increased urine output; cool, clammy skin
    D. hypotension; weak pulse; cool, clammy skin

124. The cardiac vascular nurse just started at a new facility and questions some of the practices of the organization. Which one of the following practices would be considered a HIPAA violation?
    A. giving information about the patient's condition over the phone to an approved family member
    B. leaving a printout of the patient's history and physical in plain view at the nurse's station
    C. faxing the patient's medical record to a new physician caring for the patient
    D. informing the billing department of the reason for the patient's visit

125. A patient is admitted to the ED after complaining of acute chest pain radiating down the left arm. She is diaphoretic, anxious, and has dyspnea. In addition to troponin, which laboratory study should the nurse anticipate?
    A. potassium
    B. lactic acid
    C. INR
    D. CK-MB

126. A patient being admitted for ACS tells the nurse that her father also had ACS and took multiple cardiac medications, but he died at age 40 from a heart attack. Where is the MOST appropriate place to chart this information?
    A. medication history
    B. social history
    C. past medical history
    D. family history

127. The cardiac vascular nurse is preparing to discharge a patient who has been started on warfarin during hospital admission and will be continuing this medication at home. Which part of the patient's social history would the nurse need to discuss with the patient prior to discharge?
    A. marital status
    B. upcoming plans to travel overseas
    C. daily alcohol consumption
    D. occupation of machinist

128. The nurse notes red, flat, and painless lesions on a patient's palms. Which one of the following diagnoses does she suspect?
    A. PAD
    B. heart failure
    C. endocarditis
    D. Wellens syndrome

129. Which one of the following is the BEST choice of non-pharmacological venous thromboembolism (VTE) prophylaxis for a hospitalized cardiac patient?
    A. heparin injections
    B. intermittent pneumatic compression devices
    C. massage
    D. bed rest

130. The nurse is assisting a cardiac patient with dietary planning. Which one of the following meals should be avoided?
    A. turkey meatballs with pasta sauce
    B. grilled chicken, baked potato, and green beans
    C. canned soup with a grilled ham and cheese sandwich
    D. salmon, brown rice, and salad

131. The nurse is prioritizing care after receiving the morning shift report. Which one of the following patients requires immediate intervention and should be seen first?
    A. a patient admitted the night before for an NSTEMI who is requesting pain medication
    B. a new admission who is alert and oriented with a history of diabetes and who needs a blood sugar check before breakfast
    C. a patient with a new troponin lab result of 0.05 ng/ml, decreased from the previous troponin level of 0.10 ng/ml
    D. a patient admitted for hypertension who has a new complaint of severe back pain

132. A patient who experiences a sudden cardiac arrest in the cardiac care unit cannot be resuscitated. Two of the patient's family members are at the bedside and very emotional. What should the nurse do to help provide a therapeutic environment for the patient's family?
    A. ask the family if they would like a chaplain to visit
    B. discuss organ donation with the family
    C. escort the family to the waiting room so the patient can be prepared for transport to the morgue
    D. call additional family members to notify them of the patient's death so they can come stay with family already at the hospital

133. The nurse is caring for a patient on a heparin drip. The aPTT lab results come back as a critically high value. After stopping the heparin drip, what medication does the nurse anticipate administering?
    A. digoxin immune fab
    B. protamine sulfate
    C. vitamin K
    D. acetylcysteine

134. The nurse is applying an Unna boot to a patient with venous stasis in the lower extremities. Which one of the following should the nurse ensure during this procedure?
    A. that the leg is moist to activate the gauze dressing
    B. that the dressing stops mid-calf to allow for vascular checks
    C. that the dressing is not used in a bed-bound patient
    D. that the dressing should be wrapped tightly to provide compression

135. The cardiac vascular nurse is caring for a patient after a heart catheterization in which the radial artery was used. The nurse knows that which one of the following is the BEST reason to use a radial compression device?
    A. to assist the puncture wound in healing faster
    B. to obtain a more accurate blood pressure reading
    C. to reduce the risk of blood clots after a transradial procedure
    D. to achieve hemostasis and prevent arterial damage

136. The nurse is caring for a STEMI patient who is receiving tPA. Which one of the following is a priority for the nurse?
    A. monitoring the patient for bleeding
    B. administering pain medications through the intramuscular route
    C. assessing the patient for edema
    D. auscultating heart sounds

137. The nurse is evaluating the medication list of an infant diagnosed with tetralogy of Fallot. Which one of the following medications would he expect to be ordered?
    A. adenosine
    B. dopamine
    C. digoxin
    D. potassium

138. Which of the following diet plans is the MOST appropriate for the nurse to recommend to a patient with hypertension?
    A. intermittent fasting
    B. DASH
    C. low carbohydrate
    D. gluten-free

139. The cardiac vascular nurse administers bumetanide to a patient who has been admitted for heart failure. The nurse would expect which one of the following when evaluating whether the medication was effective?
    A. decreased edema
    B. increased work of breathing
    C. wheezing lung sounds
    D. improved pain

140. A patient complaining of chest pain is administered a 0.4-mg nitroglycerin sublingual tablet. Upon reevaluation, the patient complains of a headache. Which of the following is the MOST appropriate action for the nurse to take?
    A. immediately notify the physician and discontinue the order for nitroglycerin
    B. administer acetaminophen for the headache
    C. switch the patient to an IV route of nitroglycerin
    D. prepare the patient for CT to rule out a brain hemorrhage

141. The cardiac vascular nurse is preparing to teach a patient about endocarditis. The first step is to assess which one of the following?
    A. the patient's current knowledge
    B. the patient's IV drug use habits
    C. the patient's social history
    D. the patient's lab results

142. The cardiac vascular nurse is discharging a patient who has been in the hospital for the last 5 days. The patient tells the nurse she will be flying out of the country. What is the MOST important discharge information the nurse can provide?
    A. suggesting she keep an exercise journal of her physical activity
    B. providing her with a list of heart-healthy foods for her trip
    C. giving her a physician's note in case she is stopped by airport security
    D. reminding her to stretch her legs and walk around occasionally while on the flight

143. A nursing student working with the cardiac vascular nurse is assisting with an ECG. The nurse determines that the patient has an inferior wall MI. The student asks the nurse how she knows which wall was affected. Which response by the nurse answers the student's question?
    A. "The patient's troponin level came back at 2.5."
    B. "Elevation is present in leads II, III, and aVF."
    C. "The patient had symptoms that correlated with an inferior wall MI."
    D. "The patient has a family history of an inferior wall MI."

144. The cardiac vascular nurse is working on the pediatric unit with a student nurse who is caring for a stable 1-year-old who is in SVT. The nurse knows that the student nurse is aware of the proper treatment of this abnormal heart rhythm when he goes to the break room and returns with which one of the following?
    A. a straw
    B. juice
    C. several bags of ice
    D. crackers

145. A local politician has a heart attack and is admitted to the cardiac care unit. A member of a local news station calls the nursing unit to ask for an update on the patient's status. Providing this information would be considered which one of the following?
    A. negligence
    B. defamation
    C. a HIPAA violation
    D. non-maleficence

146. Two weeks post-left-sided MI, a patient presents to the ED with dyspnea and cough with hemoptysis. The nurse should suspect that the patient has developed which one of the following?
    A. pneumonia
    B. over-coagulation
    C. pulmonary edema
    D. ruptured ventricle

147. Which of the following labs would the nurse use to evaluate a patient who is suspected of a pulmonary embolism?
    A. troponin
    B. D-dimer
    C. platelets
    D. aPTT

148. A patient being treated for hemorrhagic stroke is determined to be brain dead, but his life can be sustained for organ procurement. The patient is identified as an organ donor. Which one of the following is the next step for the nurse?
    A. notify the local organ procurement organization
    B. remove all life-supporting interventions
    C. perform postmortem care on the patient
    D. complete the death certificate

149. The cardiac vascular nurse is precepting a student nurse on her first day on the unit. A patient with heart failure begins to experience respiratory distress. Which task is MOST appropriate to assign to the student nurse?
    A. drawing an arterial blood gas
    B. applying oxygen to the patient
    C. calling the attending physician for orders
    D. preparing an IV infusion of normal saline

150. When evaluating the effect of nitroglycerin administration, the nurse knows that the primary action of this medication works to relieve pain by doing which one of the following?
    A. decreasing plaque formation on vessel walls
    B. increasing preload
    C. reducing venous return by vasodilating the coronary arteries
    D. increasing heart rate and the strength of heart muscle contraction

Answer Explanations

1. A: A myocardial contusion is the most likely diagnosis, as it usually occurs after a direct injury to the chest and presents with tachycardia, hypotension, and shortness of breath.

2. B: The patient should be instructed to tell airport security that he has an ICD prior to going through a metal detector. Carrying a note from the physician may also be helpful during travel. Most patients can fly within a few weeks after having had this procedure.

3. B: Recent phosphodiesterase use is a contraindication to administering nitrates, as it can result in severe hypotension. An inferior wall infarction would also be a contraindication. Nitrates are not contraindicated in patients with ST elevation or beta blocker use.

4. D: Dopamine (Intropin) is a positive inotrope, which will increase cardiac contractility and cardiac output, decrease the myocardial workload, and improve myocardial oxygen delivery.

5. A: The NHLBI notes that stress can trigger an MI. Stress reduction techniques, such as meditation and moderate exercise, are recommended.

6. C: Reducing the number of people who die from strokes is a Healthy People 2030 objective. Other Healthy People 2030 objectives include increasing (not reducing) the proportion of adults who get a referral to a rehab program after having survived a heart attack, increasing (not reducing) the proportion of stroke survivors who go on to take part in rehabilitation services, and raising the proportion of patients suffering a stroke who get IV reperfusion therapy within 3 hours (not 4 hours) of the onset of symptoms

7. B: Collaborative care that includes the patient in the decision-making process has been shown to increase compliance with the plan of care and reduce readmission rates. Providing too much information for patients can overwhelm them. Completing a discharge survey does not reduce readmission rates. Patients should not be kept in the hospital longer than necessary.

8. D: The combined use of St. John's Wort and digoxin can result in toxic effects. St. John's Wort can cause excessive bleeding—not excessive clotting—when combined with anticoagulants.

9. D: Having A-fib increases a patient's risk of stroke. Blood pools in the heart's chambers, causing clots that might move to the brain and cause a stroke. Patients with A-fib are not at greater risk of developing arthralgia, influenza, or DIC.

10. C: The nurse should ensure that a qualified interpreter explains any changes in the treatment plan. Asking family members to translate medical care is not appropriate. Hospital employees cannot translate medical care unless they are designated as qualified translators. The administration of the new medication should not wait until a shift change. A language line is the most appropriate intervention, as the nurse can speak directly to an interpreter and have the information translated immediately without delaying care.

11. C: A history of hypertension will cause an increase in afterload. Diabetes will cause complications with microvascular disease, leading to poor cardiac function. Endocrine disorders will cause an increase in cardiac workload. Marfan syndrome causes the cardiac muscle to stretch and weaken.

12. C: The cardiac vascular nurse can delegate appropriate tasks to LPNs, patient care techs, or medical assistants. The respiratory therapist is in an entirely different scope of practice, so it is not appropriate for the nurse to delegate tasks to this staff member.

13. C: In the United States, approximately 20% of adults read below the fifth-grade level and 54% of adults read below the sixth-grade level; therefore, printed materials should be prepared at the fourth-to-fifth grade levels to ensure maximum comprehension. The Joint Commission recommends that all patient-printed texts be at the fifth-grade level or lower. In addition, narrative text should be limited, and short sentences in plain language without medical jargon should be used to convey information. Texts should include illustrations, pictures, and diagrams when possible.

14. A: Magnesium sulfate is a CNS depressant and can cause marked bradycardia and respiratory depression. The nursing priority is to monitor the patient's vital signs for CNS depression after this drug is administered. Tachycardia and hyperventilation are not side effects of magnesium sulfate. A Swan-Ganz catheter and synchronized cardioversion are not indicated.

15. C: ST elevation in the II, III, and aVF leads indicates an inferior MI. An anterior MI would have elevation in leads V1 – V4; a lateral MI would have elevation in I, aVL, V5, and V6; and a posterior MI would show ST depression in V1 and V2, and tall R waves.

16. C: The patient should be reassured that she will be monitored for any changes in her post-procedure condition. The nurse should not give the patient false reassurance or provide results of the procedure. Anxiety medication may be indicated but is not the priority. Telling the patient that the physician will meet her soon does not address the patient's immediate concern.

17. B: Elderly people tend to have decreased renal function. Digoxin is eliminated primarily in the kidneys, which increases the likelihood of digoxin toxicity.

18. D: A patient's psychosocial and spiritual needs should be addressed in order to ensure that a therapeutic environment is provided. Administering medications and assigning the same nurse to the patient each day are not part of creating a therapeutic environment.

19. A: SMART goals should be specific, measurable, attainable, realistic, and timely. Option A defines a set amount of time, and this goal can be easily measured.

20. B: Advance directives are used to help with difficult questions and the decision-making process for patients who are unable to make decisions for themselves. An alert and oriented patient can make decisions, so advance directives are not applicable. A stable patient who is being extubated after open heart surgery would not need advance directives unless he begins to decline and is not able to communicate. Every patient who is discharged to a long-term facility does not necessarily need advance directives.

21. B: The patient is in V-fib and is pulseless. After CPR is started, the next priority intervention is defibrillation. Epinephrine should not be administered until after defibrillation. Inserting an advanced airway may be indicated but is not the priority. A fluid bolus is not a priority for a patient in V-fib.

22. C: A DNR order indicates that no heroic measures should be taken to prolong the patient's life. This includes chest compressions, defibrillation, and advanced airway placement. Administering oxygen is the most noninvasive option. The physician should be notified of the patient's status.

23. B: A patient's goal should be specific and measurable (having a pain level of 5 or less), timely (by the end of the shift), and attainable (this is likely achievable by the end of the shift). Being pain-free is an

Answer Explanations

unrealistic goal. Taking all scheduled pain medication and taking less pain medication than was taken during the prior shift are not specific goals.

24. A: Fluid boluses of 1 to 2 L normal saline should be used to treat hypotension. The patient is dehydrated at the cellular level and needs fluid resuscitation. Furosemide is used as a diuretic and would further dehydrate the patient, exacerbating the issue. Inotropes, such as dopamine, are used to promote cardiac contractility and will not hydrate the patient. D5W is not indicated because it is not an isotonic solution that will add to the systemic fluid volume.

25. A: The use of nitrates is contraindicated in patients who have taken phosphodiesterase inhibitors (erectile dysfunction medications) because the combination can cause a dangerous drop in blood pressure.

26. B: Health promotion activities are intended to help people maintain their health and functional abilities. Different types of health promotion include the following:

- Primary (to prevent disease): stop-smoking campaigns, physical activity programs, healthy eating campaigns
- Secondary (to identify and reduce the impact of disease): screening (e.g., blood pressure checks, cholesterol tests, diabetes screening with A1C), and monitoring
- Tertiary (to prevent disease progression): cardiac rehabilitation, medical management, surgical procedures
- Quaternary (to prevent complications and avoid overtreatment): medication and monitoring and polypharmacy management, end-of-life care, reduction of unnecessary testing

27. A: The PT/INR level should be drawn first to determine how the warfarin has affected the patient's ability to clot. An aPTT lab monitors the effects of heparin. Administration of FFP or vitamin K may be necessary depending on the results of the PT/INR.

28. A: Pericarditis has a typical friction rub, or "leathery" sound. Crackles would be heard in pulmonary edema or pneumonia. Wheezing would be heard with asthma. An S3 gallop may be heard with mitral regurgitation.

29. A: A patient with increased LDL and triglyceride levels should avoid foods high in saturated fats. The other options would not directly affect cholesterol levels.

30. A: The best technique for active listening is to sit facing the patient while making eye contact. Speaking clearly is important, but it is not necessary to speak loudly and slowly. Asking open-ended questions is not a component of active listening. Moving around the room is not a component of active listening.

31. C: Personally identifiable information (PII), such as a patient's Social Security number, first and last name, and medical record numbers, should be kept confidential. A date of birth, with no other identifying information, is not considered PII.

32. B: Palliative care is focused on relieving the symptoms to help improve a patient's quality of life, and it can be used at any time. A patient does not have to be terminal to receive palliative care, and it can be used in combination with other treatments. Palliative care can last more than 3 months, if needed.

33. C: The hospital volunteer is an appropriate choice to wheel the patient to his car. The patient's wife or daughter should not be given this task. A ride-sharing service is not appropriate to assist in helping the patient to his car.

34. B: The float nurse should be assigned patients who are similar to those she usually cares for. In this situation, postsurgical patients would be the most appropriate. Nurses from other units may not be familiar with the specific protocols for cardiac patients, but they can still care for them.

35. A: Patients with DVT should be on bed rest to prevent the movement of the DVT and the pressure changes that occur with walking and other weight-bearing activities. The affected extremity should be elevated. Placing the bed in reverse Trendelenburg will increase pressure on the affected extremity. Walking is contraindicated for patients with DVT, and while preventing hospital-acquired pneumonia is important, patient safety takes priority over pneumonia prevention in this situation. The patient may still use an incentive spirometer and practice coughing and deep breathing to clear the lungs without ambulating. Sitting up in a chair is also contraindicated until the DVT has resolved and the health care provider has prescribed activity for the patient.

36. C: Increased risk factors for heparin-induced thrombocytopenia (HIT) include being female and heparin use for postsurgical thromboprophylaxis. HIT is more common in patients who have been on unfractionated heparin or who have used heparin for longer than 1 week. Enoxaparin is a low-molecular-weight heparin, which carries a lower risk of causing HIT. It is often prescribed for patients with unstable angina to help increase blood flow through the heart.

37. B: Left-sided heart failure manifestations include pulmonary symptoms such as crackles and dyspnea. Right-sided heart failure causes systemic congestion, leading to hepatomegaly, dependent edema, jugular vein distention, and ascites.

38. C: Pericarditis has a characteristic friction rub sound on auscultation due to inflammation, and pain is typically relieved when leaning forward.

39. C: Smoking is one of the main risk factors for cardiovascular disease. The cardiac vascular nurse should provide patients with smoking cessation resources and encourage them to quit smoking. Gender and age are nonmodifiable risk factors. Regular exercise improves heart health.

40. A: Mitral stenosis causes increased pressure and increased blood volume in the left atrium, which causes enlargement. The enlarged atrium can lead to A-fib because the heart cannot pump as effectively.

41. D: A defining characteristic of a first-degree block is a prolonged PR interval >0.20.

42. A: Travel that requires long periods of immobility, such as plane or car rides, is associated with an increased risk of blood clot formation due to physical inactivity.

43. A: The nurse should acknowledge the patient's feelings and then attempt to discuss the results and diagnosis. The nurse should avoid blaming the other physician or facility or downplaying the diagnosis by telling the patient not to worry. The nurse should avoid telling the patient what to do and focus on why the patient is upset.

44. C: When the nurse signs as a witness on a consent form, the nurse is only stating that she has observed the patient sign that form. It is the role of the physician to explain the procedure and ensure that the patient understands the risks and benefits. The patient can be educated on medications he will receive, but this is not a prerequisite to completing a consent form.

Answer Explanations

45. C: The faith community nurse, or parish nurse, is the best option to provide health care using a holistic approach by focusing on spirituality and faith-based care.

46. B: HDL cholesterol is considered "good cholesterol," and higher levels can lower cardiovascular diseases. Cholesterol can be lowered by maintaining an exercise program, quitting smoking, and taking certain medications.

47. C: To promote population health, the cardiac vascular nurse could participate in a free community blood pressure screening event because hypertension is the number one risk factor for cardiovascular disease. Organizing team-building activities, running in a 5k, and participating in a research study do not help improve population health.

48. D: The patient is stable in SVT, so the most noninvasive treatment (vagal maneuvers) should be performed first. Adenosine is the first drug of choice if vagal maneuvers are unsuccessful. Defibrillation is not used in conscious patients with organized heart rhythms. Synchronized cardioversion is not indicated for a stable patient in SVT.

49. C: Adrenaline, dopamine, digoxin, and dobutamine are all positive inotropes and can be helpful in the management of heart failure; however, digoxin is not recommended in the treatment of acute heart failure in an 80-yearold patient because older patients are more susceptible to digoxin toxicity.

50. A: Pocket-sized portable EKG devices that use finger electrodes typically produce a single-lead EKG. These devices are simple to use and provide rapid results but provide limited data regarding heart activity. With the KardiaMobile, for example, the patient places the index fingers on the device's electrodes. These portable devices connect to a smartphone or tablet directly or through Bluetooth technology and can detect bradycardia, tachycardia, abnormal rhythms, and atrial fibrillation. Single-lead EKG devices cannot diagnose structural heart conditions, such as a myocardial infarction.

51. B: Hyperkalemia will cause bradycardia and tall peaked T waves. Patients with hypokalemia will have ventricular dysrhythmias, such as PVCs, V-tach or V-fib, or the presence of U waves. Hyponatremia can cause neurologic effects, such as a decreased level of consciousness or seizure activity.

52. D: The nurse should provide the patient with as much information as possible regarding his diagnosis and treatment plan so that he can make an informed decision regarding his care. A competent patient cannot be forced to stay and has the right to refuse tests or leave the hospital. Having the business office discuss a payment plan may be helpful, but it is not the best action for the nurse to take in this situation.

53. C: Discussing beneficial reasons for the patient to quit smoking is an example of motivational interviewing. Giving statistics and consequences for smoking may be helpful for some patients, but this is not an example of motivational interviewing. Telling the patient to use a prescription-strength medication might be an option for a patient wanting to stop smoking, but it is not an example of motivational interviewing.

54. A: Asking about special cultural needs is the appropriate action when caring for a patient from a different culture. The nurse should make every attempt to accommodate the patient's needs. The nurse should not assume the patient would like a chaplain to pray with unless requested. The nurse may be able to make an exception to the visitor policy if it is for a cultural purpose, but this statement does not help provide culturally competent care.

55. C: Patients in the young adult age group generally prefer learning strategies focused on technology. Role-playing is more appropriate for younger age groups. Older generations may prefer classroom or self-paced learning by reading.

56. D: The priority intervention is to use a Doppler to confirm if pulses are present. If pulses are not present using the Doppler, a call to the physician would be appropriate. An ultrasound or CT may be appropriate but is not the priority.

57. B: The American Heart Association currently recommends a 1,500 mg limit of sodium intake for cardiac patients to improve hypertension and heart health.

58. A: Patients who are competent can still make decisions regarding their care; doing so would override POA documentation. In this instance, the patient is within his rights to revoke his son as POA, and the patient can alter the POA documentation as long as he is mentally capable of doing so.

59. D: The main purpose of a Doppler ultrasound is to measure the patient's blood flow and help identify any blocked arteries; it does not identify cardiovascular disease. Time and cost are not the main reasons to have a Doppler. A lower-extremity Doppler will not rule out an aneurysm.

60. D: Hypercoagulability, venous stasis, and endothelial damage (also known as Virchow's triad) are the main factors that predispose an individual to clot formation. A heart murmur is not part of Virchow's triad and is not considered a major contributing factor to clot formation.

61. A: Administration of adenosine can cause a brief period of asystole on the monitor, followed by conversion to a normal sinus rhythm.

62. B: Evidence has demonstrated that a family member at the bedside for resuscitation is a preference for patients and families and should be offered when possible and appropriate. Family members should be present only if they are not disruptive to patient care.

63. D: The Zio XT Patch (iRhythm) is a wearable cardiac monitoring device that is applied to the left chest with medical-grade adhesive. It can be left in place for up to 14 days. Patients are allowed to shower or bathe but should avoid submerging the device, and showers should be brief with no soap or lotion contact with the device. Patients may exercise but should avoid excessive perspiration, which may loosen skin contact with the device. Electronic devices do not interfere with the Zio XT Patch, and patients can go through airport security.

64. A: Monitoring the patient's weight every morning is the best way to evaluate fluid and electrolyte balance. A weight gain of more than 2 pounds a day or 5 pounds in a week should be reported. Weight gain is considered the first sign of worsening heart failure. Foley catheters should be avoided when possible to prevent urinary tract complications. Reducing sodium intake is necessary for heart failure patients but does not help evaluate fluid/electrolyte balance.

65. B: The handheld iSTAT 1 (Abbott) point-of-care blood analyzer is often used in emergency situations for rapid assessment of laboratory values. Testing requires only two to three drops of blood, and results are usually available within 2 minutes. The iSTAT 1 can carry out tests for lactate, blood gases, electrolytes, blood chemistries, cardiac markers, coagulation, hematology, and endocrinology. Different cartridges are used depending on the desired test. The blood sample is applied to a sample well in the cartridge, which is then inserted into the device, triggering automatic analysis.

66. B: The elevated blood pressure is a critical finding and is considered objective data because it can be measured. The troponin level is an example of objective data, but it is a normal finding that does not need to be reported. The patient complaint of dizziness or a family member reporting that the patient seems more depressed should be followed up on, but these are considered subjective data.

67. D: In the teach-back method, the nurse has the patient demonstrate or repeat back what he has learned. Procedural education is given before a procedure so that the patient knows what to expect before, during, and after the event. Adherence is how compliant the patient is with the plan of care. Memorization means committing something to memory.

68. A: In order to sign informed consent, a patient must be alert, oriented, and deemed competent to make her own medical decisions. The patient does not need to have her insurance verified or a complete history and physical completed before the procedure. The patient should be informed of the benefits and risks of the procedure before signing the consent form. If a patient refuses the procedure, another family member cannot sign on the patient's behalf.

69. A: Abnormalities in magnesium levels may put the patient at risk for ventricular dysrhythmia. A hypomagnesemia level of 0.8 mEq/L would be of concern (normal range is 1.5 – 2.5 mEq/L). The other values are within normal ranges.

70. D: Patients with heart failure have difficulty with exertional activity, such as walking up stairs. Beta blockers are used for hypertension, but they do not indicate or contribute to heart failure. Pulmonary emboli may affect the heart but not in a chronic way like heart failure. Chest pain is not commonly associated with heart failure.

71. B: The patient is unstable in a third-degree or complete heart block, so TCP is indicated.

72. D: Wellness counseling is a holistic approach to helping individuals make healthy choices and lifestyle changes. Wellness counseling typically begins with a thorough health assessment that focuses on physical, emotional, social, intellectual, spiritual, and occupational wellness. Wellness counseling is client-centered and helps a client identify areas for improvement, such as a more making changes for a more nutritious diet or starting to exercise. The client is assisted with setting short- and long-term goals, and is provided with ongoing support.

73. D: The nurse should never share passwords under any circumstances. The nurse should properly log out of the computer when he is finished so that no one else can access the information. Any paper documents that are no longer needed should be shredded. The nurse can ask the HIPAA compliance officer questions or state concerns regarding HIPAA policies.

74. D: Sudden back pain and dyspnea indicate rupture of the aneurysm, which is an emergency. The nurse should notify the health care provider, monitor neurological and vital signs, and remain with the patient. Yellow-tinted vision is a finding of digitalis toxicity. Hemoptysis a sign of pulmonary edema. Urinary output of 75 mL/hr is normal.

75. C: The new graduate CV nurse should be prepared to insert an IV, administer epinephrine, and prepare the patient for defibrillation. Intubating the patient is typically not done by the bedside nurse and should not be done by a new graduate nurse.

76. D: Denial means refusing to accept or believe something. Passive coping describes feeling helpless to deal with the stress or change required to cope with a situation. Active coping is characterized by problem solving and seeking support to deal with an issue. Avoidance involves changing one's behavior to keep from thinking about a problem.

77. A: The nurse should assess the apical pulse for a full minute before administering digoxin. If the pulse is less than 60 bpm, the nurse should hold the dose and notify the physician. The chest X-ray results and glucose levels are not related to administering digoxin. Digoxin can affect the blood pressure, but it primarily affects the heart rate.

78. D: Asking the patient about her goals is an example of an open-ended question that may help the nurse gather more information from the patient. The other questions can all be answered with a "yes" or "no."

79. B: Morphine is the pain medication of choice for an acute MI because it decreases the oxygen demand of the heart. The half-life of morphine is 2 – 4 hours. Morphine does not reduce ST elevation.

80. B: The initial survey includes a rapid assessment to identify emergent conditions and includes LOC, breathing pattern, and skin color.

81. C: Documentation for any change in patient status is always necessary and should be as descriptive as possible. Documentation should not include a suspected diagnosis.

82. D: A recent MI would place the patient in a higher risk category for cardiac surgery. A creatinine level of 1.3 mg/dL is normal. An allergy to latex and history of asthma would not place the patient at a higher risk for cardiac surgery.

83. A: Patients who are allergic to the iodine dye used in contrast CT studies may need a different exam or may need to be premedicated before the CT.

84. D: Classic signs of cardiac tamponade include muffled heart tones, JVD, and hypotension (symptoms known as Beck's triad). Auscultating heart sounds would be helpful in identifying the presence of muffled heart tones.

85. C: Decreased CO usually occurs with increasing age due to cardiac muscles hardening, which results in decreased filling and emptying of the heart. Drug metabolism is typically reduced, and blood pressure usually increases with age.

86. C: The most likely cause of bradycardia in pediatric patients is hypoxia, so reoxygenation should be the priority intervention for any pediatric patient in bradycardia.

87. B: Tetralogy of Fallot is a congenital heart defect in which blood flow to the lungs is reduced. Oxygen-poor blood flows to the right atrium and ventricles and is then pumped through the aorta to the rest of the body. This shunting of oxygen-poor blood causes cyanosis. Infants experiencing cyanotic events are said to be having "tet spells."

88. D: IVC filters are used to prevent clots from causing a pulmonary embolism. They can be removed when necessary but are not routinely replaced every 6 months. Patients can eat a normal diet with IVC filters in place.

89. B: The patient with a new ICD should monitor the incision for signs and symptoms of infection and report them to the physician. The appropriate wound care for the incision is a dry dressing change. Patients should be taught about post-surgery activity restrictions, including limiting heavy lifting with the affected arm. The importance of handwashing should be emphasized both before and after dressing changes.

90. C: Prior to synchronized cardioversion, patients should be sedated so that they do not feel the pain associated with the electrical shock. Patients should only be awake if they are unstable and there is no time for sedation. The procedure should not need to be repeated. The patient has a choice in refusing the procedure, but should be made aware that her condition may deteriorate without it.

Answer Explanations

91. C: Telehealth can expedite care and allow the nurse to discuss patient changes with the physician remotely to develop a new plan of care. A code blue should only be called for a cardiac arrest. A patient in a second-degree, type 2 heart block should be immediately reported to the physician, and staff should take steps to prepare to transcutaneous pace.

92. A: Patients need anticoagulation therapy to prevent clots after a surgical cardiac procedure such as an LVAD. Patients typically need to stay in the ICU postoperatively and should plan on staying in the hospital for approximately 2 weeks. Several medications will be prescribed to keep the heart functioning properly. Chest compressions should not be performed on a patient with an LVAD unless it is an absolute last resort, as it may cause the LVAD to become dislodged.

93. A: Increasing the frequency of bystanders who use an AED when confronted with cardiac arrests in public places would be community-oriented health promotion strategy that aligns with the Healthy People 2030 objectives.

94. A: Patients with heart failure should be instructed to weigh themselves daily to monitor fluid balance. They should also be taught about sodium reduction, not complete restriction. Patients who have difficulty breathing should be taught to go to the ED. Patients who notice pedal edema should report this finding to their providers, as it may indicate worsening heart failure.

95. C: An HgbA1C of 9.0 is elevated and reflects poor blood sugar control over the prior 3 months. The nurse and the patient should develop a plan of care to improve diet, exercise, and medication compliance.

96. D: Goal setting is part of the planning process. Auscultating heart sounds is part of the assessment, evaluating lab results is part of the evaluation process, and checking a patient's blood pressure is part of the intervention phase.

97. B: Heparin is an anticoagulant that is commonly administered to a patient having an MI. Aspirin and clopidogrel are antiplatelet medications. Nitrates are vasodilators.

98. B: Hypocalcemia can cause a prolonged QT interval. Hypomagnesemia would cause a prolonged PR interval and widenings of the QRS complex. Hyperkalemia can cause peaked T waves. Hyponatremia does not typically cause ECG changes.

99. D: Marfan syndrome causes connective tissue to degenerate. As a result, blood vessel walls can weaken due to stretching and cause an aneurysm.

100. A: The priority intervention for any patient with chest discomfort or pressure is to obtain a 12-lead ECG. Expert consultation would not be needed at this time. A health history and review of admission policies are important but are not the priority.

101. C: Hypertension puts continuous pressure on the vessel walls, which causes them to weaken and form an aneurysm. Blood pressure control should be a priority for a patient with an AAA.

102. A: The patient feeling down, having trouble sleeping, and reporting decreased energy levels warrants a depression screening. Depression is a known risk factor for cardiac disease. All cardiac patients are recommended to be screened for depression.

103. D: A troponin of greater than 0.05 indicates cardiac damage and should be followed up on. This patient would need serial cardiac enzymes to ensure that the troponin does not continue to increase.

104. C: The nurse should anticipate that a patient in a second-degree, type II heart block could progress to a third-degree block and need transcutaneous pacing. Synchronized cardioversion is not indicated for this patient. The nurse should not continue to monitor the patient without intervention, as this type of heart block can progress to a complete heart block.

105. D: Short-term goals should be measurable and specific. Using an exercise log to record 15-minute daily walks at least 4 times a week is a clear, specific, and measurable goal. Cutting out processed foods, wearing a nicotine patch, and intermittently checking blood pressure are not specific and measurable goals.

106. C: Baked chicken with vegetables is a healthy, low-sodium option for a cardiac patient. Canned soups, deli meats and cheeses, and pizza are high-sodium foods that should be avoided or eaten sparingly.

107. D: The patient who has been following his treatment plan for hypertension would be expected to have a normal blood pressure. A patient stating that he feels better is subjective, whereas measuring that patient's blood pressure is an objective way of determining compliance. Not refilling medication is a sign of noncompliance. A patient complaint of intermittent chest pain does not necessarily indicate compliance, and the patient will need follow-up.

108. B: Before giving out any patient information, the nurse should make sure that the patient has given permission to discuss her care with the person who is asking for it. This can be done using a security code or HIPAA password that is given only to people approved by the patient. Verifying the name, birth date, and room number are not valid reasons to give out patient information. In order to protect the patient's privacy, even vague information should not be given out. Information can be given over the phone if the patient has given permission and the caller's identity is confirmed.

109. B: Cardiac rehabilitation helps provide a support system for patients during their recovery. It may not be covered fully by all insurance plans and is not required for cardiologists to treat patients with follow-up care. While cardiac rehabilitation reduces the chance of having subsequent heart attacks, it does not completely prevent them from occurring.

110. C: To access the results, the nurse should have her husband sign a release form. The nurse may not access information for any patient who is not under her care. The physician should not provide results regarding her husband's care. Asking a friend who is working to access the chart is considered a breach of confidentiality.

111. A: Increased WBCs and an increased sedimentation rate are expected findings in a patient diagnosed with endocarditis due to inflammation. Elevated lactic acid, troponin, and BNP are not expected findings for endocarditis.

112. A: Increased heart rate, increased blood volume, and increased CO are expected changes for a patient who is pregnant. Blood pressure should not be affected and can be dangerous if elevated.

113. A: Assisting a patient to the bathroom is the most appropriate task for unlicensed assistive personnel (UAP), such as patient care technicians. Patient care technicians can also assist with vital signs, but assisting the patient to the bathroom is more appropriate. It is not appropriate for patient care technicians to hang IV fluids or insert catheters.

114. A: The priority nursing diagnosis would be focused on addressing breathing issues. Activity intolerance, urinary issues, or renal perfusion may be considered in patients with heart failure, but ineffective breathing due to excess fluid would be the priority focus.

115. B: Administration of a fibrinolytic should result in the resolution of ST elevation. The effectiveness of the fibrinolytic would not be based on troponin levels, a new bundle branch block, or a decrease in pain level.

116. A: An expected outcome for a patient on day 3 of admission is to achieve a controlled pain level.

117. C: Planning for a health fair should usually begin 5 or 6 months ahead of the event because the venue, date, time, promotion activities, and budget must be determined. Vendors, sponsors, and other participants should be invited 60 to 90 days prior to the event date so that they have adequate time to prepare and communicate their needs in terms of such things as display space and electricity. This also gives the event planners time to designate spaces and provide any necessary equipment.

118. B: Airway patency is the priority for any patient following synchronized cardioversion, as the patient has likely been sedated and will need airway monitoring. The other options are important, but airway patency takes priority.

119. C: The nurse should address any specific needs the patient may have. Placing necessary items within reach can help the patient feel safer and more comfortable.

120. B: A common side effect of an ACE inhibitor is a dry cough, and patients should be informed of this before starting the medication.

121. C: The nurse should first apply oxygen by the least invasive means possible. Asking the patient to bear down could cause bradycardia and worsen oxygenation.

122. B: The patient was not harmed, so it is unlikely that he would be successful in suing the nurse for negligence. Notifying the physician and patient, monitoring for side effects, and proper documentation are all important; however, the extent of the patient injury is the determining factor.

123. D: Classic signs of cardiogenic shock include a rapid pulse that weakens; cool, clammy skin; and decreased urine output. Hypotension is another classic sign.

124. B: Leaving a printout of the patient's personal information in plain view at the nurse's station where it could be read by any staff member or visitor is a HIPAA violation. Information about a patient's status can be given over the phone if the patient has given approval. Faxing patient information to another physician who is caring for the patient is necessary for continuity of care. Giving pertinent information to the billing department is permitted.

125. D: Creatine kinase muscle/blood (CK-MB) is a cardiac enzyme specific to heart muscle and should be drawn along with troponin for any patient with complaints of chest pain. A potassium level may be indicated but is not the priority. An INR level is not necessary.

126. D: The most appropriate place to chart information about a family member's health history is in the family history section. Medication history includes which medications the patient is on; past medical history includes the patient's medical history diagnoses. Social history includes details about the patient's personal life that may be pertinent (e.g., occupation or recreational activities).

127. C: Increased alcohol consumption can increase the effect of warfarin and cause excessive bleeding. The patient should be instructed to abstain from alcohol consumption while taking this medication.

128. C: One physical sign of endocarditis is red, flat, and painless lesions known as Janeway lesions. These are often seen in patients with endocarditis along with fever, chest pain, petechiae, and flu-like symptoms.

129. B: Intermittent pneumatic compression devices use cuffs that wrap around the legs and intermittently fill with air to squeeze the legs to increase blood flow. Heparin is a pharmacological type of VTE prophylaxis. Massage and bed rest are not considered best practice for VTE prophylaxis.

130. C: Canned soup and sandwiches with processed meats and cheeses are typically high in sodium and should be avoided on a cardiac diet.

131. D: The patient with hypertension and severe back pain (especially if described as "tearing") could have an AAA rupture, which is emergent. A patient needing a blood sugar check can be delegated to a UAP. A decreased troponin result is an improvement and does not require immediate intervention. A patient requesting pain medicine can be covered by another RN or seen after the patient who has tearing pain is assessed.

132. A: Arranging for a chaplain can help meet the psychosocial and spiritual needs of the family after a loss. The nurse should not discuss organ donation with the family members at this time. The family should be allowed to stay with the patient and not rushed to leave after the patient's death.

133. B: The antidote for heparin is protamine sulfate. Vitamin K is the antidote for warfarin. Digoxin immune fab is the antidote for digoxin. Acetylcysteine is the antidote for acetaminophen.

134. C: The Unna boot moves fluid with activity to improve venous flow and is therefore not recommended for patients who are bed-bound. The leg should be dry before the boot is applied. The dressing should not stop mid-calf or be wrapped too tightly, as there should be room for natural swelling to occur.

135. D: A radial compression device is often used after a transradial procedure to achieve hemostasis and prevent arterial damage.

136. A: Any patient receiving a thrombolytic should be monitored for signs of bleeding. Intramuscular injections should be avoided since the patient is at risk for bleeding. Assessing the patient for edema and auscultating heart sounds are not priorities for a patient who is receiving tPA.

137. C: An infant with tetralogy of Fallot would be ordered digoxin to slow down and control the heart rate.

138. B: The Dietary Approaches to Stop Hypertension (DASH) diet is composed of fruits, vegetables, and low-fat dairy products. It features low cholesterol, low fat, and low sodium and is recommended for patients with hypertension.

139. A: Bumetanide is a diuretic, so decreased edema is an expected result if the medication is effective. The work of breathing should improve due to reduced fluid in the heart and lungs. Wheezing is a lower-airway obstruction and is not expected when administering bumetanide. Improved pain is not an expected side effect.

140. B: A headache is a common side effect of nitroglycerin, which causes vasodilation. Acetaminophen can be administered to help with a headache.

141. A: The nurse should first assess what the patient already knows about endocarditis. The patient's social history, IV drug habits, and lab results are important but are not the priority when performing patient education.

142. D: A patient who has been hospitalized for several days and then takes a long flight is at risk for a DVT. She should be encouraged to stretch her legs and walk around the airplane occasionally to increase blood flow and prevent clots. Although heart-healthy foods and exercise logs are important, preventing a DVT takes priority.

143. B: Elevation in leads II, III, and aVF on an ECG indicates an inferior wall MI. Troponin levels will not indicate which wall is affected. Symptoms and family history do not correlate to the specific wall affected.

144. C: A stable 1-year-old in SVT is treated with ice to the face to stimulate the vagal nerve. A straw can be used to stimulate the vagal nerve in older children who can follow directions. Returning with juice and crackers would not indicate that the student has knowledge of treating SVT.

145. C: Disclosing personal patient information to parties who do not have a need to know and to whom the patient has not given permission is considered a HIPAA violation. Negligence is failure to act as another nurse reasonably would in the same situation. Defamation is providing information that damages someone's reputation. Nonmaleficence means doing no harm.

146. C: The patient is experiencing symptoms of pulmonary edema, a complication of left-sided heart failure. Coagulation is not a secondary effect of MI. Pneumonia is not generally related to post–MI concerns. A ruptured ventricle would present symptoms closer to the time of injury.

147. B: The D-dimer can help diagnose the presence of a clot. A patient with an elevated D-dimer level should be further assessed with a CT of the chest to rule out a pulmonary embolism.

148. A: When an organ donor patient dies, the nurse should first contact the organ procurement organization because of time sensitivity. Life-supporting interventions, such as ventilators and medications, should be continued until the organ procurement agency arrives. Postmortem care and completing the death certificate can be performed after organ procurement has taken place.

149. B: The most appropriate task to assign to a student nurse on his first day would be a simple one, such as applying oxygen. Performing a procedure, such as an arterial blood gas, or calling the physician are not appropriate tasks for a student. A patient in heart failure would not be administered fluids.

150. C: Nitroglycerin works through vasodilation that improves blood flow and helps reduce venous return. Nitroglycerin reduces preload and does not increase the heart rate or reduce plaque formation

Appendix A – Signs and Symptoms Glossary

angioedema: edema of subcutaneous tissues

aphasia: impairment in ability to speak, write, and understand others

apnea: temporary cessation of breathing

arthralgias: joint pain

ascites: abdominal swelling caused by fluid in the peritoneal cavity

bradycardia: slow heart rate

bradypnea: slow respiration rate

carotid bruits: murmur heard over the carotid artery

cardiomegaly: enlarged heart

cyanosis: blueish skin

diaphoresis: excessive sweating

dysarthria: slurred speech caused by muscle weakness

dyspnea: difficulty breathing

ecchymosis: bruising

edema: swelling caused by excess fluid

effusion: accumulation of fluid

epistaxis: bleeding from the nose

erythema: redness of the skin

erythema multiforme: skin rash characterized by target-shaped lesions

hematuria: blood in urine

hemoptysis: blood in expectorate from respiratory tract

hepatomegaly: enlargement of liver

Homans' sign: discomfort behind the knee or increased resistance in response to dorsiflexion of the foot

hypertension: high blood pressure

hypotension: low blood pressure

hypoxemia: low levels of oxygen in the blood

hypoxia: lack of oxygen supplied to tissues

ileus: lack of movement in the intestines

ischemia: restricted blood flow to tissue

jaundice: yellowing of the skin or sclera

Kussmaul respirations: deep, labored breathing

Levine's sign: a clenched fist held over the chest in response to ischemic chest pain

nocturia: excessive urination at night

oliguria: low urine output

orthopnea: dyspnea that occurs while lying flat

orthostatic (postural) hypotension: decrease in blood pressure after standing

pallor: pale appearance

palpitations: sensation of the heart racing, fluttering, or pounding

paresthesia: abnormal dermal sensation, such as burning or "pins and needles"

petechiae: tiny red or brown spots on the skin caused by subcutaneous bleeding

poikilothermia: inability to regulate body temperature

polydipsia: excessive thirst

polyphagia: excessive hunger

polyuria: abnormally high urine output

pulsus alternans: alternating strong and weak pulse

stenosis: narrowing of a passage

stridor: high-pitched wheezing sound caused by a disruption in airflow

syncope: temporary loss of consciousness

tachycardia: fast heart rate

tachypnea: fast respiratory rate

varicose veins: swollen veins

Appendix B - Abbreviations

A

AAA: abdominal aortic aneurysm (triple A)

AACVPR: American Association of Cardiovascular and Pulmonary Rehabilitation

ABCM: American Board of Cardiovascular Medicine

ABCs: airway, breathing, circulation

ABG: arterial blood gas

ABI: ankle-brachial index

ACC: American College of Cardiology

ACE-Is or ACE inhibitors: angiotensin-converting enzyme inhibitors

ACLS: advanced cardiovascular life support

ACPE: acute cardiogenic pulmonary edema

ACS: acute coronary syndrome

ADHD: attention deficit hyperactivity disorder

ADLs: activities of daily living

ADP: adenosine diphosphate

ADPIE model: assessment, diagnosis, planning, intervention, evaluation

A-fi b: atrial fibrillation

AHA: American Heart Association

ALP: alkaline phosphatase

ALT: alanine aminotransferase

AMA: against medical advice

ANA: American Nurses Association

ANCC: American Nurses Credentialing Center

AND: allow natural death

aPTT: activated partial thromboplastin time

AR: aortic regurgitation

ARB: angiotensin II receptor blocker

AS: aortic stenosis

ASAP: as soon as possible

ASCVD: atherosclerotic cardiovascular disease

ASD: atrial septal defect

AST: aspartate aminotransferase

AV: atrioventricular

aVF: augmented vector foot (ECG lead)

aVL: augmented vector left (ECG lead)

aVR: augmented vector right (ECG lead)

B

BBB: bundle branch block

BHV: bioprosthetic heart valves

BiPAP: bilevel positive airway pressure

BMI: body mass index

BNP: B-type natriuretic peptide

BP: blood pressure

BPEG: British Pacing and Electrophysiology Group (pacemaker codes)

BPH: benign prostatic hyperplasia

bpm: beats per minute

BPM: breaths per minute

BUN: blood urea nitrogen

C

CABG: coronary artery bypass graft

CAD: coronary artery disease

cAMP: cyclic adenosine monophosphate

CAOD: carotid artery occlusive disease

CBC: complete blood count

CEA: carotid endarterectomy

CI: cardiac index

CK: creatine kinase

CK-MB: creatine kinase–muscle/brain

CLL: chronic lymphocytic leukemia

CML: chronic myelogenous leukemia

CMP: comprehensive metabolic panel

CNS: central nervous system

CO: cardiac output

COBRA: Consolidated Omnibus Budget Reconciliation Act

COPD: chronic obstructive pulmonary disease

CPR: cardiopulmonary resuscitation

CRT: capillary refill time

CT scan: computed tomography scan

CV nurse: cardiac vascular nurse

CVA: cerebrovascular accident

CVD: cardiovascular disease

CVI: chronic venous insufficiency

CVP: central venous pressure

CVRN: cardiac vascular registered nurse

D

D5W: dextrose 5% in water

DASH: dietary approaches to stop hypertension

DBP: diastolic blood pressure

DCCM: dilated congestive cardiomyopathy

DNI: do not intubate

DNR: do not resuscitate

DOB: date of birth

DVT: deep vein thrombosis

E

ECG: electrocardiogram

ED: emergency department

EMTALA: Emergency Medical Treatment and Active Labor Act

EPS: electrophysiology studies

EVAR: endovascular aneurysm repair

F

FDP: fibrin degradation products

FFP: fresh frozen plasma

FSP: fibrin split products

G

GCS: Glasgow Coma Scale

GGT: gamma-glutamyltransferase

GI: gastrointestinal

H

Hct: hematocrit

HCM: hypertrophic cardiomyopathy

HDL: high-density lipoprotein

HDL-C: high-density lipoprotein cholesterol

HF: heart failure

HFpEF: heart failure with preserved ejection fraction

HFrEF: heart failure with reduced ejection fraction

HgB: hemoglobin

HIPAA: Health Insurance Portability and Accountability Act

HIT: heparin-induced thrombocytopenia

HR: heart rate

I

IABP: intra-aortic balloon pump

IADLs: instrumental activities of daily living

ICD: implantable cardioverter defibrillator

ICM: insertable cardiac monitor
ICP: intracranial pressure
ID: identification
INR: international normalized ratio
IV: intravenous
IVC: inferior vena cava

J

JNC: Joint National Committee on Prevention, Detection, Evaluation, and Treatment of High Blood Pressure
JVD: jugular vein distention

L

LAD: left anterior descending (artery)
LBBB: left bundle branch block
LD (or LDH): L-lactate dehydrogenase
LDL: low-density lipoprotein
LDL-C: low-density lipoprotein cholesterol
LLQ: left lower quadrant
LMWH: low molecular weight heparin
LOC: level of consciousness
LPN: licensed practical nurse
LUQ: left upper quadrant
LV: left ventricle
LVAD: left ventricle assist device
LVEDP: left ventricular-end diastolic pressure
LVN: licensed vocational nurse

M

MAP: mean arterial pressure
MCH: mean corpuscular hemoglobin
MCHC: mean corpuscular hemoglobin concentration
MCT: mobile cardiac telemetry
MCV: mean corpuscular volume
mEq: milliequivalent
MHV: mechanical heart valves
MI: myocardial infarction
MONA: morphine, oxygen, nitroglycerin, aspirin
MR: mitral regurgitation
MRA: magnetic resonance angiography
MRI: magnetic resonance imaging
MS: mitral stenosis

N

NASPE: North American Society of Pacing and Electrophysiology (pacemaker codes)
NHLBI: National Heart, Lung, and Blood Institute
NIH: National Institutes of Health
NIHSS: National Institutes of Health Stroke Scale
NPH: neutral protamine Hagedorn (insulin)
NPO: nil per os (nothing by mouth)
NSAID: nonsteroidal anti-inflammatory drug
NSTEMI: non-ST-elevation myocardial infarction
NVS: Newest Vital Signs

P

PAD: peripheral artery disease
PAH: pulmonary arterial hypertension
PAOP: pulmonary artery occlusion pressure
PAP: pulmonary artery pressure
PCI: percutaneous coronary intervention
PCWP: pulmonary capillary wedge pressure
PDA: patent ductus arteriosus
PE: pulmonary embolism
PEA: pulseless electrical activity

PERRLA: pupils equal, round, and reactive to light and accommodation (motor function assessment)

PET: positron emission tomography

PFO: patent foramen ovale

PH: pulmonary hypertension

PHI: protected health information

PII: personally identifiable information

PO: per os (by mouth)

POA: power of attorney

PQRST: provoking, quality, region, severity, timing (to assess pain in a patient)

PRN: pro re nata (as needed)

PSVT: paroxysmal supraventricular tachycardia

PT: prothrombin time

PTA: percutaneous transluminal angioplasty

PTCA: percutaneous transluminal coronary angioplasty

PT/INR: prothrombin time and international normalized ratio

PTT: partial thromboplastin time

PVD: peripheral vascular disease

PVR: pulmonary vascular resistance

R

RA: right atrial

RAP: right atrial pressure

RBBB: right bundle branch block

RBC: red blood cell

RCA: right coronary artery

RCM: restrictive cardiomyopathy

REALM: Rapid Estimate of Adult Literacy in Medicine

RHD: rheumatic heart disease

RLQ: right lower quadrant

RR: respiration rate

RUQ: right upper quadrant

RV: right ventricle

RVEDP: right ventricular end-diastolic pressure

S

SA: sinoatrial

SBAR: situation, background, assessment, recommendations

SBP: systolic blood pressure

SCD: sequential compression devices

SIADH: syndrome of inappropriate antidiuretic hormone secretion

S-ICD: subcutaneous implantable cardioverter defibrillator

SMART: specific, measurable, attainable, realistic, time-restricted

SND: sinus node dysfunction

SSS: sick sinus syndrome

STEMI: ST-elevation myocardial infarction

SV: stroke volume

SVN Society for Vascular Nursing

SVR: systemic vascular resistance

SVT: supraventricular tachycardia

T

TCP: transcutaneous pacing

TEE: transesophageal echocardiogram

TED: thromboembolic deterrent stockings

TF: tissue factor

TIA: transient ischemic attack

TOFHLA: Test of Functional Health Literacy in Adults

tPA: tissue plasminogen activator

TTE: transthoracic echocardiogram

TV-ICD: transvenous implantable cardioverter defibrillator

U

UAP: unlicensed assistive personnel

ULQ: upper left quadrant

URQ: upper right quadrant

UTI: urinary tract infection

V

V-fib: ventricular fibrillation

V-tach: ventricular tachycardia

VAD: ventricular assist device

VSD: ventricular septal defect

VTE: venous thromboembolism prophylaxis

vW: von Willebrand factor

W

WBC: white blood cell

WHO: World Health Organization

Appendix C – Diagnostic Tests and Critical Values

Test	Description	Normal Range
Basic Metabolic Panel		
Potassium (K+)	electrolyte that helps with muscle contraction and regulates water and acid-base balance	3.5 – 5.2 mEq/L
Sodium (Na+)	maintains fluid balance and plays a major role in muscle and nerve function	135 – 145 mEq/L
Calcium (Ca+)	plays an important role in skeletal function and structure, nerve function, muscle contraction, and cell communication	8.5 – 10.3 mg/dL
Chloride (Cl$^-$)	electrolyte that plays a major role in muscle and nerve function	98 – 107 mEq/L
Blood urea nitrogen (BUN)	filtered by the kidneys; high levels can indicate insufficient kidney function	7 – 20 mg/dL
Creatinine	filtered by the kidneys; high levels can indicate insufficient kidney function	0.6 – 1.2 mg/dL
BUN to creatinine ratio	increased ratio indicates dehydration, AKI, or GI bleeding; decreased ratio indicates renal damage	10:1 – 20:1
Glucose	tests for hyper- and hypoglycemia	non-fasting: 140 mg/dL fasting: 70 – 99 mg/dL
Bicarbonate (HCO$_3$ or CO$_2$)	measures amount of CO_2 in the blood; decreased levels indicate acidosis or kidney damage; increased levels indicate alkalosis or lung damage	23 – 29 mEq/L
Other Serum Tests		
Magnesium	electrolyte that regulates muscle, nerve, and cardiac function	1.8 – 2.5 mg/dL
Glomerular filtration rate (GFR)	volume of fluid filtered by the renal glomerular capillaries per unit of time; decreased GFR rate indicates decreased renal function	men: 100 – 130 mL/min/1.73m^2 women: 90 – 120 mL/min/1.73m^2

		GFR 60 mL/min/1.73m² is common in adults >70 years of age
Total cholesterol (LDL and HDL)	a steroid produced by the liver that is needed to build and maintain animal cell membranes and that has protective properties for the heart; goals for low-density lipoprotein (LDL) and high-density lipoprotein (HDL) levels are based on the patient's risk factors for cardiovascular disease	200 mg/dL LDL: 100 mg/dL HDL (men): 40 – 50 mg/dL HDL (women): 50 – 59 mg/dL
Triglycerides	stores fat	150 mg/dL
B-type natriuretic peptide (BNP)	protein produced by the heart; high levels can indicate heart failure	100 pg/ml
Highly selective CRP test for C-reactive protein	marker for inflammation used to determine a patient's risk for heart disease	low risk: 1.0 mg/L average risk: 1.0 – 3.0 mg/L high risk: >3.0 mg/L
Homocysteine	an amino acid used as a marker for heart disease and vitamin deficiency (B_6, B_{12}, and folate)	4 – 14 mol/L
Prostate-specific antigen (PSA)	enzyme produced by prostate gland; high levels can indicate prostate cancer, prostatitis, or BPH	4 ng/mL
Erythrocyte sedimentation rate (ESR, or sed rate)	measures rate at which RBCs sediment (fall); increased ESR may indicate inflammation, anemia, or infection; decreased ESR may indicate heart failure or liver or kidney disease; ESR increases with age	men: 12 – 14 mm/h women: 18 – 21 mm/h
Ammonia	produced by bacteria in the intestines during the breakdown of proteins; increased levels may indicate liver or kidney damage; decreased levels are associated with hypertension	15 – 45 mcg/dL
Serum lipase (LPS)	protein secreted by the pancreas that helps break down fats; increased levels can indicate damage to the pancreas	0 – 160 U/L
Amylase	enzyme produced by pancreas and salivary glands; increased levels may indicate damage to the pancreas	23 – 85 U/L
Complete Blood Count (CBC)		

White blood cells (WBCs)	number of WBCs in blood; an increased number of WBCs can be an indication of inflammation or infection	4,500 – 10,000 cells/mcL
Red blood cells (RBCs)	carry oxygen throughout the body and filter carbon dioxide	men: 5 – 6 million cells/mcL women: 4 – 5 million cells/ mcL
Hemoglobin (HgB)	protein that holds oxygen in the blood	men: 13.8 – 17.2 g/dL women: 12.1 – 15.1 g/dL
Hematocrit (Hct)	percentage of the blood composed of red blood cells	men: 41% – 50% women: 36% – 44%
Red blood cell indices	mean corpuscular volume (MCV): average size of the red blood cells mean corpuscular hemoglobin (MCH): average amount of hemoglobin per RBC mean corpuscular hemoglobin concentration (MCHC): average concentration of hemoglobin in RBCs	MCV: 80 – 95 fL MCH: 27.5 – 33.2 pg MCHC: 334 – 355 g/L
Platelets	play a role in the body's clotting process	150,000 – 450,000 cells/mcL
Coagulation Studies		
Prothrombin time (PT)	tests how long it takes blood to clot	10 – 13 seconds
International normalized ratio (INR)	determines the effectiveness of an anticoagulant in thinning blood	healthy adults: 1.1 patients receiving anticoagulants: 2.0 – 3.0
Partial thromboplastin time (PTT)	assesses the body's ability to form blood clots	60 – 70 sec
Activated partial thromboplastin time (aPTT)	measures the body's ability to form blood clots using an activator to speed up the clotting process	20 – 35 sec
Cardiac Biomarkers		
Troponin I (cTnI) and troponin T (cTnT)	proteins released when the heart muscle is damaged; high levels can indicate a myocardial infarction but may also be due to other conditions that stress the heart (e.g., renal failure, heart failure, PE); levels peak 24 hours	cTnI: cutoff values for MI vary widely between assays cTnT: possible MI: >0.01 ng/mL

	post MI and can remain elevated for up to 2 weeks	
Creatine kinase (CK)	responsible for muscle cell function; an increased amount indicates cardiac or skeletal muscle damage	22 – 198 U/L
Creatine kinase–muscle/brain (CK-MB or CPK-MB)	cardiac marker for damaged heart muscle; often used to diagnose a second MI or ongoing cardiovascular conditions; a high ratio of CK-MB to CK indicates damage to heart muscle (as opposed to skeletal muscle	5 – 25 IU/L possible MI: ratio of CK-MB to CK is 2.5 – 3
Urinalysis		
Leukocytes	presence of WBCs in urine indicates infection	negative
Nitrate	presence of nitrates in urine indicates infection by gram-negative bacteria	negative
Urobilinogen	produced during bilirubin reduction; presence in urine indicates liver disease, bilinear obstruction, or hepatitis	0.2 – 1 mg
Protein	presence of protein in the urine may indicate nephritis or eclampsia	negative
pH	decreased (acidic) pH may indicate systemic acidosis or diabetes mellitus; increased (alkali) pH may indicate systemic alkalosis or UTI	4.5 – 8
Blood	blood in urine may indicate infection, renal calculi, neoplasm, or coagulation disorders	negative
Specific gravity	concentration of urine; decreased may indicate diabetes insipidus or pyelonephritis; increased may indicate dehydration or SIADH	1.010 – 1.025
Ketone	ketones are produced during fat metabolism; presence in urine may indicate diabetes, hyperglycemia, starvation, alcoholism, or eclampsia	negative
Bilirubin	produced during the breakdown of heme; presence in urine may indicate liver disease, biliary obstruction, or hepatitis	negative
Glucose	presence of glucose in urine indicates hyperglycemia	0 – 15 mg/dL
Urine hCG	determination of pregnancy	N/A
Urine culture and sensitivity	study of urine with growth on a culture medium to determine which pathogenic	N/A

	bacteria is present and which antibiotic the pathogen is sensitive to	
Liver Function Tests		
Albumin	a protein made in the liver; low levels may indicate liver damage	3.5 – 5.0 g/dL
Alkaline phosphatase (ALP)	an enzyme found in the liver and bones; increased levels indicate liver damage	45 – 147 U/L
Alanine transaminase (ALT)	an enzyme in the liver that helps metabolize protein; increased levels indicate liver damage	7 – 55 U/L
Aspartate transaminase (AST)	an enzyme in the liver that helps metabolize alanine; increased levels indicate liver or muscle damage	8 – 48 U/L
Total protein	low levels of total protein may indicate liver damage	6.3 – 7.9 g/dL
Total bilirubin	produced during the breakdown of heme; increased levels indicate liver damage or anemia	0.1 – 1.2 mg/dL
Gamma-glutamyltransferase (GGT)	an enzyme that plays a role in antioxidant metabolism; increased levels indicate liver damage	9 – 48 U/L
L-lactate dehydrogenase (LD or LDH)	an enzyme found in most cells in the body; high levels may indicate liver damage, cancer, or tissue breakdown	adult: 122 – 222 U/L
pH	measure of blood pH	7.35 – 7.45
Partial pressure of oxygen (PaO_2)	amount of oxygen gas in the blood	75 – 100 mm Hg
Partial pressure of carbon dioxide ($PaCO_2$)	amount of carbon dioxide gas in the blood	35 – 45 mm Hg
Bicarbonate (HCO_3)	amount of bicarbonate in the blood	22 – 26 mEq/L
Oxygen (O_2) saturation	measurement of the amount of oxygen-saturated hemoglobin relative to unsaturated hemoglobin	94 – 100%
Lactate	molecule produced during anaerobic cellular respiration; high levels indicate lack of available oxygen in cells	4.5 – 14.4 mg/dL

Dear CVRN test taker,

Great job completing this study guide. The hard work and effort you put into your test preparation will help you succeed on your upcoming CVRN exam. Thank you for letting us be a part of your education journey!

We have other study guides and products that you may find useful. Search for us on Amazon.com or let us know what you are looking for. We offer a wide variety of study guides that cover a multitude of subjects.

If you would like to share your success stories with us, or if you have a suggestion, comment, or concern, please send us an email at support@triviumtestprep.com.

Thanks again for choosing us!
Happy Testing
Ascencia Test Prep Team

Online Resources

We include online resources with the purchase of this study guide to help you fully prepare for your exam.

Practice Test
In addition to the practice test in the book, there is an online practice test.

Flash Cards
Our flash cards allow you to review important terms easily on your computer or smartphone.

Cheat Sheets
Review the core skills you need to master the exam with easy-to-read Cheat Sheets.

From Stress to Success Video
Watch "From Stress to Success," a brief but insightful video that offers the tip and tricks you need to score higher on your exam.

Scan the QR code or go to this link: **ascenciatestprep.com/cvrn-online-resources**

If you need assistance, contact support@ascenciatestprep.com.

www.ingramcontent.com/pod-product-compliance
Lightning Source LLC
Chambersburg PA
CBHW081152290426
44108CB00018B/2523